An Introduction To The Study Of Wave Mechanics

Louis De Broglie, HT Flint

AN INTRODUCTION TO THE STUDY OF WAVE MECHANICS

AN INTRODUCTION TO THE STUDY OF WAVE MECHANICS

BY

LOUIS DE BROGLIE

DOCTEUR ÈS-SCIENCES, PROFESSOR IN THE HENRI POINCARÉ INSTITUTE, PARIS

TRANSLATED FROM THE FRENCH BY

H. T. FLINT, D.Sc., Ph.D.

WITH FOURTEEN DIAGRAMS

METHUEN & CO. LTD.

36 ESSEX STREET W.C.

First Published in 1930

CONTENTS

AN INTRODUCTION TO THE STUDY OF WAVE MECHANICS

GENERAL INTRODUCTION [1]

THE new wave mechanics has received during the past two years the firm support of experiment, thanks to the discovery of a striking phenomenon completely unknown previously, viz.: the diffraction of electrons by crystals. From one point of view it may be said that this discovery is the exact counterpart of the older discovery of the photo-electric effect, since it shows that for matter as for light we have hitherto neglected one of the aspects of physical reality.

The discovery of the photo-electric effect has taught us that the undulatory theory of light, firmly established by Fresnel and subsequently developed by Maxwell as the electromagnetic theory, although it contains a large body of truth, is, nevertheless, insufficient, and that it is necessary, in a certain sense, to turn again to the corpuscular conception of light proposed by Newton.

Planck, in his famous theory of black body radiation, was led to assume that radiation of frequency ν is always emitted and absorbed in equal and finite quantities, in quanta of magnitude $h\nu$, h being the constant with which the name of Planck will always be associated. In order to explain the photo-electric effect, Einstein had only to adopt the hypothesis, which is quite in conformity with the ideas of Planck, that light consists of corpuscles and that the energy of the corpuscles of light of frequency ν is $h\nu$. When a light corpuscle in its passage through matter encounters an electron at rest, it can impart to it its energy $h\nu$ and the electron thus set in

[1] This introduction is the reproduction of a communication made by the author at the meeting of the British Association for the Advancement of Science held in Glasgow in September, 1928.

motion will leave the matter with kinetic energy equal in amount to the difference between the energy $h\nu$, which it has received, and the work it has had to expend to get out of the matter. Now, this is precisely the experimental law of the photo-electric effect in the form which has been verified in succession for all the radiations from the ultra-violet region to X- and γ-rays.

Einstein, in developing his idea, has shown that if the hypothesis of light corpuscles or light quanta be accepted, it is necessary to attribute to each of these corpuscles a momentum $p = \frac{h\nu}{c}$ together with energy $W = h\nu$. These two relations define mechanically the light corpuscle of frequency ν. More recently the corpuscular theory of Einstein has been confirmed by the discovery of the Compton effect. This effect may be described in the following way; a beam of X-rays falling on matter may undergo a lowering of frequency, while electrons are set in more or less rapid motion. The phenomenon is readily explained if it be admitted that there is an encounter, or impact, between a light corpuscle and an electron initially at rest in the matter. During the impact the electron takes up energy from the light corpuscle and is set in motion. The light corpuscle has thus lost a part of its energy, and as the relation $W = h\nu$ must always be maintained, the frequency of the light quantum will be less after the impact than before it. The theory of the Compton phenomenon, based on the two equations $W = h\nu$ and $p = \frac{h\nu}{c}$, has been developed by Compton himself and by Debye: experiment has confirmed the theory quantitatively, and this has provided another brilliant success for the hypothesis that light has a granular structure.

In spite of these successes the theory of light quanta would not by itself be completely satisfactory. In the first place, those phenomena described by the terms diffraction and interference demand the introduction of the concept of waves, and, further, the two relations $W = h\nu$ and $p = \frac{h\nu}{c}$ imply the existence of a frequency ν.

This is sufficient to show that light cannot consist of simple

corpuscles

particles in motion. Nevertheless, the discovery of the photo-electric effect confirmed by the Compton effect has shown the necessity of introducing into optics the idea of corpuscles side by side with the idea of waves. A curious duality of Nature appears to be revealed here.

But if for a century we have neglected too much the corpuscular aspect in the theory of light in our exclusive attachment to waves, have we not erred in the opposite direction in the theory of matter? Have we not wrongly neglected the point of view of waves and thought only of corpuscles? These are the questions the author of this book set himself some years ago in reflecting upon the analogy between the principle of least action and the principle of Fermat and upon the meaning of the mysterious quantum conditions introduced into intra-atomic dynamics by Planck, Bohr, Wilson and Sommerfeld.

By reasoning which will be studied in this volume, we may arrive at the conviction that it is necessary to introduce waves into the theory of matter and to do it in the following way. Let a material particle (e.g. an electron) of mass m be considered which is moving freely with a constant velocity v. If we adopt the expressions given by the theory of Relativity, its energy and momentum are:

$$W = \frac{mc^2}{\sqrt{1-\beta^2}}, \quad p = \frac{mv}{\sqrt{1-\beta^2}} = \frac{Wv}{c^2}, \quad \left(\beta = \frac{v}{c}\right), \qquad (1)$$

c being the velocity of light in empty space.

According to the new conception it is necessary to associate with this particle a wave travelling in the direction of motion of which the frequency is:

$$\nu = \frac{W}{h} \qquad (2)$$

and of which the phase velocity is:

$$V = \frac{c^2}{v} = \frac{c}{\beta}, \qquad (3)$$

hence:

$$\frac{h\nu}{V} = \frac{W}{c^2}v = p \qquad (4)$$

and consequently if λ is the wave-length of the associated wave,

$$\lambda = \frac{V}{\nu} = \frac{h}{p}. \quad \quad \quad \quad (5)$$

If we seek to apply these formulæ, not only to a material particle but also to a light particle, we must write $v = c$, and then we find:

$$W = h\nu, \quad p = \frac{h\nu}{c}. \quad \quad \quad \quad (6)$$

These are exactly the fundamental formulæ of the theory of light quanta. Our formulæ (2) to (5) are thus general; they apply equally well to matter and radiation, and they are the expression of the necessity in both cases of introducing side by side the ideas of corpuscle and of wave.

As follows, in particular, from the elegant works of Schrodinger, and as we shall show in detail in the course of these studies, the old mechanics corresponds to the case in which the propagation of the associated wave proceeds according to the laws of geometrical optics In this case the corpuscle or particle may be regarded as describing one of the rays of the wave with a velocity equal to Lord Rayleigh's group velocity. Thus we may under these circumstances consider the particle as constituted by a group of waves of neighbouring frequencies and this gives a physical picture of the particle which would be very satisfactory were it possible to generalise it, unfortunately, this is not the case.

It is to be noted that, if the associated wave is propagated according to the laws of geometrical optics no experiment can prove the existence of associated waves, because the result of an experiment can then always be regarded as proving only the exactness of the laws of the old mechanics. But it is quite another matter when the conditions of propagation of the associated wave are such that the approximations of geometrical optics are no longer sufficiently accurate to describe the process. According to the new ideas, we must then expect to observe phenomena which the old mechanics is quite powerless to predict and which are characteristic of the new undulatory conception of dynamics.

In the domain proper to the new dynamics, the principle

which appears best established is that the square of the amplitude of the wave, i.e. its intensity, must measure at each point of space and at each instant of time the probability that the associated particle is at that point at that instant. A little reflection will show that this principle is necessary to account for the phenomena of interference and diffraction of light, for in optics the maximum luminous energy is found in the places where the Fresnel wave has the greatest intensity. Since we are following as our guide the idea of bringing together as closely as possible the theory of light and that of matter, it is quite natural to extend the principle which is necessary in the case of light to the case of particles of matter.

We thus arrive at the idea that material particles will give rise to phenomena analogous to those of interference and diffraction of light and that the methods of calculation must be closely alike in the two cases. Thus a cloud consisting of electrons with the same velocity must be associated with a plane monochromatic wave. Let us suppose that this cloud falls on a medium with regular structure, such as occurs in the case of a crystal. If the distances between the elements of this structure are of the same order of magnitude as the wavelength of the incident wave, diffraction will occur, and in certain directions, which may be readily found by calculation, the amplitude of the diffracted wave will have maximum values. In accordance with this, we must expect that the electrons will be concentrated along certain directions. We shall thus have the exact analogy with Laue's experiment on X-rays, and if the result agrees with the theoretical deduction we shall obtain a very direct and a very strong proof that it is necessary, even in the case of matter, to complete our conception of a particle by the addition of that of a wave.

These experiments have been realised by various methods under different conditions by Davisson and Germer in New York, by Professor G. P. Thompson in Aberdeen, and by Rupp in Göttingen. The agreement between theory and experiment is excellent; the deviations which had been established in the first experiments of Davisson and Germer appear to receive a very natural explanation by taking account of the refractive index of the waves in the crystal. Rupp has, indeed, been able quite recently to diffract a beam of electrons at grazing incidence on an ordinary lined grating. Thus, experimental confirmation is as satisfactory as could be desired.

In this way a collection of magnificent experimental results has clearly established the necessity of introducing simultaneously particles and waves into the whole domain of physics.

But what does this duality of waves and particles mean? This is a very difficult question and one which is still far from being very clearly elucidated.

The simplest idea is that which Schrödinger put forward at the beginning of his work, viz. that the particle or the electron is constituted by a group of waves; it is a "wave packet." We have seen that this can be maintained so long as mechanical phenomena are considered which are in harmony with the old dynamics, that is to say in the new language, phenomena in which the propagation of the associated wave obeys the laws of geometrical optics. Unfortunately, when we pass to the domain proper of the new theory it appears scarcely possible to support this idea which is so attractive on account of its simplicity. In an experiment like that of the diffraction of an electron by a crystal the wave packet would be completely dispersed and destroyed; as a result no particles would be found in the diffracted bundles. In other words, if they were simple wave packets the particles would have no stable existence.

If it appears impossible to maintain Schrödinger's view in all its consequences, neither is it easy to develop another opinion with which the author has for a long time associated himself and according to which the particle is a singularity in a wave phenomenon. In the special case of the uniform motion of a particle it is possible to find a solution of the wave equation showing a moving singularity and capable of representing the particle. But it is very difficult to make the generalisation to the case of non-uniform motion, and there are serious objections to this point of view, we shall not discuss this difficulty any further in this volume.

The author has also made another suggestion which is published in his report to the Fifth Solway Congress.[1] We have seen that we must always associate a wave with a

[1] "Electrons et photons," Gauthier Villars, editeur, Paris, 1928.

particle, and so the idea which is in best agreement with the older views of physics is to consider the wave as a reality and as occupying a certain region of space, while the particle is regarded as a material point having a definite position in the wave. This is the basis of the suggestion Since it is necessary, as we have said above, that the intensity of the wave should be proportional at each point to the probability of the occurrence of the particle at that point, we must attempt to connect the motion of the particle with the propagation of the wave so that this relation is automatically realised in every case. It is, in fact, actually possible to establish a connection between the motion of the particle and the propagation of the wave, so that if at an initial instant the intensity of the wave measures the required probability the same is true at all later instants. We may thus suppose that the particle is guided by the wave which plays the part of a pilot-wave. This view permits of an interesting visualization of the corpuscular motion in wave mechanics without too wide a departure from classical ideas. Unfortunately, we encounter very serious objections to this view also, and these will be pointed out in the course of the book. It is not possible to regard the theory of the pilot-wave as satisfactory. Nevertheless, since the equations on which this theory rests are sound, we may preserve some of its consequences by giving to it a modified form in agreement with ideas developed independently by Kennard.[1] Instead of speaking of the motion and of the trajectory of the particles, we speak of the motion and of the trajectory of the "elements of probability" and in this way the difficulties noted are avoided.

Finally, there is a fourth point of view developed by Heisenberg and Bohr which is most favoured at present. This point of view is a little disconcerting at first sight, but yet it appears to contain a large body of truth. According to this view, the wave does not represent a physical phenomenon taking place in a region of space; rather it is simply a symbolic representation of what we know about the particle. An experiment or observation never permits us to say exactly that this particle occupies this position in space and that it has this particular velocity. All that experiment can show us

[1] "Physical Review," 31, 1928, p. 876.

R′ vanishes just as the expectation of an event which is not realized vanishes. This shows very clearly the non-physical character of the wave in the conceptions of Bohr and Heisenberg.

To sum up, the physical interpretation of the new mechanics remains an extremely difficult question. Nevertheless, one great fact is now well established; this is that for matter and for radiation the dualism of waves and particles must be admitted, and that the distribution of the particles in space can only be foreseen by the consideration of waves. Unfortunately the profound nature of the two members in this duality and the precise relation existing between them still remain a mystery.

CHAPTER I

THE OLD SYSTEMS OF MECHANICS OF

1. Hamilton's Principle

THERE are two systems of mechani describe under the term " old mechaı these, and the older of the two, is th tonian mechanics ; the second is the relati Einstein. Newtonian mechanics remainec sufficient for the needs of science, but the pı of Einstein have shown that it must be system is obtained which coincides with t velocity of the particle is small compared c, of light in empty space, but which deviat velocity is comparable with c.

The two old systems of mechanics, in sp between them, at the same time resemble portant particulars ; the general equati form, they are both derivable from the saı least action, and there are other analogie it is easy to describe at the same time tl of the two systems. The essential point is of Newtonian mechanics can be deduced of Einstein by supposing that the veloci space is infinitely great ; in other words, are always obtained from the relativity fc ment in a series in powers of $\beta\left(=\frac{v}{c}\right)$ and l of higher orders.

We shall consider first the dynamics that is to say, we shall study the motion of force which is assumed to be given.

field of force by a potential function $F(x, y, z, t)$ of the co-ordinates of space and time. In the old mechanics we consider particles or corpuscles as having a definite position in space so that we can record their position by means of three co-ordinates. Thus, since the particle has a definite situation in space at each instant, we may evidently define its velocity as the limit of the ratio of the space described along the trajectory and the time taken when the latter tends to zero. If the position of the particle is recorded by means of rectangular co-ordinates, we have :

$$v = \sqrt{\dot{x}^2 + \dot{y}^2 + \dot{z}^2},$$

where the dots denote differentiation with respect to time. In the general case, where curvilinear co-ordinates (q_1, q_2, q_3) are employed, the velocity is expressed by a certain function of the q's and $\dot{q}$'s.

The fundamental principle of the two old dynamics is Hamilton's principle of stationary action. Let it be supposed that at the instant t_0 the particle is situated at a point M_0 of space and that at a later instant t_1 it is at M_1. The problem arising in the dynamics of a particle is to determine the motion in the interval of time between t_0 and t_1. Hamilton's principle states that a certain function $L(q, \dot{q}, t)$ exists, which is a function of the q's, $\dot{q}$'s, and the time, with the property that the integral $\int_{t_0}^{t_1} L dt$ is smaller for the actual motion than for any other infinitesimally varied motion which takes the particle from M_0 at time t_0 to M_1 at time t_1.

The integral $\int_{t_0}^{t_1} L dt$ is the Hamiltonian integral of action. The function L is called the Lagrangian function and sometimes the kinetic potential.

Hamilton's principle of least action is thus described by the formula :

$$\delta \int_{t_0}^{t_1} L(q, \dot{q}, t) dt = 0, \qquad . \quad . \quad . \quad (1)$$

t_0 and t_1 being invariable, and the symbol denoting an infinitesimal change in the form of the function $q(t)$, and consequently in $\dot{q}(t)$, with the condition that their initial and final values are unchanged.

2. The Equations of Lagrange

The general procedure of the calculus
lead to the equations of Lagrange. If we ch
q for each value of t so that it becomes $q +$
will become $\dot{q} + \delta\dot{q}$, and we obtain :

$$\delta L = \sum_{n=1}^{n=3}\Big(\frac{\partial L}{\partial q_n}\delta q_n + \frac{\partial L}{\partial \dot{q}_n}\delta\dot{q}_n$$

and in consequence, since t_0 and t_1 are fixed,

$$\delta\int_{t_0}^{t_1} L dt = \int_{t_0}^{t_1}\delta L dt = \int_{t_0}^{t_1}\sum_{n=1}^{n=3}\Big(\frac{\partial L}{\partial q_n}\delta q_n + \frac{\partial}{\partial}$$

But $\delta\dot{q} = \delta\Big(\frac{dq}{dt}\Big) = \frac{d}{dt}(\delta q)$, so that by int

$$\int_{t_0}^{t_1}\sum_{n=1}^{n=3}\frac{\partial L}{\partial \dot{q}_n}\delta\dot{q}_n dt = \Big[\sum_{n=1}^{n=3}\frac{\partial L}{\partial \dot{q}_n}\delta q_n\Big]_{t_0}^{t_1} - \int_{t_0}^{t_1}$$

whence we obtain for Hamilton's principle

$$\int_{t_0}^{t_1}\sum_{n=1}^{n=3}\delta q_n\Big[\frac{\partial L}{\partial q_n} - \frac{d}{dt}\Big(\frac{\partial L}{\partial \dot{q}_n}\Big)\Big]dt$$

Since the δq's are arbitrary, it follows that

$$\frac{d}{dt}\Big(\frac{\partial L}{\partial \dot{q}_n}\Big) - \frac{\partial L}{\partial q_n} = 0 \quad (n = 1,$$

These are the equations of Lagrange. Th
of the particle as a function of 6 arbitr
may be the three initial co-ordinates and t
of the initial velocity.

3. The Lagrangian Function. Moment

Up to this point our dynamical theor
were, a blank form, since we have not st
function L in the q's, $\dot{q}$'s and t. It is just
mechanics of Newton and Einstein diver
of L is different.

In the Newtonian system

$$L(q, \dot{q}, t) = \tfrac{1}{2}mv^2 - F(q, t), \qquad . \quad . \quad (7)$$

m being a characteristic constant of the particle considered, called its mass. The function $F(q, t)$ is the potential function, and v is the velocity of the particle which must be expressed in terms of the q's and $\dot{q}$'s.

In Einstein's system

$$L(q, \dot{q}, t) = -mc^2\sqrt{1-\beta^2} - F(q, t). \qquad . \quad (8)$$

Since $\sqrt{1-\beta^2} = 1 - \tfrac{1}{2}\beta^2 + \ldots$, we see that by neglecting the unwritten terms, we have :

$$L = -mc^2 + \tfrac{1}{2}mv^2 - F(q, t), \qquad . \quad . \quad (9)$$

so that the relativistic form of the function with this degree of approximation differs from the classical form only in the constant term $-mc^2$. In the integral (1) this term gives rise to $-mc^2(t_1 - t_0)$, which is not subject to variation and may consequently be neglected. In this way we readily appreciate the point mentioned above that these two systems of mechanics coincide when we neglect the higher powers of β.

Now that we know how we must fill in our blank Hamiltonian form in order to obtain the one or the other old system of dynamics, let us return to the equations of Lagrange.

We shall define certain quantities p by the equations :

$$p_n = \frac{\partial L}{\partial \dot{q}_n} \quad (n = 1, 2, 3) \qquad . \quad . \quad . \quad (10)$$

and we shall describe p_n as the conjugate momentum of q_n

The equations of Lagrange then give :

$$\frac{dp_n}{dt} = \frac{\partial L}{\partial q_n}. \qquad . \quad . \quad . \quad . \quad (11)$$

Let us consider briefly the particular case where the co-ordinates are rectangular. We have then :

$$q_1 = x, \quad q_2 = y, \quad q_3 = z, \quad \text{and } v^2 = \dot{x}^2 + \dot{y}^2 + \dot{z}^2.$$

With the Newtonian form of L we find :

$$p_1 = m\dot{x}, \quad p_2 = m\dot{y}, \quad p_3 = m\dot{z}. \qquad . \quad . \quad (12)$$

The p's are thus the components of the mon
the relativistic form of L,

$$p_1 = \frac{m\dot{x}}{\sqrt{1-\beta^2}}, \quad p_2 = \frac{m\dot{y}}{\sqrt{1-\beta^2}}, \quad p_3$$

The p's will then be components of moment
is defined to be equal to

$$\frac{m\mathbf{v}}{\sqrt{1-\beta^2}}.$$

Moreover, in both cases the choice of recta
has the effect of making L depend upon t
the function F. Hence:

$$\frac{\partial L}{\partial q} = -\frac{\partial F}{\partial q}$$

If we consider the vector $-$ grad F with

$$\left(-\frac{\partial F}{\partial x}, \quad -\frac{\partial F}{\partial y}, \quad -\frac{\partial F}{\partial z}\right.$$

and if we call this vector the force app
denoting it by $\mathbf{f}$, the equations (11) give th

$$\frac{dp_1}{dt} = f_x, \quad \frac{dp_2}{dt} = f_y, \quad \frac{dp_3}{dt}$$

which are applicable in both the old dyn

Let us now introduce the conception
purpose we begin with the general forn
equations of Lagrange:

$$\frac{d}{dt}\left(\frac{\partial L}{\partial \dot{q}_n}\right) = \frac{dp_n}{dt} = \frac{\partial L}{\partial q_n}. \quad (n =$$

Now let us consider the quantity:

$$W = \sum_{n=1}^{n=3} p_n\dot{q}_n - L,$$

and obtain its time derivative:

$$\frac{dW}{dt} = \sum_{n=1}^{n=3}\left[\dot{q}_n\frac{dp_n}{dt} + p_n\frac{d\dot{q}_n}{dt} - \frac{\partial L}{\partial q_n}\dot{q}_n - \right.$$

The first and third terms of the right-hand side of (18) cancel on account of the equations of Lagrange, the second and fourth on account of the definition of p_n. Thus :

$$\frac{dW}{dt} = -\frac{\partial L}{\partial t}, \qquad (19)$$

whence the theorem ; if the function L does not depend explicitly on the time, the quantity W remains constant. W is called the energy of the particle.

Let us examine the expression for the energy in classical dynamics. We have in this case $L = \frac{1}{2}mv^2 - F$, and whatever the co-ordinates chosen, the term $\frac{1}{2}mv^2$ is a homogeneous quadratic function of the q's for $v^2 = \dot{x}^2 + \dot{y}^2 + \dot{z}^2$, and each of the terms $\dot{x}$, $\dot{y}$, z is a linear function of the $\dot{q}$'s. Thus, if $T = \frac{1}{2}mv^2$, we obtain, by means of Euler's theorem,

$$2T = \sum_{n=1}^{n=3} q_n \frac{\partial T}{\partial \dot{q}_n} = \sum_{n=1}^{n=3} \dot{q}_n \frac{\partial L}{\partial \dot{q}_n} = \sum_{n=1}^{n=3} p_n \dot{q}_n, \qquad (20)$$

since L depends on the q's through T only.

We therefore obtain :

$$W = 2T - L = 2T - (T - F) = T + F. \qquad (21)$$

The energy is the sum of $T(= \frac{1}{2}mv^2)$, called the kinetic energy, and of F, called the potential energy.

Let us pass now to the dynamics of relativity where

$$L = -mc^2\sqrt{1 - \beta^2} - F.$$

We can no longer follow exactly the same argument, since $\sqrt{1 - \beta^2}$ is not a homogeneous quadratic function of the $\dot{q}$'s, but we can write :

$$\sum_{n=1}^{n=3} p_n \dot{q}_n = \sum_{n=1}^{n=3} \dot{q}_n \frac{\partial L}{\partial \dot{q}_n} = \sum_{n=1}^{n=3} \dot{q}_n \frac{m}{2\sqrt{1 - \beta^2}} \frac{\partial v^2}{\partial q_n} \qquad (22)$$

and since v^2 is a homogeneous quadratic function of the $\dot{q}_n$'s, we have :

$$2v^2 = \sum_{n=1}^{n=3} \dot{q}_n \frac{\partial v^2}{\partial \dot{q}_n}$$

and by (22):

$$\sum_{n=1}^{n=3} p_n \dot{q}_n = \frac{mv^2}{\sqrt{1-\beta^2}}.$$

Thus:

$$W = \sum_{n=1}^{n=3} p_n \dot{q}_n - L = \frac{mv^2}{\sqrt{1-\beta^2}} + mc^2\sqrt{1 -$$

$$=$$

The term $\frac{mc^2}{\sqrt{1-\beta^2}}$ represents the energy motion in the dynamics of relativity. If tl the term has the value mc^2, which is the en at rest, that is, its internal energy correspon m and equal to the product of the rest ma the velocity of light. When the partic energy becomes $\frac{mc^2}{\sqrt{1-\beta^2}}$, which is equal

and the quantity $\frac{m}{\sqrt{1-\beta^2}}$, which may be of the particle in motion. It is impoı particle with a proper mass different fr have a speed lower than that of light, sir infinity when β tends to unity.

If we develop $\frac{mc^2}{\sqrt{1-\beta^2}}$ in a series of higher powers, we find:

$$W = mc^2 + \tfrac{1}{2}mv^2 +$$

and we see that the relativistic enerı approximation equal to that of Newton by the term mc^2. We must never los difference, and must remember that c matically neglects the internal energy

4. Another form of Hamilton's Prin Maupertuis

We proceed to show that it is possi integral of action the form of an inte this purpose let us consider an abstract four dimensional space formed by the union of the three co-ordinates q and the time t. The motion of the particle is represented in this space by a certain curve, since this motion is expressed by three relations of the type :

$$q_n = f_n(t).$$

This curve is what is called in the theory of relativity the world line of the moving particle ; along this curve each co-ordinate q_n is a certain function of the time.

By (17) Hamilton's integral may be written :

$$\int_{P_0}^{P_1}\left(\sum_{n=1}^{n=3} p_n dq_n - W\,dt\right), \quad . \quad . \quad . \quad (26)$$

the points P_0 and P_1 corresponding to the times t_0 and t_1 on the world line. The principle of stationary action asserts that this line integral is stationary for all infinitely small deformations from the curve of integration, the extremities of the curve being kept fixed, which means that neither the initial and final instants nor the initial and final positions are varied.

In the case of constant fields of force the principle of stationary action takes a particularly important form. In fact, we have : $\frac{\partial F}{\partial t} = 0$, and consequently $\frac{\partial L}{\partial t} = 0$. The energy is constant, and we can give to the principle a celebrated form of expression which is due to Maupertuis. This permits of the determination of the trajectory without the necessity of considering the way in which the particle describes it. It is only for fields of force which are constant in time that such a separation between the study of the trajectory and the study of the motion can be realised ; this may be readily understood by the following consideration.

To pass from Hamilton's principle, which is always true, to the principle of Maupertuis, which is restricted to constant fields, it is necessary to establish a formula sometimes called the principle of varied action. Instead of considering a variation in which the initial and final times and co-ordinates are fixed, let us cause them to vary also by very small amounts δt_0, δt_1 and $(\delta q_n)_0$, $(\delta q_n)_1$. The variation of Hamilton's integral

is the sum of what it would be if the lin
and of the variation due to change of the
Thus :

$$\delta\int_{t_0}^{t_1} L\,dt = \int_{t_0}^{t_1} \delta L\,dt + \Big[\sum_{n=1}^{n=3} p_n \delta q_n$$

for when the initial instant is varied by
co-ordinates by $(\delta q_n)_0$, the integral, consider
evidently changes by

$$-\Big[\sum_{n=1}^{n=3} (p_n)_0(\delta q_n)_0 - W_0 \delta t_0\Big]$$

while for variations at the upper limit, the change is

$$\Big[\sum_{n=1}^{n=3} (p_n)_1(\delta q_n)_1 - W_1 \delta t_1\Big].$$

The first term of (27) is zero according to Hamilton's principle, so that :

$$\delta\int_{t_0}^{t_1} L\,dt = \Big[\sum_{n=1}^{n=3} p_n \delta q_n - W\,\delta t\Big]_0^1 . \quad \quad (28)$$

This formula is the expression of the principle of varied action. Denote by S Hamilton's integral, and by S_1 the curvilinear integral,

i.e. $$S_1 = \int_{M_0}^{M_1} \sum_{n=1}^{n=3} p_n dq_n \quad \quad (29)$$

taken along the trajectory from the initial point M_0 to the final point M_1. The integral (29) is the integral of action of Maupertuis. Since in the case of a constant field the formulæ (21) and (24) allow the velocity, and consequently the p's, to be expressed as a function of the constant energy and of the co-ordinates q, the integral of Maupertuis does not depend upon the time. We have :

$$S = S_1 - \int_{t_0}^{t_1} W\,dt \quad \quad (30)$$

and consequently in general for any variation whatsoever :

$$\delta S = \delta S_1 - \int_{t_0}^{t_1} \delta W \, dt - \Big[W \, \delta t \Big]_0^1. \quad . \quad . \quad (31)$$

By comparison with (28) we find :

$$\delta S_1 = \Big[\sum_{n=1}^{n=3} p_n \delta q_n \Big]_0^1 + \int_{t_0}^{t_1} \delta W \, dt. \quad . \quad . \quad (32)$$

If, therefore, we restrict ourselves to variations of the trajectory in which the ends M_0 and M_1 are unchanged, while the energy is unaltered, the integral of action of Maupertuis is stationary. This is the principle of Maupertuis.

Let us consider the case where the q's are rectangular co-ordinates so that :

$$\sum_{n=1}^{n=3} p_n dq_n = p_x dx + p_y dy + p_z dz \quad . \quad . \quad (33)$$

and we see that the integral S_1 has the following interpretation. It is the integral of momentum along the trajectory, and has the value $\int mvds$ in classical mechanics and $\int \frac{mv}{\sqrt{1 - \beta^2}} ds$ in relativistic mechanics, ds denoting the element of arc of the trajectory.

5. The Hamiltonian Canonical Equations

We proceed to show that the dynamical equations can be put into a form well known as Hamilton's canonical equations. Since the function L depends on the q's, $\dot{q}$'s and t, we may, by means of (10), express the p's as a function of these variables, and consequently write in general :

$$\dot{q}_n = f_n(q, p, t), \quad (n = 1, 2, 3) \quad . \quad . \quad (34)$$

where f_n denotes a function which can be calculated in any particular case.

We may thus choose as our variables the q's, p's and t in the place of the q's, $\dot{q}$'s and t. Let $H(q, p, t)$ denote the energy expressed in terms of these variables which are often described as the canonical variables. We have by the definition of energy :

$$H(q, p, t) = \sum_{n=1}^{n=3} p_n\dot{q}_n - L(q, \dot{q}, t), \quad . \quad . \quad (35)$$

where, on the right-hand side, we must suppose that the $\dot{q}$'s are expressed as functions of the p's, q's and t by means of (34). If we determine the derivatives $\frac{\partial H}{\partial p_m}$ and $\frac{\partial H}{\partial q_m}$, where m has a definite value 1, 2 or 3,

$$\frac{\partial H}{\partial p_m} = \dot{q}_m + \sum_{n=1}^{n=3} p_n \frac{\partial f_n}{\partial p_m} - \sum_{n=1}^{n=3} \frac{\partial L}{\partial \dot{q}_n}\frac{\partial f_n}{\partial p_m}$$

$$= \dot{q}_m \quad . \quad . \quad . \quad . \quad . \quad . \quad (36)$$

$$\frac{\partial H}{\partial q_m} = \sum_{n=1}^{n=3} p_n \frac{\partial f_n}{\partial q_m} - \frac{\partial L}{\partial q_m} - \sum_{n=1}^{n=3} \frac{\partial L}{\partial \dot{q}_n}\frac{\partial f_n}{\partial q_m}$$

$$= -\frac{\partial L}{\partial q_m} = -\frac{dp_m}{dt} \text{ by the equations of Lagrange.} \quad (37)$$

We have thus obtained the system of Hamiltonian canonical equations :

$$\frac{dq_n}{dt} = \frac{\partial H}{\partial p_n}, \quad \frac{dp_n}{dt} = -\frac{\partial H}{\partial q_n} \quad (n = 1, 2, 3) \quad . \quad (38)$$

It is easy to deduce the theorem of conservation of energy, and it suffices to determine $\frac{dH}{dt}$.

$$\frac{dH}{dt} = \frac{\partial H}{\partial t} + \sum_{n=1}^{n=3}\left(\frac{\partial H}{\partial p_n}\frac{dp_n}{dt} + \frac{\partial H}{\partial q_n}\frac{dq_n}{dt}\right)$$

$$= \frac{\partial H}{\partial t} \quad . \quad . \quad . \quad . \quad . \quad (39)$$

According to the definition of energy given in (35), it appears that if L does not contain the time explicitly, the same is true of H and $\frac{\partial H}{\partial t} = 0$ Thus the energy is constant, a result already obtained.

We proceed to consider in detail Hamilton's equations in both the old systems of dynamics.

Let us take first the case of classical mechanics with rectangular co-ordinates.

We have :

$$p_x = mv_x, \quad p_y = mv_y, \quad p_z = mv_z,$$

$$v^2 = v_x^2 + v_y^2 + v_z^2 = \frac{1}{m^2}(p_x^2 + p_y^2 + p_z^2), \quad . \quad . \quad (40)$$

whence

$$\mathrm{H} = \frac{1}{2}mv^2 + \mathrm{F} = \frac{1}{2m}(p_x^2 + p_y^2 + p_z^2) + \mathrm{F}(q, t). \quad (41)$$

The equations $\frac{dq_n}{dt} = \frac{\partial \mathrm{H}}{\partial p_n}$ are immediately verified, since we have, for example :

$$\frac{dx}{dt} = v_x = \frac{p_x}{m} = \frac{\partial \mathrm{H}}{\partial p_x}. \quad . \quad . \quad . \quad (42)$$

The equations $\frac{dp_n}{dt} = -\frac{\partial \mathrm{H}}{\partial q_n}$ now become :

$$m\frac{dv_x}{dt} = -\frac{\partial \mathrm{F}}{\partial x}, \text{ etc.} \quad . \quad . \quad (43)$$

These are the fundamental Newtonian equations.

Let us now take the relativity theory with rectangular axes.

In this case :

$$p_x = \frac{m}{\sqrt{1-\beta^2}}v_x, \quad p_y = \frac{m}{\sqrt{1-\beta^2}}v_y, \quad p_z = \frac{m}{\sqrt{1-\beta^2}}v_z, \quad (44)$$

$$\mathrm{H} = \frac{mc^2}{\sqrt{1-\beta^2}} + \mathrm{F}(q, t). \quad . \quad . \quad (45)$$

It is necessary first of all to express H as a function of the q's, p's and t.

We have :

$$p_x^2 + p_y^2 + p_z^2 = \frac{m^2v^2}{1-\beta^2},$$

whence

$$\frac{1}{m^2c^2}(p_x^2 + p_y^2 + p_z^2) = \frac{\beta^2}{1-\beta^2}. \quad . \quad . \quad (46)$$

If we add unity to each side and take the square root, we obtain :

$$\frac{1}{\sqrt{1-\beta^2}}=\frac{1}{mc}\sqrt{m^2c^2+p_x^2+p_y^2+p_z^2} \quad . \quad (47)$$

and

$$H(q, p, t)=c\sqrt{m^2c^2+p_x^2+p_y^2+p_z^2}+F(q, t) \quad (48)$$

We have therefore :

$$\frac{\partial H}{\partial q_n}=\frac{\partial F}{\partial q_n}, \qquad \frac{\partial H}{\partial p_n}=\frac{cp_n}{\sqrt{m^2c^2+\sum_1^3 p_n^2}}=\frac{p_n}{m}\sqrt{1-\beta^2}, \quad (49)$$

where the suffixes 1, 2, 3 are to be identified with x, y, z respectively. The equations $\frac{dq_n}{dt}=\frac{\partial H}{\partial p_n}$ are again identically satisfied in this case, since we have :

$$\frac{dx}{dt}=v_x=\frac{p_x}{m}\sqrt{1-\beta^2}, \text{ etc.} \quad . \quad . \quad (50)$$

The equations $\frac{dp_n}{dt}=-\frac{\partial H}{\partial q_n}$ give the equations of motion of the dynamics of Einstein's theory :

$$\frac{d}{dt}\left[\frac{mv_x}{\sqrt{1-\beta^2}}\right]=-\frac{\partial F}{\partial x}, \text{ etc.} \quad . \quad . \quad (51)$$

6. Contact Transformations

Hamilton's equations are expressed in terms of seven variables, the time t, the three co-ordinates q_n, and the three momenta p_n. Let the variables q_n and p_n be replaced by new variables α_n and $\beta_n (n = 1, 2, 3)$, defined by relations such as :

$$\alpha_n=f_n(p, q, t), \quad \beta_n=\phi_n(p, q, t). \quad . \quad . \quad (52)$$

We do not at present attribute any particular dynamical significance to the α's and β's, they are merely six new variables. The relations (52) may be written :

$$p_n=F_n(\alpha, q, t), \quad \beta_n=\Phi_n(\alpha, q, t). \quad . \quad . \quad (53)$$

We may then obtain the theorem that if it is possible to find a function $S(\alpha, q, t)$ such that:

$$\sum_{n=1}^{n=3} p_n dq_n - \sum_{n=1}^{n=3} \beta_n d\alpha_n = -(dS)_t, \quad . \quad . \quad (54)$$

where $(dS)_t$ denotes a variation in which t is constant, then the variables α and β satisfy the canonical equations:

$$\frac{d\alpha_n}{dt} = \frac{\partial K}{\partial \beta_n}, \quad \frac{d\beta_n}{dt} = -\frac{\partial K}{\partial \alpha_n} \quad (n = 1, 2, 3) \quad . \quad (55)$$

where $K = H - \frac{\partial S}{\partial t}$.

In order to prove this, we note that

$$\frac{\partial S}{\partial \alpha_n} = \beta_n, \quad \frac{\partial S}{\partial q_n} = -p_n, \quad (dS)_t = dS - \frac{\partial S}{\partial t}dt \quad . \quad (56)$$

and in consequence, by (54),

$$\sum_{n=1}^{n=3} p_n dq_n - H\,dt = \sum_{n=1}^{n=3} \beta_n d\alpha_n - H\,dt - dS + \frac{\partial S}{\partial t}dt \quad (57)$$

$$= \sum_{n=1}^{n=3} \beta_n d\alpha_n - K\,dt - dS.$$

Let the initial and final positions be characterised by times t_0 and t_1 and by co-ordinates $(q_n)_0$ and $(q_n)_1$ respectively.

Consider space of four dimensions in which the co-ordinates are the four variables (q_n, t). Hamilton's principle shows that if the motion of the particle is represented in this space by a curve C joining M_0 with co-ordinates $(q_n)_0$, t and M_1 with co-ordinates $(q_n)_1$, t, the integral

$$\int_{M_0}^{M_1} \left(\sum_{n=1}^{n=3} p_n dq_n - H\,dt \right)$$

taken along this curve does not vary to the first order of small quantities if the curve is deformed while keeping M_0 and M_1 fixed. We have:

$$\int_{M_0}^{M_1} \delta\left(\sum_{n=1}^{n=3} p_n dq_n - H\,dt \right) = 0.$$

Let us consider also the four-dimensional space formed by the time and the three variables x_n. A curve Γ in this new space then corresponds to the curve C, for at each point of the latter there are definite values, not only of q_n and t, but also of p_n; in consequence, by (52), each point of C corresponds to a point of Γ. Let $(\alpha_n)_0$ at t_0, and $(\alpha_n)_1$ at t_1 be the co-ordinates of the extremities of Γ. When the curve C is varied with fixed extremities in order to apply Hamilton's principle, the curve Γ varies in consequence, but in general its extremities are not fixed, since the initial and final values of the p's are, in general, affected by the variation of C, and on this account a change occurs in $(\alpha_n)_0$ and $(\alpha_n)_1$.

Thus:

$$\int_{(q_n)_0}^{(q_n)_1} \delta\Big(\sum_{n=1}^{n=3} p_n dq_n - \mathrm{H}\,dt\Big) = \int_{(\alpha_n)_0}^{(\alpha_n)_1} \delta\Big(\sum_{n=1}^{n=3} \beta_n d\alpha_n - \mathrm{K}\,dt\Big) + \Big[\sum_{n=1}^{n=3} \beta_n \delta\alpha_n\Big]_0^1 - \delta\Big[\mathrm{S}\Big]_0^1 \quad (58)$$

since $\int_0^1 d\mathrm{S} = \Big[\mathrm{S}\Big]_0^1$, and since the q_0's and the q_1's are fixed, we have:

$$\delta\Big[\mathrm{S}\Big]_0^1 = \Big[\sum_{n=1}^{n=3} \frac{\partial \mathrm{S}}{\partial \alpha_n}\delta\alpha_n\Big]_0^1 \quad . \quad . \quad . \quad (59)$$

The last two terms of (58) cancel one another by (56) and (59), and finally:

$$\int_{(q_n)_0}^{(q_n)_1} \delta\Big(\sum_{n=1}^{n=3} p_n dq_n - \mathrm{H}\,dt\Big) = \int_{(\alpha_n)_0}^{(\alpha_n)_1} \delta\Big(\sum_{n=1}^{n=3} \beta_n d\alpha_n - \mathrm{K}\,dt\Big), \quad (60)$$

where the variation of the right-hand side is subject to the condition that the initial and final values of the α's are fixed. Since the left-hand side is zero by Hamilton's principle, the same is true of the right-hand side, and since the β's, α's, and the function K play the same part as the p's, q's and H, we conclude that the equations (55) are verified.

In short we may say that the change of variables expressed by (54), and known as a contact transformation, preserves the form of Hamilton's equations, provided that the original H is replaced by $\mathrm{K} = \mathrm{H} - \frac{\partial \mathrm{S}}{dt}$.

CHAPTER II

THE THEORY OF JACOBI

1. The Equation of Jacobi

THE theorem on contact transformations will enable us to obtain at once the Jacobian equation. Let it be supposed that we have found a contact transformation such that $K = 0$. Then the new canonical variables α_n and β_n will satisfy the Hamiltonian equations :

$$\frac{d\alpha_n}{dt} = 0, \quad \frac{d\beta_n}{dt} = 0. \quad (n = 1, 2, 3) \quad . \quad . \quad (1)$$

The α's and β's will thus be constants Now K is equal to $H - \frac{\partial S}{\partial t}$, and p_n to $-\frac{\partial S}{\partial q_n}$. Thus, by expressing the energy in

of the q's, p's and t, and by replacing p_n by $-\frac{\partial S}{\partial q_n}$, the

$K = 0$ is equivalent to :

$$H(q, -\frac{\partial S}{\partial q}, t) = \frac{\partial S}{\partial t}. \quad . \quad . \quad . \quad (2)$$

n in the partial derivatives of S is the

n integral of this equation is found

onstants, α_n, that is to say, the

nction $S(q_n, \alpha_n, t)$ will define a

variables q_n, p_n, t and the

$K = 0.$

W

$$\beta_n = \frac{\partial S}{\partial \alpha_n} = \text{constant.} \quad . \quad (3)$$

We may thus derive Jacobi's theorem that if it is possible to find a complete integral $S(q, \alpha, t)$ of the first order partial differential equation :

$$H(q, -\frac{\partial S}{\partial q}, t) = \frac{\partial S}{\partial t} \quad . \quad . \quad . \quad (4)$$

we shall have :

$$p_n = \frac{\partial S}{\partial q_n}, \quad \frac{\partial S}{\partial \alpha_n} = \beta_n. \quad . \quad . \quad . \quad (5)$$

The β's being three new constants, the equations (5), which define the six quantities q_n, p_n as functions of the time and the six constants α_n. β_n, give completely the motion of the particle.

2. Hamilton's Integral and Jacobi's Function

In the theory of contact transformations given above, the variables α_n, β_n are six variables, of which the dynamical significance is not defined. We can thus suppose that the α's are co-ordinates, the β's being the momenta. Since the α's are constants in the function $S(q, \alpha, t)$, we are naturally led to consider them as initial co-ordinates of the particle. In order to examine this in detail let us consider not a single particle but a cloud of identical particles, all situated in the same field of force and without mutual reactions. The motion of this cloud, taken altogether, represents a whole assembly of possible motions of the same particle in the given field. The motion of the cloud between the instant t_0 and the instant t has the effect of transforming the initial co-ordinates $(q_n)_0$ of the particles of the cloud at time t_0 to the final co-ordinates (q_n) at the instant t.

Let us now consider Hamilton's integral :

$$I = \int\left(\sum_{n=1}^{n=3} p_n dq_n - H\,dt\right)$$

along the trajectory of the particle from $(q_n)_0$ to q_n. It is a function of the co-ordinates q_n, $(q_n)_0$, and of the time which satisfies the equations :

$$\frac{\partial I}{\partial q_n} = p_n, \quad \frac{\partial I}{\partial (q_n)_0} = -(p_n)_0, \quad . \quad . \quad (6)$$

the quantities $(p_n)_0$ denoting the initial values of the p's. The function I with its sign changed thus defines a contact transformation between the variables q_n, p_n, and the variables $(q_n)_0$, $(p_n)_0$. Moreover, the function $S(q, (q)_0, t) = -I$ satisfies Jacobi's equation, for

$$S(q, (q)_0, t) = \int_0^1 \left(H\,dt - \sum_{n=1}^{n=3} p_n dq_n\right) \quad . \quad (7)$$

and consequently:

$$\frac{\partial S}{\partial t} = H(q, p, t), \quad \frac{\partial S}{\partial q_n} = -p_n, \quad . \quad (8)$$

thus:

$$\frac{\partial S}{\partial t} = H\left(q, -\frac{\partial S}{\partial q}, t\right) \quad . \quad . \quad . \quad (9)$$

According to Jacobi's theorem the co-ordinates $(q_n)_0$ must be constants in the course of the motion, which is in agreement with their character as initial values of the co-ordinates, and the quantities $(p_n)_0$ must therefore be constants; they are the initial momenta.

3. The Reduced Function of Jacobi

The α's are not necessarily the values of the initial co-ordinates. We can also find a complete integral depending upon the initial momenta, or even of other constants.

Whenever such an integral is found, we have:

$$p_n = -\frac{\partial S}{\partial q_n}, \quad \frac{\partial S}{\partial \alpha_n} = \beta_n = \text{constant} \quad . \quad (10)$$

and these equations will determine the motion.

A special case of importance is that of constant fields. In this case, as we have seen, the energy is constant. Denoting this constant by W, the Hamiltonian integral is

$$\int \left(\sum_{n=1}^{n=3} p_n dq_n - W\,dt\right),$$

and if we adopt for S this integral with the sign changed we have:

$$\frac{\partial S}{\partial t} = W.$$

Moreover, if we write :

$$S_1 = \int \sum_{n=1}^{n=3} p_n dq_n \qquad . \quad . \quad . \quad (11)$$

we have .

$$S = Wt - S_1, \; \frac{\partial S}{\partial q_n} = - \frac{\partial S_1}{\partial q_n} \qquad . \quad . \quad (12)$$

Finally, H does not contain the time explicitly, so that S_1, which we call the reduced function of Jacobi, satisfies the equation :

$$H\left(q, \frac{\partial S_1}{\partial q}\right) = W. \qquad . \quad . \quad . \quad (13)$$

If a complete integral, which will depend upon W and two arbitrary constants α_1 and α_2, be found for (13), the function $S = Wt - S_1(q, \alpha_1, \alpha_2, W)$ will be a complete integral with three arbitrary constants α_1, α_2, $\alpha_3 (= W)$ of the complete Jacobian equation, and from Jacobi's theorem we know that the motion is defined by the relations .

$$p_n = \frac{\partial S_1}{\partial q_n}, \quad \frac{\partial S_1}{\partial \alpha_1} = -\beta_1 = \text{constant}, \quad \frac{\partial S_1}{\partial \alpha_2} = -\beta_2 = \text{constant},$$

$$\frac{\partial S}{\partial W} = t - \frac{\partial S_1}{\partial W} = -\beta_3 = \text{constant}. \quad (14)$$

Let us write $\beta_3 = -t_0$, so that the last equation gives

$$\frac{\partial S_1}{\partial W} = t - t_0. \quad . \quad . \quad . \quad . \quad (15)$$

This equation, the only one that contains the time, gives the law of motion, while the two equations : $\frac{\partial S_1}{\partial \alpha_1} =$ const. and $\frac{\partial S_1}{\partial \alpha_2} =$ const. depend upon the q's, and define the form of the trajectory. Here we find the separation of the study of the motion and the study of the trajectory which is characteristic of constant fields.

4. Different Forms of Jacobi's Equation

Before studying concrete examples, we will consider in detail the form that Jacobi's equation takes in classical mechanics and in the mechanics of Einstein, taking the classical case first For the sake of generality we suppose the co-ordinates chosen are of any kind whatsoever. In classical mechanics the kinetic energy T is a homogeneous quadratic function of the velocities $\dot{q}$.

Thus :

$$T = \tfrac{1}{2}\sum m_{kl}\dot{q}_k\dot{q}_l, \qquad . \quad . \quad . \quad (16)$$

where the summation is actually double and extends over the values (1, 2, 3) for k and l, and where $m_{kl} = m_{lk}$, these being functions of the q's only From (16) we deduce :

$$L = T - F = \tfrac{1}{2}\sum m_{kl}\dot{q}_k\dot{q}_l - F(q, t) \quad . \quad . \quad (17)$$

$$W = T + F = \tfrac{1}{2}\sum m_{kl}\dot{q}_k\dot{q}_l + F(q, t) \quad . \quad . \quad (18)$$

By definition :

$$p_n = \frac{\partial L}{\partial \dot{q}_n} = \sum_{k=1}^{k=3} m_{kn}\dot{q}_k. \quad (n = 1, 2, 3) \quad . \quad (19)$$

If we solve the linear equations (19) with respect to the $\dot{q}$'s, we find :

$$\dot{q}_n = \sum_{k=1}^{k=3} \frac{M_{kn}}{|m_{kl}|} p_k \quad (n = 1, 2, 3) \quad . \quad . \quad (20)$$

where $|m_{kl}|$ denotes the determinant formed by the co-efficients m_{kl}, and where M_{kn} denotes the minor correspondng to the element m_{kn} of this determinant.

Let us write
$$\frac{M_{kn}}{|m_{kl}|} = m^{kn},$$

so that :

$$\dot{q}_n = \sum_{k=1}^{k=3} m^{kn} p_k \quad (n = 1, 2, 3) \quad . \quad . \quad (21)$$

Replacing the $\dot{q}$'s by the values (21), and substituting in (16) we find :

$$T = \tfrac{1}{2}\sum m_{kl} m^{kn} p_n m^{lr} p_r, \quad . \quad . \quad . \quad (22)$$

where the summation is to be made over the values (1, 2, 3) for k, l, n and r. By the properties of determinants :

$$\sum_{k=1}^{k=3} m_{kl} m^{kn} = \sum_{k=1}^{k=3} m_{kl} \frac{M_{kn}}{|m_{kl}|} = 1 \text{ or } 0, \quad . \tag{23}$$

according as $l = n$ or $l \neq n$.

Thus:

$$T = \tfrac{1}{2} \sum m^{lr} p_l p_r, \quad . \quad . \quad . \tag{24}$$

where, again, the summation is a double one over l and r.

Consequently the energy expressed as a function of the q's, p's and t is:

$$H(q, p, t) = \tfrac{1}{2} \sum m^{lr} p_l p_r + F(q, t). \quad . \quad . \tag{25}$$

We then obtain for Jacobi's equation:

$$\frac{\partial S}{\partial t} = \frac{1}{2} \sum m^{lr} \frac{\partial S}{\partial q_l} \frac{\partial S}{\partial q_r} + F(q, t). \quad . \quad . \tag{26}$$

In the special case of rectangular co-ordinates we have:

$$T = \tfrac{1}{2} m(\dot{x}^2 + \dot{y}^2 + z^2) \quad . \quad . \quad . \tag{27}$$

so that:

$$m_{kk} = m, \quad m_{kl} = 0, \quad \text{when } k \neq l.$$

Hence:

$$m^{kk} = \frac{1}{m}, \quad m^{kl} = 0, \quad \text{for } k \neq l, \quad . \quad . \tag{28}$$

and Jacobi's equation takes the simple classical form:

$$\frac{\partial S}{\partial t} = \frac{1}{2m} \left[\left(\frac{\partial S}{\partial x} \right)^2 + \left(\frac{\partial S}{\partial y} \right)^2 + \left(\frac{\partial S}{\partial z} \right)^2 \right] + F(x, y, z, t) \tag{29}$$

Let us now pass to the dynamics of relativity. As we shall not make many applications of these dynamics in this work we will limit ourselves to the case of rectangular co-ordinates. We have found (Chap. I (48)):

$$H(q, p, t) = c\sqrt{m^2c^2 + p_x^2 + p_y^2 + p_z^2} + F(x, y, z, t). \tag{30}$$

This expression for H leads to the relativity equation of Jacobi:

$$\frac{\partial S}{\partial t} = c\sqrt{m^2c^2 + \left(\frac{\partial S}{\partial x} \right)^2 + \left(\frac{\partial S}{\partial y} \right)^2 + \left(\frac{\partial S}{\partial z} \right)^2} + F(x, y, z, t), \tag{31}$$

$$\frac{1}{c^2} \left(\frac{\partial S}{\partial t} - F \right)^2 - \left(\frac{\partial S}{\partial x} \right)^2 - \left(\frac{\partial S}{\partial y} \right)^2 - \left(\frac{\partial S}{\partial z} \right)^2 = m^2c^2. \tag{32}$$

5. Jacobi's Function in the case of Uniform Rectilinear Motion

We proceed to find the form of Jacobi's function in two simple and important cases, which will be useful later on. We will content ourselves with classical dynamics and begin with the case of the uniform rectilinear motion of a particle in the absence of a field. Thus $\mathrm{F} = 0$ and equation (29) becomes :

$$\frac{1}{2m}\left[\left(\frac{\partial S}{\partial x}\right)^2 + \left(\frac{\partial S}{\partial y}\right)^2 + \left(\frac{\partial S}{\partial z}\right)^2\right] = \frac{\partial S}{\partial t}. \quad . \quad (33)$$

It is easy to verify that a complete integral is given by :

$$S(x, y, z, x_0, y_0, z_0, t) = -\frac{m}{2t}[(x - x_0)^2 + (y - y_0)^2 + (z - z_0)^2]. \quad (34)$$

By Jacobi's theorem we have :

$$p_x = -\frac{\partial S}{\partial x} = \frac{m}{t}(x - x_0) \quad . \quad . \quad . \quad (35)$$

and

$$\frac{\partial S}{\partial x_0} = \frac{m}{t}(x - x_0) = \text{constant}, \quad . \quad . \quad (36)$$

with similar equations in y and z.

The constants occurring are thus equal to the constant values of p_x, p_y, p_z and the equations of the motion take the well-known form :

$$x = x_0 + v_x t, \quad y = y_0 + v_y t, \quad z = z_0 + v_z t. \quad . \quad (37)$$

It appears that the three arbitrary constants x_0, y_0, z_0 of the complete integral are in this case the three co-ordinates of the particle at $t = 0$. The integral (34) is simply Hamilton's integral with the sign changed. We can, in fact, write Hamilton's integral in the form :

$$\int_0^t \mathrm{T}\,dt = \int_0^t \tfrac{1}{2}mv^2 dt = \tfrac{1}{2}mv^2 t \quad . \quad . \quad (38)$$

Now, since the motion is uniform,

$$v_x = \frac{x - x_0}{t}, \quad v_y = \frac{y - y_0}{t}, \quad v_z = \frac{z - z_0}{t} \quad . \quad (39)$$

and

$$v^2 = v_x^2 + v_y^2 + v_z^2 = \frac{1}{t^2}[(x - x_0)^2 + (y - y_0)^2 + (z - z_0)^2]. \quad (40)$$

It thus appears that Hamilton's integral is exactly (34) with the opposite sign.

In the case of no field we can also find a complete integral of Jacobi's equation where the arbitrary constants are the three momenta, which are in this case constant, instead of the three initial co-ordinates. This complete integral is ·

$$S(x, y, z, t, p_x, p_y, p_z) = \frac{1}{2m}(p_x^2 + p_y^2 + p_z^2)t - p_x x - p_y y - p_z z. \quad (41)$$

The equations $\frac{\partial S}{\partial x} = p_x$, etc., are identically satisfied. The other three Jacobian relations are :

$$\frac{\partial S}{\partial p_x} = \frac{1}{m}p_x t - x = \text{constant}, \quad . \quad . \quad (42)$$

together with the equations in y and z.

If we denote the three constants by $-x_0$, $-y_0$, $-z_0$, we obtain again the equations of motion (37) The solution (41) may be derived also from Hamilton's integral, since for the latter, except for an additive constant, we have in this case :

$$p_x x + p_y y + p_z z - Wt.$$

Since

$$p_x = mv_x, \quad p_y = mv_y, \quad p_z = mv_z,$$

and

$$W = \frac{1}{2}mv^2 = \frac{1}{2m}(p_x^2 + p_y^2 + p_z^2),$$

Hamilton's integral with change of sign gives (41).

Finally, we have seen that in constant fields, where the field alone plays a dominant part, we could write Jacobi's function in the form $Wt - S_1(x, y, z, \alpha_1, \alpha_2, W)$, S_1 being an integral of equation (13). In order to put the function in this form we shall note that it is possible to express one of the momenta, for example p_z, in terms of W and the other two, since

$$p_z^2 = 2mW - p_x^2 - p_y^2. \quad . \quad . \quad . \quad (43)$$

By substituting this value of p_z into Hamilton's integral with the sign changed, we obtain :

$$S(x, y, z, t, W, p_x, p_y) = Wt - p_x x - p_y y - z\sqrt{2mW - p_x^2 - p_y^2} \quad (44)$$

and

$$S_1(x, y, z, p_x, p_y, W) = p_x x + p_y y + z\sqrt{2mW - p_x^2 - p_y^2}. \quad (45)$$

The equations of motion (14) and (15) give :

$$\left.\begin{aligned} &\frac{\partial S_1}{\partial p_x} = x - \frac{p_x z}{\sqrt{2mW - p_x^2 - p_y^2}} = \text{constant, with a similar equation in } y, \\ &\text{and} \\ &\frac{\partial S_1}{\partial W} = \frac{mz}{\sqrt{2mW - p_x^2 - p_y^2}} = t - t_0 \end{aligned}\right\} \quad (46)$$

The first two give the rectilinear trajectories defined by

$$\frac{x - x_0}{p_x} = \frac{y - y_0}{p_y} = \frac{z - z_0}{p_z}. \quad . \quad . \quad . \quad (47)$$

The third equation of (46) defines the motion on the trajectory, i.e. it gives z as a function of t :

$$z = \frac{t - t_0}{m}\sqrt{2mW - p_x^2 - p_y^2} = \frac{p_z}{m}(t - t_0), \quad . \quad (48)$$

where t_0 evidently denotes the time corresponding to $y = 0$.

6. Jacobi's Function in a Uniform Constant Field

Let us now take the case which, after that of no field, is next in order of simplicity. This is the case where a uniform constant field exists. Let k_x, k_y, k_z, denote the force components, which have the same values everywhere.
Then

$$F(x, y, z) = -\sum k_x x, \quad . \quad . \quad . \quad (49)$$

since $f_x = -\dfrac{\partial F}{\partial x} = k_x$, and there are similar equations in y and z.

Jacobi's equation in this case is :

$$\frac{1}{2m}\left[\left(\frac{\partial S}{\partial x}\right)^2 + \left(\frac{\partial S}{\partial y}\right)^2 + \left(\frac{\partial S}{\partial z}\right)^2\right] - \sum k_x x = \frac{\partial S}{\partial t} \quad . \quad . \quad (50)$$

The following is a complete integral of this equation :

$$S(x, y, z, t, x_0, y_0, z_0) =$$
$$-\frac{m}{2t}\sum(x - x_0)^2 - \frac{1}{2}t\sum k_x(x + x_0) + \frac{1}{24m}t^3\sum k_x^2. \quad (51)$$

It is easy to verify this solution by substitution, and we find, from the equations of Jacobi's theory,

$$p_x = -\frac{\partial S}{\partial x} = \frac{m}{t}(x - x_0) + \frac{1}{2}k_x t \quad . \quad . \quad (52)$$

together with similar equations in y and z.

These equations may be verified, since in the case of uniformly-accelerated motion we have :

$$x = x_0 + v_{0x}t + \frac{1}{2}\frac{k_x}{m}t^2 \quad . \quad . \quad . \quad (53)$$

and

$$v_x = v_{0x} + \frac{k_x}{m}t, \quad . \quad . \quad . \quad (54)$$

again with similar equations in y and z.

From these :

$$p_x = mv_x = \frac{m}{t}(x - x_0) + \frac{1}{2}k_x t,$$

which is the same as (52).

The other three relations : $\frac{\partial S}{\partial \alpha_n}$ = constant, are in this particular case :

$$\frac{\partial S}{\partial x_0} = \frac{m}{t}(x - x_0) - \frac{1}{2}k_x t = \text{constant} \quad . \quad . \quad (55)$$

and the similar equations in y and z.

If x_0, y_0, z_0 are initial co-ordinates, $\frac{\partial S}{\partial x_0}, \frac{\partial S}{\partial y_0}, \frac{\partial S}{\partial z_0}$ r the initial momenta $mv_{0x}, mv_{0y}, mv_{0z}$, and we obtair dx equations (53) for uniformly-accelerated motion. $, -p_z^2\}^{\frac{1}{2}}$. (68)

We will now show that the complete integral (51) can be obtained from Hamilton's integral. The latter, with a change of sign, is in fact :

$$\int(\mathrm{W}dt - \sum p_x dx) = \int[(\tfrac{1}{2}mv^2 - \sum k_x x)dt - \sum mv_x dx] \qquad (56)$$

where the integration extends from the initial to the final time and position.

But the formulæ (53) and (54) for uniformly accelerated motion give :

$$v^2 = v_x^2 + v_y^2 + v_z^2 = \sum\left(\frac{x - x_0}{t} + \frac{1}{2}\frac{k_x}{m}t\right)^2 \quad . \quad (57)$$

and substituting in (56) we find, for the right-hand side ·

$$\int\left[\left\{\tfrac{1}{2}m\sum\left(\frac{x - x_0}{t} + \frac{1}{2}\frac{k_x}{m}t\right)^2 - \sum k_x x\right\}dt - \sum m\left(\frac{x - x_0}{t} + \frac{1}{2}\frac{k_x}{m}t\right)dx\right]. \quad (58)$$

We note that the coefficient of dt when partially differentiated with respect to x gives the result obtained by differentiating the coefficient of dx partially with respect to t, and a similar remark is true for those of dy and dz. Thus the quantity under the sign of integration is a perfect differential. On evaluating the integral, we find that it has the value (51) so that, except for the sign, (51) is equal in this case also to Hamilton's integral.

As in the case of uniform motion, we can obtain a complete integral of Jacobi's equation, in which the three arbitrary constants are the initial momenta instead of the initial co-ordinates. These initial momenta are :

$$p_{0x} = mv_{0x}, \quad p_{0y} = mv_{0y}, \quad p_{0z} = mv_{0z}. \quad . \quad (59)$$

n 'f we again change the sign of Hamilton's integral and make coı e of the equations (54), we obtain .

ponε Then $$\int\left[\left\{\frac{1}{2m}\sum(p_{0x} + k_x t)^2 - \sum k_x x\right\}dt - \sum(p_{0x} + k_x t)dx\right]. \quad (60)$$

condition of integrability is verified at once, since :

since $f_x = -$ $$\ldots_{0x} + k_x t)^2 - \sum k_x x\right\} = -k_x = -\frac{\partial}{\partial t}(p_{0x} + k_x t) \quad (61)$$

with similar equations in y and z, and the integral (60) has the value :

$$S(x, y, z, t, p_{0x}, p_{0y}, p_{0z}) = \frac{1}{6m}\sum\frac{(p_{0x} + k_x t)^3}{k_x} - \sum(p_{0x} + k_x t)x \quad (62)$$

We may easily verify a result which follows from the second paragraph of this chapter, i e that the function (62) satisfies Jacobi's equation (50). The equations $p_n = \frac{\partial S}{\partial q_n}$ are identically satisfied, because of the manner in which (62) was obtained. The equations $\frac{\partial S}{\partial \alpha_n}$ = constant give :

$$\frac{\partial S}{\partial p_{0x}} = \frac{1}{2m}\frac{(p_{0x} + k_x t)^2}{k_x} - x, \quad . \quad . \quad (63)$$

with the equations in y and z.

Since $\frac{p_{0x}^2}{2mk_x}, \frac{p_{0y}^2}{2mk_y}, \frac{p_{0z}^2}{2mk_z}$ are constants, we can also write :

$$x = \frac{p_{0x}}{m}t + \frac{1}{2}\frac{k_x}{m}t^2 + \text{constant}, \quad . \quad . \quad (64)$$

and similar expressions for y and z, and obtain again the classical equations (53). Finally, we seek a complete integral of (50) having the form :

$$S(x, y, z, t, \alpha_1, \alpha_2, W) = Wt - S_1(x, y, z, \alpha_1, \alpha_2, W), \quad (65)$$

which we know is possible, since the field is constant in time. We shall obtain this function by once more calculating Hamilton's integral and changing the sign, but to simplify the calculations we will take the direction of the uniform field as the axis of x. Then $k_y = k_z = 0$, and the momenta p_y and p_z are constant. The energy expression

$$W = \frac{1}{2m}(p_x^2 + p_y^2 + p_z^2) - k_x x, \quad . \quad . \quad (66)$$

gives us :

$$p_x = \sqrt{2m(W + k_x x) - p_y^2 - p_z^2}, \quad . \quad . \quad (67)$$

and consequently the negative Hamilton integral is :

$$\begin{aligned} Wt &- \int(p_x dx + p_y dy + p_z dz) \\ &= Wt - p_y y - p_z z - \int\sqrt{2m(W + k_x x) - p_y^2 - p_z^2}\,dx \\ &= Wt - p_y y - p_z z - \frac{1}{3mk_x}\{2m(W + k_x x) - p_y^2 - p_z^2\}^{\frac{3}{2}}. \quad (68) \end{aligned}$$

By equating this to (65) we deduce ·

$$S_1(x, y, z, \alpha_1, \alpha_2, W) = p_y y + p_z z + \frac{1}{3mk_x}\{2m(W + k_x x) - p_y^2 - p_z^2\}^{\frac{3}{2}}, \quad (69)$$

where

$$p_y = \alpha_1, \quad p_z = \alpha_2$$

The other expressions of the theory give ·

$$\frac{\partial S_1}{\partial p_y} = y - \frac{p_y}{mk_x}\sqrt{2m(W + k_x x) - p_y^2 - p_z^2} = \text{constant}, \quad (70)$$

and a similar expression for $\frac{\partial S_1}{\partial p_z}$. These define the trajectory, which in this case is a parabola.

Also

$$\frac{\partial S_1}{\partial W} = \frac{1}{k_x}\sqrt{2m(W + k_x x) - p_y^2 - p_z^2} = t - t_0, \quad . \quad (71)$$

or

$$p_x = k_x(t - t_0) \equiv k_x t + p_{0x}, \quad . \quad . \quad (72)$$

where p_{0x} denotes the initial value of p_x, and the equation gives the well-known relation between the velocity and time (cf. 54).

CHAPTER III

THE CONCEPTIONS UNDERLYING WAVE MECHANICS

1. The Point of Departure

THE point of departure in wave mechanics was the wish always to associate the idea of a particle with that of periodicity in such a way as to bind inseparably the idea of the motion of a particle with that of wave propagation.

We shall first examine the simplest case, that of a corpuscle moving freely outside any field of force, and we shall see that the connection to be established between wave and particle is then in some measure imposed by the fundamental principles of relativity.

We remind ourselves in the first place that a Galilean system of axes is a rectangular system at rest or in uniform rectilinear motion with respect to the fixed stars ; it is for systems of this kind that the equations of dynamics are valid. The principle of inertia, which is of the nature of a definition in disguise, teaches that if a particle is subject to no forces it is necessarily at rest or in uniform rectilinear motion in a Galilean system.

Of the infinite number of Galilean systems let us consider two in particular. The first with respect to which the particle possesses the velocity v ($= \beta c$) is so oriented that the particle describes the axis of z. The second, called the " proper system " of the particle, moves with respect to the first with the velocity $\mathbf{v}$ in magnitude and direction, and its z axis slides over that of the first system. We will denote by x_0, y_0, z_0 the co-ordinates of a point in the proper system, while x, y, z denote those of the point in the second system.

Before Einstein's theory came into being the existence of an absolute time was accepted with the property that an observer bound to the system (x, y, z) was supposed to make use of the same time co-ordinate as an observer bound to the proper system. The variables of space and time were therefore supposed to be related by the Galilean group of formulæ :

$$x = x_0, \quad y = y_0, \quad z = z_0 + vt, \quad t = t_0. \qquad (1)$$

The profound researches of Einstein have led us to think that it is necessary to substitute instead of (1) the following Lorentz group :

$$x = x_0, \quad y = y_0, \quad z = \frac{z_0 + vt_0}{\sqrt{1-\beta^2}}, \quad t = \frac{t_0 + \frac{\beta}{c}z_0}{\sqrt{1-\beta^2}}, \qquad (2)$$

from which we deduce inversely :

$$x_0 = x, \quad y_0 = y, \quad z_0 = \frac{z - vt}{\sqrt{1-\beta^2}}, \quad t_0 = \frac{t - \frac{\beta}{c}z}{\sqrt{1-\beta^2}}. \qquad (3)$$

We shall adopt the formulæ (2) and (3) without entering here into any further discussion of the ideas of the theory of relativity, which would be out of place in the present work.

Let us place ourselves in the system of reference (x_0, y_0, z_0) which is bound to the particle. Since it is our aim to associate a wave with the particle, it is quite natural to suppose that this wave has the form of a stationary wave in the proper system, that is to say, that its mathematical expression depends only on the time through a factor $\cos 2\pi\nu_0(t_0 - \tau_0)$, and we can place $\tau_0 = 0$, since this depends only upon a convenient choice of the origin in time. We shall describe the constant ν_0 by the term " proper frequency " of the particle.

Let us now change our point of view by placing ourselves in the system (x, y, z) with respect to which the particle has the velocity βc along the z-axis. The essential point is to determine what will be the form of the wave associated with the particle in the system (x, y, z). In the proper system the phase factor was $\cos 2\pi\nu_0 t_0$, so that according to the last of equations (3) in the system (x, y, z) it will be $\cos 2\pi\nu_0 \frac{t - \frac{\beta}{c}z}{\sqrt{1-\beta^2}}$.

Let us write :

$$\nu = \frac{\nu_0}{\sqrt{1-\beta^2}}, \quad V = \frac{c}{\beta} = \frac{c^2}{v}, \qquad (4)$$

so that the phase factor is $\cos 2\pi\nu\left(t - \frac{z}{V}\right)$. The wave will thus appear to the observer of the system (x, y, z) as a wave of frequency ν propagated along the axis of z with phase velocity V. This appears as a simple direct consequence of the way in which the time variable is transformed according to the theory of relativity in passing from one Galilean system to another.

The phase velocity of the wave associated with the particle is inversely proportional to the velocity of the particle itself; it is infinite in the proper system where the particle velocity is zero. We have already remarked that according to the dynamics of relativity a particle can never be made to move with a velocity greater than that of light; we have always:

$$\beta < 1, \quad V > c. \qquad \qquad (5)$$

The sign of equality cannot apply except when the mass is zero, which is the case when the particles are light corpuscles. We shall return to this point later.

2. An Alternative Method of Obtaining the Preceding Results

The foregoing results with regard to the phase of the associated wave may also be obtained by the use of a rather more concrete method which gives precision to certain points.

Since the wave has by hypothesis the same frequency and phase at each point of the proper system, we can represent the phase distribution by imagining that synchronous clocks of period, $T_0 = \frac{1}{\nu_0}$, are situated at all points of the system. In the system (x, y, z) each of these clocks will be moving with velocity βc, and will be subject to the relativity retardation. This retardation arises because the clock has a co-ordinate z_0 fixed in the proper system, but in the system (x, y, z) its z co-ordinate increases by vt in time t. Thus the variation of t_0 recorded by the clock is connected with the variation of t by the fourth of Lorentz's formulæ:

$$\delta t_0 = \frac{\delta t - \frac{\beta}{c}\delta z}{\sqrt{1-\beta^2}} = \frac{\delta t(1-\beta^2)}{\sqrt{1-\beta^2}} = \delta t\sqrt{1-\beta^2}. \qquad (6)$$

When the clock has completed an oscillation, the lapse of time is $\delta t_0 = T_0$ in the proper system, and consequently in the system (x, y, z) the interval is measured by :

$$T_1 = \frac{T_0}{\sqrt{1 - \beta^2}} > T_0. \quad . \quad . \quad . \quad (7)$$

The observer in the latter system attributes to the clock a longer period than that recorded by an observer in the system bound to the clock. This explains the relativity retardation

Let us pass from periods to frequencies. Each clock has a frequency :

$$\nu_1 = \frac{1}{T_1} = \nu_0\sqrt{1 - \beta^2} < \nu_0, \quad . \quad . \quad (8)$$

but at the same time it is in motion with velocity v.

We shall see that in this motion it remains constantly in phase with the wave :

$$\psi = a \cos 2\pi\nu\left(t - \frac{z}{V}\right) \quad . \quad . \quad (9)$$

To show this, let us suppose that at a certain instant when $t = t_1$ the clock agrees in phase with the wave ψ, as judged by an observer in the system (x, y, z).

Then :

$$2\pi\nu\left(t_1 - \frac{z_1}{V}\right) = 2\pi\nu_1 t_1, \quad . \quad . \quad . \quad (10)$$

where z_1 is the value of z at time t_1. At a later time t_2 the clock occupies the position $z_2 = z_1 + v(t_2 - t_1)$, so that the phase of the wave at this point is $2\pi\nu\left(t_2 - \frac{z_2}{V}\right)$, while the phase of the clock is $2\pi\nu_1 t_2$. In order that the agreement in phase may persist, it is necessary that

$$\nu_1 t_2 = \nu\left(t_2 - \frac{z_2}{V}\right), \quad . \quad . \quad . \quad (11)$$

which by (10) may be written :

$$\nu_1(t_2 - t_1) = \nu(t_2 - t_1) - \frac{\nu}{V}(z_2 - z_1)$$

$$= \nu\left(1 - \frac{v}{V}\right)(t_2 - t_1), \quad . \quad . \quad (12)$$

or

$$\nu_1 = \nu(1 - \beta^2). \quad . \quad . \quad . \quad . \quad (13)$$

But this equation is identically satisfied on account of the definitions of ν and ν_1 in equations (4) and (8).

3. Refractive Index. Fundamental Theorem on the Group-Velocity of the ψ-waves

The phase velocity V may be used to define an index of refraction for the ψ-waves in the system (x, y, z). We define this index by the usual relation :

$$n = \frac{c}{V}, \quad . \quad . \quad . \quad . \quad (14)$$

which gives by (4)

$$n = \beta. \quad . \quad . \quad . \quad . \quad (15)$$

Thus, by substituting (15) in the first of the formulæ (4)

$$n = \sqrt{1 - \frac{\nu_0^2}{\nu^2}}. \quad . \quad . \quad . \quad (16)$$

This formula may be considered as defining the dispersion of space for the ψ-waves associated with a particle the nature of which is characterised by the constant ν_0. In other words, if we consider the assembly of possible uniform rectilinear motions of the particle in the system (x, y, z), the frequency and phase velocity of the associated wave are always connected by the equation (16).

The dispersion formula just established leads to a very important theorem, but before stating it we must consider the meaning of the term "group velocity," which was introduced by Lord Rayleigh in connection with the propagation of waves in a dispersive medium. A plane monochromatic wave of frequency ν which is propagated in a certain direction, which we may take along the axis of x, is represented by the function $a \cos 2\pi\nu\left(t - \frac{nx}{c}\right)$, where n is the refractive index of the medium for the frequency ν. Instead of a single plane monochromatic wave, let us consider a very large number of waves of this kind travelling along the axis of x with frequencies lying in the small range $\nu - \delta\nu$ to $\nu + \delta\nu$; this is what is called a group of waves. An element of the group may be represented by :

$$a_{\nu+\epsilon}d\epsilon \cos 2\pi(\nu + \epsilon)\left\{t - n_{\nu+\epsilon}\frac{x}{c} + b_\epsilon\right\}, \quad |\epsilon| < \delta\nu,$$

where b_ϵ is a phase constant. If at a certain instant all the members of the group agree in phase at a certain point there will be a high resultant amplitude at the point As the medium is dispersive, which means that the phase velocities differ slightly for the various waves of the group, the waves will get out of step with one another during the propagation. We shall, however, show that a point where there is agreement of phase exists, which travels with a velocity in general different from the phase velocity.

Let there be two waves of the group characterised by the values ϵ_1 and ϵ_2. According to our assumption, the two waves agree in phase for a certain value of x and for a certain value of t. Let x and t change by amounts dx and dt respectively, so that the phase of the first wave changes by

$$2\pi(\nu + \epsilon_1)\left(dt - n_{\nu+\epsilon_1}\frac{dx}{c}\right).$$

Since ϵ_1 is very small, we may write :

$$n_{\nu+\epsilon_1} = n_\nu + \frac{dn_\nu}{d\nu}\epsilon_1, \quad . \quad . \quad . \quad (17)$$

provided that n is continuous. Thus if we neglect quantities of the second order the change in phase in the first wave is :

$$2\pi\left\{(\nu + \epsilon_1)dt - (\nu + \epsilon_1)n_\nu\frac{dx}{c} - \nu\epsilon_1\frac{dn_\nu}{d\nu} \cdot \frac{dx}{c}\right\}.$$

There is, of course, a similar expression in ϵ_2 for the second wave.

The difference of the two phase changes is :

$$2\pi(\epsilon_2 - \epsilon_1)\left(dt - n_\nu\frac{dx}{c}\right) - 2\pi(\epsilon_2 - \epsilon_1)\nu\frac{dn_\nu}{d\nu} \cdot \frac{dx}{c} \quad . \quad (18)$$

so that if dt and dx satisfy the relation :

$$dt = \left(n_\nu + \nu\frac{dn}{d\nu}\right)\frac{dx}{c}, \quad . \quad . \quad . \quad (19)$$

the two waves are still in phase.

This equation defines a velocity U given by :

$$\frac{1}{U} = \left(\frac{dx}{dt}\right)^{-1} = \frac{1}{c}\left(n_\nu + \nu\frac{dn_\nu}{d\nu}\right) = \frac{1}{c}\frac{d}{d\nu}(n_\nu \nu). \quad . \quad (20)$$

If we travel along the axis of x with velocity U, we see the two waves always in phase. But ϵ_1 and ϵ_2 are arbitrary, and our reasoning holds for all pairs of waves in the group. Thus if we travel with velocity U along the axis all the waves are seen in phase, in other words, the maximum which arises as a consequence of this agreement in phase travels along the axis with velocity U, which we describe as the group velocity.

We proceed to establish the theorem that the group velocity of the associated waves of a particle is equal to the velocity of the particle.

The equation of dispersion (16) gives,

$$n\nu = \sqrt{\nu^2 - \nu_0{}^2}, \quad . \quad . \quad (21)$$

and

$$\frac{d}{d\nu}(n\nu) = \frac{\nu}{\sqrt{\nu^2 - \nu_0{}^2}} = \frac{1}{n} \quad . \quad . \quad (22)$$

Thus, from (15) and (20),

$$U = nc = \beta c. \quad . \quad . \quad . \quad . \quad (23)$$

4. Relations Between Wave and Mechanical Quantities

Hitherto we have introduced no relation between the mechanical quantities, mass, momentum and energy, which are characteristic of the particle and the characteristics of the wave, frequency, phase velocity and index of refraction Yet if we wish the associated waves to be of use to us in the inclusion of quanta, such relations must exist and, in particular, we must expect to find the energy W of the particle and the frequency ν of its associated wave related by the formula ·

$$W = h\nu, \quad . \quad . \quad . \quad . \quad (24)$$

where h is Planck's constant, which is a relation which forms the starting point of the quantum theory.

By the theory of relativity the value of the energy of the particle is :

$$W = \frac{mc^2}{\sqrt{1-\beta^2}} \quad . \quad . \quad . \quad (25)$$

in the system (x, y, z). In the proper system its value is

$$W_0 = mc^2, \quad . \quad . \quad . \quad . \quad . \quad (26)$$

whence

$$W = \frac{W_0}{\sqrt{1-\beta^2}}. \quad . \quad . \quad . \quad . \quad (27)$$

This formula, giving the transformation from W_0 to W, is thus the same as (4) which transforms ν_0 to ν. Since this similarity in the transformations in the Galilean systems exists, we are justified in adopting the relation :

$$W = h\nu \quad . \quad . \quad . \quad (28)$$

between the energy of the particle and the frequency of the associated wave, where h is a constant of proportionality, which is naturally taken to be Planck's constant.

We pass to consider the momentum which is a vector tangential to the trajectory, and has the value,

$$\mathbf{p} = \frac{m\mathbf{v}}{\sqrt{1-\beta^2}}, \quad . \quad . \quad . \quad . \quad (29)$$

in the dynamics of relativity.

From (25) and (29) it appears that the magnitude of this vector is :

$$|p| = \frac{W}{c^2}v. \quad . \quad . \quad . \quad . \quad . \quad (30)$$

If we replace W by $h\nu$ and $\frac{c^2}{v}$ by V, we see that it is possible to describe momentum as a vector in the direction of the phase velocity of magnitude :

$$|p| = \frac{h\nu}{V} = \frac{h\nu}{c}n. \quad . \quad . \quad . \quad . \quad (31)$$

It is of interest to introduce also at this point the wave length, λ, of the associated wave, by writing as usual :

$$\lambda = \frac{V}{\nu}. \quad . \quad . \quad . \quad . \quad . \quad (32)$$

Formula (31) gives :

$$|p| = \frac{h}{\lambda}. \quad . \quad . \quad . \quad . \quad . \quad (33)$$

5. The Principle of Least Action and Fermat's Principle

We may sum up these points by saying that a particle of mass m, moving in a certain direction with velocity v $(=\beta c)$, must be associated with a wave of frequency $\nu = \frac{mc^2}{h\sqrt{1-\beta^2}}$, travelling in the same direction with phase velocity $V\left(=\frac{c^2}{v}\right)$. The wave length is:

$$\lambda = \frac{h}{p} = \frac{h\sqrt{1-\beta^2}}{mv},$$

and the group velocity is v.

When β^2 is negligible with respect to unity, as in Newtonian mechanics, it is sufficient to write:

$$\nu = mc^2 + \tfrac{1}{2}mv^2 \quad \text{and} \quad \lambda = \frac{h}{mv}.$$

We conclude this chapter with the consideration of an important point. In a medium of refractive index n, the rays in geometrical optics are limited by the condition, which is Fermat's principle, that the ray which passes through two points A and B must have a form such that the line integral

$$\int_A^B \frac{\nu}{V} dl = \frac{\nu}{c}\int_A^B n\,dl$$

is a minimum. In our case the index is constant in space and the principle states that the ray joining A and B is a curve of minimum length or a straight line. The rays are rectilinear and the waves are plane. The important point is that, $\frac{\nu}{V}$ being equal to $\frac{p}{h}$, the Fermat integral may be written

$$\frac{1}{h}\int p\,dl = \frac{1}{h}\int (p_x dx + p_y dy + p_z dz)$$

and it is thus identical with the principle of Maupertuis, except for the constant $\frac{1}{h}$. An analogy between this principle for the particle and Fermat's principle for the associated waves thus appears. We have, in this chapter, established the connection between waves and particles only in the very simple case where there is no field of force. It will be necessary to seek a generalisation of this connection in the case when the particle moves in a field of force. In order to attain this goal we shall rely upon the analogy which we have just pointed out, and this makes it necessary to study rather more closely the question of wave propagation.

CHAPTER IV

GENERAL REMARKS ON WAVE PROPAGATION

1. The Propagation of Waves in a Permanent Homogeneous Medium

WE will first consider the simplest case; that of wave propagation in a space which is homogeneous and has permanent properties. This is the familiar case, for example, of the propagation of light waves in a homogeneous refracting medium. The conditions of propagation are then characterised by a certain quantity, the refractive index n, constant in space and time. If the velocity of light in empty space is denoted by the constant c ($= 3 \times 10^{10}$ cms. per sec.) the wave equation has most frequently the well-known form:

$$\nabla^2\psi = \frac{\partial^2\psi}{\partial x^2} + \frac{\partial^2\psi}{\partial y^2} + \frac{\partial^2\psi}{\partial z^2} = \frac{n^2}{c^2}\frac{\partial^2\psi}{\partial t^2}. \qquad (1)$$

A solution of this equation in the form:

$$\psi(x, y, z, t) = a \cos 2\pi\left\{\nu t - \frac{n\nu}{c}(\alpha x + \beta y + \gamma z)\right\} \qquad (2)$$

will be said to represent a simple sinusoidal or plane monochromatic wave.

The constants a and ν are respectively the amplitude and frequency of the wave, α, β, γ are direction cosines, and satisfy the relation

$$\alpha^2 + \beta^2 + \gamma^2 = 1.$$

The phase of the plane monochromatic wave is defined by:

$$\Phi(x, y, z, t) = \nu t - \frac{n\nu}{c}(\alpha x + \beta y + \gamma z). \qquad (3)$$

It is easy to verify that (2) is a solution of (1). In the first place, $\frac{\partial^2\psi}{\partial t^2} = -4\pi^2\nu^2\psi$, so that we can write (1) in the form:

$$\nabla^2\psi + \frac{4\pi^2 n^2\nu^2}{c^2}\psi = 0. \qquad (4)$$

Moreover,

$$\frac{\partial^2\psi}{\partial x^2} = -\frac{4\pi^2 n^2\nu^2}{c^2}\alpha^2\psi, \qquad (5)$$

and similarly for y and z, so that equation (4) is immediately verified on account of the direction cosine relation.

We shall write:

$$\Phi_1(x, y, z, t) = \frac{n\nu}{c}(\alpha x + \beta y + \gamma z). \qquad (6)$$

At a particular instant the phase (3) will be constant on the planes:

$$\Phi_1 = \text{constant or } \alpha x + \beta y + \gamma z = \text{constant.}$$

These are planes of constant phase, and the quantities (α, β, γ) are the direction cosines of the normals to these planes.

As the time passes, the values of the phase Φ progress in space, passing from one equiphase plane to another. We may say that the phase travels in the direction (α, β, γ) which we call the direction of wave propagation. The parallel straight lines with direction cosines (α, β, γ) are the rays, and we can easily calculate the phase velocity, that is the velocity with which it is necessary to travel along the ray to keep up with a certain phase value. Let dl denote the element of length along the ray, so that:

$$dl = \alpha dx + \beta dy + \gamma dz \qquad (7)$$

and the change in phase for the given values of dt and dl is thus:

$$d\Phi = \nu\, dt - \frac{n\nu}{c}dl. \qquad (8)$$

This variation will be zero if we travel along the ray with velocity

$$V = \frac{dl}{dt} = \frac{c}{n}. \qquad (9)$$

V is the phase velocity.

The wave-length λ is defined in a similar way; it is the length which must be traversed along the ray at a particular instant in order to obtain a variation in Φ of amount unity, which restores to ψ its original value. We find at once:

$$\lambda = \frac{c}{n\nu} = \frac{V}{\nu}. \qquad (10)$$

2. Dispersion

In the foregoing discussion we have supposed n constant, but it is often necessary to consider n as a function of ν in equation (4), that is to say, that n, although independent of x, y, z and t, is a function of the frequency of the simple sinusoidal wave considered. We say, then, that there is dispersion and the relation between n and v is called the dispersion formula. In a special case, this occurs when the wave equation in its general form has, instead of (1), the form:

$$\nabla^2\psi - \frac{1}{c^2}\frac{\partial^2\psi}{\partial t^2} = K\psi, \qquad (11)$$

where K is a constant, for then, on substitution of (2), we can write (11) in the form:

$$\nabla^2\psi + \left(\frac{4\pi^2\nu^2}{c^2} - K\right)\psi = 0, \qquad (12)$$

and to obtain (4) we must write:

$$n^2 = 1 - \frac{Kc^2}{4\pi^2\nu^2} = f(\nu), \qquad (13)$$

so that n depends upon ν.

3. Trains and Groups of Waves

The plane monochromatic wave must in a certain sense be considered as an abstraction, for it would fill the whole of space and last throughout all time In practice a wave always occupies a limited region of space at a particular instant, and at any particular point it has a beginning and an end. A wave thus limited is known as a wave train.

To represent a wave train we consider not merely a single

plane monochromatic wave but an assembly of such waves, representing the assembly by

$$\psi(x, y, z, t) = \sum a(\nu, \alpha, \beta, \gamma)$$
$$\cos 2\pi\left\{\nu t - \frac{n}{c}\nu(\alpha x + \beta y + \gamma z) + \Delta(\nu, \alpha, \beta, \gamma)\right\}, \quad (14)$$

where Δ denotes that the individual plane monochromatic waves have, in general, different phases. If α, β, γ are always related by the equation $\alpha^2 + \beta^2 + \gamma^2 = 1$, it follows as above (§ 1) that each individual wave satisfies the wave equation, and on account of the linearity of this equation, the sum of the waves is a solution. Instead of a sum of a finite number of terms we may also consider the integral .

$$\psi(x, y, z, t) = \iiint a(\nu, \alpha, \beta)$$
$$\cos 2\pi\left\{\nu t - \frac{n\nu}{c}(\alpha x + \beta y + \gamma z) + \Delta(\nu, \alpha, \beta)\right\}d\nu\, d\alpha\, d\beta, \quad (15)$$

with $\alpha^2 + \beta^2 + \gamma^2 = 1$.

We must remember that n may be a function of ν in equations (14) and (15). In order to make it clear how one can represent a wave train by a sum of plane monochromatic waves, we shall consider the case of a train travelling along the direction of the z axis, which may be represented by :

$$\psi(x, y, z, t) = A(x, y, z, t)\cos 2\pi\left(\nu t - \frac{n\nu}{c}z\right), \quad . \quad (16)$$

with a suitable choice of the origin of time. We shall suppose, in addition, that the form of the wave train is symmetrical with respect to the z axis, i.e. A is an even function of the variables x and y.

$$A(-x, y, z, t) = A(x, y, z, t), \quad A(x, -y, z, t) = A(x, y, z, t). \quad (17)$$

Since the wave train is limited in space, at any given time the function A will be different from zero only if the variables are included between the limits (x_1, y_1, z_1) and (x_2, y_2, z_2). These limits determine the extension of the wave train in space. In order to simplify the analysis a little further we shall suppose that in the region occupied by the wave train at a given instant the value of A is appreciably constant, except at the boundaries, where it falls rapidly to zero ; in other words, for given values of y, z, and t the function A, considered as a function of x alone, is zero for $x < x_1$, passes rapidly to a constant value in the neighbourhood $x = x_1$, remains constant up to $x = x_2$, and then falls rapidly to zero (Fig. 1).

The dependence upon y and z is of the same type. In short, our wave train may be mistaken in the greatest part of its domain for a plane monochromatic wave, but it differs from it, of course, at the boundaries.

By the definition of a wave group, the assembly of waves constituting it have neighbouring frequencies and directions.

We propose to show that it is possible to represent the wave train studied by means of a group with the condition

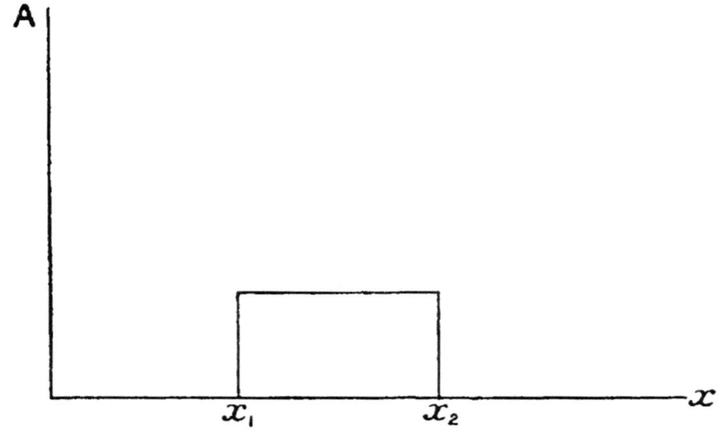

FIG 1.

that the dimensions of the train in space are large in relation to the wave-length, and that its duration at a fixed point is large in relation to the period On account of the assumed symmetry of the train about the z-axis, if we represent it by a wave group the form must be .

$$\int_{-\eta_1}^{+\eta_1} d\alpha \int_{-\eta_2}^{+\eta_2} d\beta \int_{-\eta_3}^{+\eta_3} d\epsilon \, a(\epsilon, \alpha, \beta)$$

$$\cos 2\pi \left\{ (\nu+\epsilon)t - \frac{(\nu+\epsilon)n_{\nu+\epsilon}}{c}(\alpha x + \beta y + z) + \Delta(\epsilon, \alpha, \beta) \right\}, \quad (18)$$

We have written z instead of γz, since α and β are very small and consequently $\gamma (= \sqrt{1 - \alpha^2 - \beta^2})$ differs from unity by terms of the second order only.

By limiting ourselves to quantities of the first order, we have .

$$(\nu + \epsilon)n_{\nu+\epsilon} = \nu n + \epsilon\frac{d}{d\nu}(n\nu), \quad . \quad . \quad (19)$$

and the argument of the cosine in (18) becomes :

$$2\pi\left[\nu t - \frac{\nu n}{c}(\alpha x + \beta y + z) + \epsilon\left\{t - \frac{d(n\nu)}{d\nu}\frac{z}{c}\right\} + \Delta(\epsilon, \alpha, \beta)\right]. \quad (20)$$

If we make use of the formula : $\cos(a + b) = \cos a \cos b - \sin a \sin b$, we can write (18) in the form :

$$\cos 2\pi\left(\nu t - \frac{\nu n}{c}z\right)\int_{-\eta_1}^{+\eta_1}d\alpha\int_{-\eta_2}^{+\eta_2}d\beta\int_{-\eta_3}^{+\eta_3}d\epsilon\, a(\epsilon, \alpha, \beta)$$
$$\cos 2\pi\left[\epsilon\left\{t - \frac{d(n\nu)}{d\nu}\frac{z}{c}\right\} - \frac{\nu n}{c}(\alpha x + \beta y) + \Delta(\epsilon, \alpha, \beta)\right]$$
$$- \sin 2\pi\left(\nu t - \frac{\nu n}{c}z\right)\int_{-\eta_1}^{+\eta_1}d\alpha\int_{-\eta_2}^{+\eta_2}d\beta\int_{-\eta_3}^{+\eta_3}d\epsilon\, a(\epsilon, \alpha, \beta)$$
$$\sin 2\pi\left[\epsilon\left\{t - \frac{d(n\nu)}{d\nu}\frac{z}{c}\right\} - \frac{\nu n}{c}(\alpha x + \beta y) + \Delta(\epsilon, \alpha, \beta)\right]. \quad (21)$$

In order to identify this expression for the wave group with (16) for the wave train, it is necessary, in the first place, to make the coefficient in the sine term vanish. To bring this about we shall suppose that Δ has the same value for all the monochromatic waves of the group, and we shall then write $\Delta = 0$. In addition, we shall suppose that $a(\epsilon, \alpha, \beta)$ is an even function in the three arguments ϵ, α, β. This assumption with regard to α and β corresponds to the symmetry of the wave train about the z-axis. and with regard to ϵ to a symmetry of spectral distribution in the group about the central frequency ν.

To complete the identification, it is sufficient to write :

$$A(x, y, z, t) = \int_{-\eta_1}^{+\eta_1}d\alpha\int_{-\eta_2}^{+\eta_2}d\beta\int_{-\eta_3}^{+\eta_3}d\epsilon\, a(\epsilon, \alpha, \beta)$$
$$\cos 2\pi\left[\epsilon\left\{t - \frac{d(n\nu)}{d\nu}\frac{z}{c}\right\} - \frac{\nu n}{c}(\alpha x + \beta y) + \Delta(\epsilon, \alpha, \beta)\right]. \quad (22)$$

The expression (22), when it is exact, that is to say, when the wave train can be exactly represented by a wave group, allows us to determine once more Rayleigh's group velocity.

Let us consider a straight line parallel to the direction of the z-axis. When this line is displaced by an amount dz the displacement is associated with a constant value of A if it takes a time $dt = \frac{1}{c}\frac{d(n\nu)}{d\nu}dz$, to make the displacement. We can thus consider, to the degree of approximation employed[1] that the amplitude resulting from the wave train is displaced in the direction z with velocity U defined by the formula :

$$\frac{1}{\mathrm{U}} = \frac{1}{c}\frac{d(n\nu)}{d\nu}. \quad . \quad . \quad . \quad (23)$$

This is the group velocity previously introduced. If n is independent of ν we have: $\mathrm{U} = \frac{c}{n}$, or the group velocity is identical with the phase velocity.

Thus, when (22) is applicable, A depends upon z and t through $\left(t - \frac{z}{\mathrm{U}}\right)$ only, and it is natural to introduce $z' = z - \mathrm{U}t$. For any given value of t, z' measures the value of z, except for a constant, and if z_1' and z_2' correspond to points at the beginning and end of the wave train :

$$z_1' - z_2' = z_1 - z_2. \quad . \quad . \quad . \quad (24)$$

It is easy to see that the group (22) is symmetrical in z' as in x and y. We can now write (22) in the form .

$$\mathrm{A}(x, y, z') = \int_{-\eta_1}^{+\eta_1} d\alpha \int_{-\eta_2}^{+\eta_2} d\beta \int_{-\eta_3}^{+\eta_3} d\epsilon \, a(\epsilon, \alpha, \beta) \cos 2\pi\left\{-\frac{\epsilon}{\mathrm{U}}z' - \frac{n\nu}{c}(\alpha x + \beta y)\right\}. \quad (25)$$

If we decompose the integral into a sum of products of sines and cosines, the only part which does not vanish will be that which contains the product of three cosines on account of the evenness of $a(\epsilon. \alpha, \beta)$.

Thus if we write :

$$c(\epsilon. \alpha, \beta) = 8a(\epsilon, \alpha, \beta) \quad . \quad . \quad . \quad (26)$$

[1] Actually for intervals of sufficiently long duration a wave train has always a tendency to spread. More rigorous calculations made in Chap. XIII will show this clearly.

we obtain :

$$A(x, y, z') = \int_0^{\eta_1} d\alpha \int_0^{\eta_2} d\beta \int_0^{\eta_3} d\epsilon\, c(\epsilon, \alpha, \beta)$$
$$\cos \frac{2\pi\epsilon}{U} z' \cos 2\pi \frac{n\nu}{c} \alpha x \cos 2\pi \frac{n\nu}{c} \beta y. \quad (27)$$

This is the form which A must take in order that the wave train may be represented by a wave group. But the question arises with regard to the possibility of expressing A in this way.

Fourier's theory of integrals shows that under very general conditions a function $f(x, y, z)$, which is even in x, y, z, can be expressed in the form :

$$f(x, y, z) = \int_0^{\infty} d\lambda \int_0^{\infty} d\mu \int_0^{\infty} d\nu\, p(\lambda, \mu, \nu) \cos \lambda x \cos \mu y \cos \nu z, \quad (28)$$

where

$$p(\lambda, \mu, \nu) = \frac{1}{\pi^3} \int_{-\infty}^{\infty} dx \int_{-\infty}^{\infty} dy \int_{-\infty}^{\infty} dz\, f(x, y, z) \cos \lambda x \cos \mu y \cos \nu z. \quad (29)$$

Thus the function $A(x, y, z')$, which is even in x, y, z', may be written .

$$A(x, y, z') = \int_0^{\infty} d\alpha \int_0^{\infty} d\beta \int_0^{\infty} d\epsilon\, c(\epsilon, \alpha, \beta)$$
$$\cos \frac{2\pi\epsilon}{U} z' \cos 2\pi \frac{n\nu}{c} \alpha x \cos 2\pi \frac{n\nu}{c} \beta y, \quad (30)$$

where

$$c(\epsilon, \alpha, \beta) = 8 \int_{-\infty}^{\infty} \frac{dz'}{U} \int_{-\infty}^{\infty} \frac{n\nu}{c} dx \int_{-\infty}^{\infty} \frac{n\nu}{c} dy A(x, y, z')$$
$$\cos \frac{2\pi\epsilon}{U} z' \cos 2\pi \frac{n\nu}{c} \alpha x \cos 2\pi \frac{n\nu}{c} \beta y. \quad (31)$$

But to be able to represent our wave train by a wave group we must identify (27) and (30), i e. we must reduce the intervals of integration in (30) to the very small intervals 0 to η_1, 0 to η_2, 0 to η_3. Thus it is necessary that the function $c(\epsilon, \alpha, \beta)$ defined by (31) should vanish outside these small intervals. Now, by hypothesis, A is appreciably constant for $x_1 < x < x_2$, $y_1 < y < y_2$, $z_1 < z < z_2$, and is zero elsewhere. If in (31) we consider the integral with respect to x, we have .

$$c(\epsilon, \alpha, \beta) = \text{constant} \times \int_{x_1}^{x_2} A \cos 2\pi \frac{n\nu}{c} \alpha x\, dx, \quad (32)$$

where A is appreciably constant. When the cosine has a large number of periods in the region x_1 to x_2, $c(\epsilon, \alpha, \beta)$ is approximately zero. In order that c may have an appreciable value it is necessary that:

$$\frac{\alpha}{\lambda}(x_1 - x_2) \sim 1, \qquad . \quad . \quad . \quad (33)$$

where the sign $\sim$ denotes "is of the order." In order that this should be equivalent to $\alpha \ll 1$ it is necessary that:

$$\lambda \ll x_1 - x_2. \qquad . \quad . \quad . \quad (34)$$

The dimension of the wave train in the x direction must be much greater than the average wave-length λ. We find the same result for the y direction.

For the z direction we find:

$$\frac{\epsilon}{\mathrm{U}}(z_1' - z_2') = \frac{\epsilon}{\mathrm{U}}(z_1 - z_2) \sim 1, \qquad . \quad (35)$$

and in order that $\epsilon \ll \nu$ we require:

$$z_1 - z_2 \gg \frac{\mathrm{U}}{\nu} = \mathrm{UT}. \qquad . \quad . \quad . \quad (36)$$

The product UT is not, in general, equal to the wave-length VT, but the two quantities are often of the same order. We can thus say that the wave train can be represented by a group when all its dimensions are great with respect to the wave-length. The time taken by the wave train to pass a fixed point completely is clearly:

$$t_1 - t_2 = \frac{z_1 - z_2}{\mathrm{U}} \qquad . \quad . \quad . \quad (37)$$

According to (36) this interval must be long with respect to the period According to (33), to the similar relation for y and to (35) the quantities $\frac{\eta_1}{\lambda}(x_1 - x_2)$, $\frac{\eta_2}{\lambda}(y_1 - y_2)$, and $\frac{\eta_3}{\mathrm{U}}(z_1 - z_2)$ must be at least of the order unity. Let us describe a vector **N** for a plane monochromatic wave in the direction of propagation and of magnitude equal to the number of waves per cm. by the term "vector wave number." Its components are:

$$\mathrm{N}_x = \frac{\alpha}{\lambda}, \quad \mathrm{N}_y = \frac{\beta}{\lambda}, \quad \mathrm{N}_z = \frac{\gamma}{\lambda}. \qquad . \quad . \quad (38)$$

On account of the hypotheses made with regard to α, β and γ, the maximum variations of N_x, N_y and N_z corresponding to the various monochromatic components of the wave train are :

$$\delta N_x = \frac{\eta_1}{\lambda}, \quad \delta N_y = \frac{\eta_2}{\lambda}, \quad \delta N_z = \delta\left(\frac{1}{\lambda}\right) = \frac{\partial\left(\frac{1}{\lambda}\right)}{\partial \nu}\eta_3 = \frac{\eta_3}{U}. \quad (39)$$

Let us write :

$$\delta x = x_1 - x_2, \quad \delta y = y_1 - y_2, \quad \delta z = z_1 - z_2. \quad . \quad (40)$$

These are the maximum variations of the co-ordinates throughout the extent of the wave train. We may therefore write the inequalities in order of magnitude :

$$\delta N_x \,.\, \delta x > 1, \quad \delta N_y \,.\, \delta y > 1, \quad \delta N_z \;\; \delta z > 1 \quad . \quad (41)$$

Finally, let us write ·

$$\delta t = t_1 - t_2 \quad . \quad . \quad . \quad . \quad . \quad (42)$$

for the time of passage of the wave train at a fixed point, and $\delta\nu$ for the maximum variation in frequency in the group, so that by (35) and (37)

$$\delta\nu \;\; \delta t > 1. \quad . \quad . \quad . \quad . \quad . \quad (43)$$

We shall see later the importance of (41) and (43) in the theory of Bohr and Heisenberg.

4. Propagation in a Permanent Heterogeneous Medium

Hitherto we have assumed that the index of refraction was independent of x, y and z. We will now suppose it a function of these variables, but independent of the time. This is the case occurring in optics for refracting, heterogeneous media. In general, the index depends upon the frequency or heterogeneous refracting media are dispersive.

The equation of propagation of simple sinusoidal waves will in this case be .

$$\nabla^2\psi + \frac{4\pi^2\nu^2 n^2}{c^2}\psi = 0, \quad . \quad . \quad . \quad (44)$$

where n is now a function of x, y, z.

Let us consider the sinusoidal solution :

$$\psi = a(x, y, z) \cos 2\pi\{\nu t - \Phi_1(x, y, z)\}, \quad . \quad . \quad (45)$$

where a is the amplitude and is variable from point to point.

The quantity

$$\Phi(x, y, z, t) = \nu t - \Phi_1(x, y, z) \quad . \quad . \quad (46)$$

is the phase, and is still linear in t, though no longer linear in x, y, z.

If we substitute (45) in (44) we obtain :

$$\left\{\nabla^2 a - 4\pi^2 a \sum\left(\frac{\partial \Phi_1}{\partial x}\right)^2 + \frac{4\pi^2\nu^2}{c^2} n^2 a\right\} \cos 2\pi(\nu t - \Phi_1)$$
$$+ \left(4\pi \sum \frac{\partial \Phi_1}{\partial x} \cdot \frac{\partial a}{\partial x} + 2\pi a \nabla^2 \Phi_1\right) \sin 2\pi(\nu t - \Phi_1) = 0. \quad (47)$$

Since this equation must be always satisfied, the coefficients of the sine and cosine terms are each equal to zero, so that :

$$\sum\left(\frac{\partial \Phi_1}{\partial x}\right)^2 = \frac{n^2\nu^2}{c^2} + \frac{1}{4\pi^2}\frac{\nabla^2 a}{a} \quad . \quad . \quad (48)$$

$$\sum \frac{\partial \Phi_1}{\partial x}\frac{\partial a}{\partial x} + \frac{1}{2} a \nabla^2 \Phi_1 = 0 \quad . \quad . \quad (49)$$

We shall describe as the wave-length the quantity λ where :

$$\frac{1}{\lambda} = \frac{\partial \Phi_1}{\partial l}, \quad . \quad . \quad . \quad . \quad (50)$$

where dl denotes an element of length along the normal to the surface, Φ_1 = constant, at the point under consideration. In this case, λ varies from point to point.

This definition, of course, includes the case where n is constant, for then the surfaces, $\Phi_1 = \frac{n\nu}{c}(\alpha x + \beta y + z\gamma) =$ constant, are planes of which the normal has direction cosines (α, β, γ) and

$$\frac{\partial \Phi_1}{\partial l} = \frac{n\nu}{c} = \frac{\nu}{V}.$$

As in the case of homogeneous media, we shall describe the surfaces, Φ_1 = constant, as surfaces of constant phase, and these are not, in general, plane The curves normal to these surfaces are still called rays, and we shall call the velocity with which it is necessary to move along a ray to accompany a constant value of the phase the phase velocity $V(x, y, z)$.

It is easy to determine V, for if we traverse a length dl of the ray in time dt the change in Φ_1 is $\left(\nu dt - \frac{\partial \Phi_1}{\partial l} dl\right)$, and for this to be zero we must have :

$$V = \frac{dl}{dt} = \frac{\nu}{\frac{\partial \Phi_1}{\partial l}} = \nu \div \sqrt{\sum \left(\frac{\partial \Phi_1}{\partial x}\right)^2} = \nu\lambda. \quad . \quad (51)$$

The function (45) can thus be written in the form .

$$\psi = a(x, y, z) \cos 2\pi\left(\nu t - \nu \int \frac{dl}{V}\right), \quad . \quad . \quad (52)$$

the integral being taken along the ray to the particular point $M(x, y, z)$ from a certain surface of constant phase chosen as origin. But, in general, the function $V(x, y, z)$ is not known *a priori* and its determination requires the evaluation of $a(x, y, z)$ and $\Phi_1(x, y, z)$ by means of the simultaneous partial differential equations (48) and (49).

Nevertheless, there is a very interesting case where the determination of V and of Φ_1 can be carried out at once without a determination of a. This is the case in which the medium may be considered homogeneous and the refractive index constant for variations of the order of the wave-length. We shall then have :

$$\left.\begin{array}{l} \frac{\partial a}{\partial x}\lambda \ll a, \quad \frac{\partial^2 a}{\partial x^2}\lambda^2 \ll a, \\ \text{with similar relations for } y \text{ and } z, \text{ and :} \\ \lambda^2 . \nabla^2 a \ll a \end{array}\right\} \quad . \quad . \quad (53)$$

The last of these equations taken with the definition of λ in (50) shows that in (48) the term $\frac{1}{4\pi^2}\frac{\nabla^2 a}{a}$ is negligible with respect to $\sum\left(\frac{\partial \Phi_1}{\partial x}\right)^2$, since this is equal to $\frac{1}{\lambda^2}$. Moreover, by multiplication of (49) by λ^2, and making use of (50), we find :

$$\frac{1}{a}\frac{\partial a}{\partial l}\lambda + \frac{1}{2}\lambda^2\nabla^2\Phi_1 = 0, \quad . \quad . \quad . \quad (54)$$

and by (53) the first term may be neglected.

Finally, (48) and (49) may be written :

$$\left(\frac{\partial \Phi_1}{\partial l}\right)^2 = \frac{n^2\nu^2}{c^2}, \quad \lambda^2\nabla^2\Phi_1 = 0. \qquad . \quad . \quad (55)$$

We will write in agreement with (51) :

$$V = \frac{\nu}{\frac{\partial \Phi_1}{\partial l}} = \frac{c}{n}, \quad \lambda = \frac{V}{\nu} = \frac{c}{n\nu}. \qquad . \quad . \quad (56)$$

The second equation (55) is necessarily true, since Φ_1 is appreciably linear in (x, y, z) in measurements of the order of the wave-lengths, and thus quantities such as $\sum \frac{\partial^2 \Phi_1}{\partial x^2} \cdot \lambda^2$ are negligible.

Formula (52) therefore gives in this case the approximate solution ·

$$\psi(x, y, z, t) = a(x, y, z) \cos 2\pi\left(\nu t - \nu\int\frac{ndl}{c}\right), \quad . \quad (57)$$

and the determination of Φ_1 is made *a priori*, since n is given, without the necessity of calculating a.

When the foregoing approximation is satisfactory we say that geometrical optics is applicable. We can thus say that for an extension of the order of magnitude of a wave-length the wave is plane and monochromatic, but for an extension containing many wave-lengths there is a progressive variation in the conditions of propagation appearing as a variation in amplitude and a non-linear form of the phase

5. Construction of Wave Envelopes and Fermat's Principle

We suppose that the conditions are such that geometrical optics is applicable and pass on to study the propagation of a wave. If we know one surface of constant phase we can construct others infinitely close to it by describing about each point M of it a sphere of radius ϵV_M, where ϵ is an infinitely small constant and where V_M is the value of V at the point M. The two sheets of the envelope of these small spheres are surfaces of constant phase, for they are surfaces on which at the times $(t - \epsilon)$ and $(t + \epsilon)$ we find the value of the phase which at time t is associated with the known surface. The two straight lines which join each point M to the points of contact of the sphere of which it is the centre with the envelope are elements of rays. By proceeding in this way, step by step, we can construct all the constant phase surfaces and at the same time we determine the rays as limits of broken lines

This method, known as the construction of wave envelopes, makes it possible to demonstrate Fermat's principle, which, in geometrical optics, is a postulate. According to this principle any ray passing through two points A and B is such that the line integral

$$\int_A^B \frac{dl}{V} = \int_A^B \frac{n\,dl}{c}, \qquad (58)$$

taken along the ray, has a stationary value. From the point of view of the wave this means that the time taken by the phase to go from A to B is a minimum along the ray.

To prove this let $\Phi_1(x, y, z) = C_1$ and $\Phi_1(x, y, z) = C_2$ be two constant phase surfaces through A and B respectively. Let the intermediate constant phase surfaces be represented by $\Phi_1(x, y, z) = C$, where C may have a series of infinitely close values between C_1 and C_2. The ray from A to B may be regarded as formed of small straight segments normal to this series of surfaces. Any varied curve infinitely close to the ray is formed of infinitely small straight lines having the character just described and of at least two segments not normal to the equiphase surfaces which pass through their extremities. The quantity $\frac{dl}{V}$ taken over the normal elements is equal to this quantity taken along a ray, for since the elements in each case are normal to surfaces $\Phi_1 = C$ and $\Phi_1 = C + dC$ passing through their extremities, we have for each :

$$\frac{dl}{V} = \frac{1}{\nu}\frac{\partial \Phi_1}{\partial l}\,.\,dl = \frac{dC}{\nu}.$$

If we compare a non-normal element of the varied curve with the corresponding element of the ray, the quantity $\frac{dl}{V}$ is greater for the former than for the latter, since the perpendicular is shorter than the oblique element. This proves the principle which is no longer a postulate but a theorem, valid, however, only when we can apply the principles of geometrical optics.

6. Wave Groups in a Permanent Heterogeneous Medium

We must now enquire how the conception of wave groups can be generalised in the case of permanent heterogeneous media when geometrical optics may be applied. The function Φ_1 then satisfies the equation :

$$\left(\frac{\partial \Phi_1}{\partial x}\right)^2 + \left(\frac{\partial \Phi_1}{\partial y}\right)^2 + \left(\frac{\partial \Phi_1}{\partial z}\right)^2 = \frac{\nu^2}{V^2} = \frac{n^2\nu^2}{c^2}, \quad . \quad (59)$$

which is often described as the equation of geometrical optics.

The equiphase surface which serves as the starting point in the construction of the wave envelopes is one of a family of complete integrals :

$$\Phi_1(x, y, z, a, b) = \text{constant}, \quad . \quad . \quad (60)$$

of equation (59), and the surfaces obtained by this construction belong to this family, the constant alone varying as we pass from one member of the family to another. Thus for a definite propagation the equiphase surfaces form a family with two parameters. In the special case of homogeneous media, we have . $\Phi_1 = \frac{n\nu}{c}(\alpha x + \beta y + \gamma z)$, the two parameters a and b being the direction cosines α and β, where we still take $\gamma = \sqrt{1 - \alpha^2 - \beta^2}$.

Let us consider a group of waves consisting of an infinity of simple sine waves with frequencies comprised within the small interval $(\nu - \delta\nu)$ to $(\nu + \delta\nu)$ for which the parameters a and b have values in the small intervals $(a - \delta a)$, $(a + \delta a)$ and $(b - \delta b)$, $(b + \delta b)$, and let us suppose that all the waves are in phase at the point (x_0, y_0, z_0). We enquire how this state of phase agreement will be displaced. The function Φ_1 depending upon V depends in general upon ν, and in order that the waves of the group may be all in phase at the instant t_0, at the point (x_0, y_0, z_0), it is necessary that ·

$$t_0 d\nu - \left\{\left(\frac{\partial \Phi_1}{\partial a}\right)_0 da + \left(\frac{\partial \Phi_1}{\partial b}\right)_0 db + \left(\frac{\partial \Phi_1}{\partial \nu}\right)_0 d\nu\right\} = 0, \quad (61)$$

where the suffix 0 denotes that the values are those at (x_0, y_0, z_0) and where da, db, $d\nu$ have values less than δa, δb, $\delta\nu$. If this agreement in phase is to be found at a later time t at a point (x, y, z) we require

$$td\nu - \left(\frac{\partial \Phi_1}{\partial a}da + \frac{\partial \Phi_1}{\partial b}db + \frac{\partial \Phi_1}{\partial \nu}d\nu\right) = 0, \qquad (62)$$

where the derivatives have the values at (x, y, z) and the same limits are imposed upon da, db, and $d\nu$

The relation (62) will follow from (61) if we have:

$$\frac{\partial \Phi_1}{\partial a} = C_1, \quad \frac{\partial \Phi_1}{\partial b} = C_2, \quad \frac{\partial \Phi_1}{\partial \nu} - t = C_3. \qquad (63)$$

The first two relations give the locus of the point where this phase agreement exists, and the third describes the motion of the point on its trajectory. The analogy with Jacobi's theory is obvious.

It is easy to show that the locus obtained in this way is normal to the equiphase surfaces. For by differentiation .

$$\frac{\partial^2 \Phi_1}{\partial x \partial a} dx + \frac{\partial^2 \Phi_1}{\partial y \partial a} dy + \frac{\partial^2 \Phi_1}{\partial z \partial a} dz = 0, \qquad (64)$$

$$\frac{\partial^2 \Phi_1}{\partial x \partial b} \cdot dx + \frac{\partial^2 \Phi_1}{\partial y \partial b} dy + \frac{\partial^2 \Phi_1}{\partial z \partial b} dz = 0. \qquad (64a)$$

By differentiation of equation (59) with respect to a and b:

$$\frac{\partial \Phi_1}{\partial x} \cdot \frac{\partial^2 \Phi_1}{\partial a \partial x} + \frac{\partial \Phi_1}{\partial y} \cdot \frac{\partial^2 \Phi_1}{\partial a \partial y} + \frac{\partial \Phi_1}{\partial z} \cdot \frac{\partial^2 \Phi_1}{\partial a \partial z} = 0, \qquad (65)$$

$$\frac{\partial \Phi_1}{\partial x} \cdot \frac{\partial^2 \Phi_1}{\partial b \partial x} + \frac{\partial \Phi_1}{\partial y} \cdot \frac{\partial^2 \Phi_1}{\partial b \partial y} + \frac{\partial \Phi_1}{\partial z} \cdot \frac{\partial^2 \Phi_1}{\partial b \partial z} = 0. \qquad (65a)$$

If these two systems of equations be compared, it will be seen that:

$$\frac{\partial \Phi_1}{\partial x}, \quad \frac{\partial \Phi_1}{\partial y} \text{ and } \frac{\partial \Phi_1}{\partial z}$$

are proportional respectively to dx, dy and dz taken along the trajectory. Thus this curve is normal to the surfaces $\Phi_1 =$ constant.

When geometrical optics is applicable and the dimensions are of the order of a wave-length, the propagation proceeds as if the refractive index were constant, and even in a region containing a certain number of wave-lengths the waves (45) may be considered as plane and as having a constant amplitude. But in the cases usually occurring the wave-length is much smaller than the smallest dimensions directly measurable. It will thus be possible to consider wave trains with very small dimensions, as judged by ordinary standards, but which contain a large number of wave-lengths. These trains can be represented by a wave group with neighbouring frequencies and directions which at each instant can be regarded as appreciably plane and as having a constant amplitude, but, of course, the amplitude and phase will be slowly changed during the propagation on account of the large scale variation of the refractive index.

7. Propagation of Waves in a Non-Permanent Medium

Finally, we consider the most general case where the conditions of propagation vary not only in space but also in time ; this is the case of heterogeneous, non-permanent refractive media. Let us take, for example, the equation of propagation :

$$\nabla^2\Psi = \frac{n^2}{c^2}\frac{\partial^2\psi}{\partial t^2}, \quad . \quad . \quad . \quad (66)$$

where n is a function of x, y, z and t. Since the time in this equation plays no distinctive part we can no longer eliminate it by taking a sinusoidal solution of which the phase is linear in the time

We shall thus take for the general form of the sinusoidal solution :

$$\psi(x, y, z, t) = a(x, y, z, t) \cos 2\pi\Phi\,(x, y, z, t). \quad . \quad (67)$$

If we substitute in equation (66) and equate to zero the coefficients of the sine and cosine terms we obtain

$$\sum\left(\frac{\partial\Phi}{\partial x}\right)^2 = \frac{n^2}{c^2}\left(\frac{\partial\Phi}{\partial t}\right)^2 + \frac{1}{4\pi^2 a}\left(\nabla^2 a - \frac{n^2}{c^2}\frac{\partial^2 a}{\partial t^2}\right) \quad . \quad (68)$$

$$\sum\frac{\partial\Phi}{\partial x}\frac{\partial a}{\partial x} - \frac{n^2}{c^2}\frac{\partial\Phi}{\partial t}\frac{\partial a}{\partial t} + \frac{a}{2}\left(\nabla^2\Phi - \frac{n^2}{c^2}\frac{\partial^2\Phi}{\partial t^2}\right) = 0. \quad . \quad (69)$$

We will write, as a definition of ν and λ :

$$\nu(x, y, z, t) = \frac{\partial\Phi}{\partial t}, \quad \lambda(x, y, z, t) = \left(\frac{\partial\Phi}{\partial l}\right)^{-1}, \quad . \quad (70)$$

dl being an element of the normal to $\Phi =$ constant at the point and at the instant considered. The frequency and wave-length defined in this way are in general both variable, but when n is constant they coincide with the frequency and wave-length in the usual sense of these terms. We shall say that the approximation of geometrical optics is valid if the conditions of propagation vary very little over extents in space of the order of λ or over intervals of time of the order of the period $\frac{1}{\nu}$. We can then write by (68):

$$\sum\left(\frac{\partial\Phi}{\partial x}\right)^2 = \frac{n^2}{c^2}\left(\frac{\partial\Phi}{\partial t}\right)^2 \quad . \quad . \quad (71)$$

where we consider the derivatives of the second order as zero.

Equation (71) is the form taken by the equation of geometrical optics (59) which is appropriate to the general case. Over distances of the order of the wave-length, and during intervals which are not very large with respect to the period, we can consider (67) as a plane monochromatic wave. This is the basis of the possibility of imagining in this case trains of waves of which the space and time dimensions are less than those we can measure and which still satisfy the conditions necessary for their representation by a wave group.

Let $\Phi(x, y, z, t, a, b, c)$ be a complete integral of equation (71), and let a group be formed of sinusoidal waves for which the constants a, b and c are included within the limits $a - \delta a$, $a + \delta a$; $b - \delta b$, $b + \delta b$; $c - \delta c$, $c + \delta c$.

Let all the waves be supposed in phase at the time t_0 at the point (x_0, y_0, z_0), whence:

$$\left(\frac{\partial\Phi}{\partial a}\right)_0 da + \left(\frac{\partial\Phi}{\partial b}\right)_0 db + \left(\frac{\partial\Phi}{\partial c}\right)_0 dc = 0, \quad . \quad (72)$$

where the suffix denotes that the values are appropriate to the chosen time t_0 and the point (x_0, y_0, z_0), and where da, db, dc are less than δa, δb, δc, respectively. If the agreement in phase recurs again at a point (x, y, z) at the time t, we must have:

$$\frac{\partial\Phi}{\partial a}da + \frac{\partial\Phi}{\partial b}db + \frac{\partial\Phi}{\partial c}dc = 0. \quad . \quad . \quad (73)$$

In order that (73) may be a consequence of (72) we require :

$$\frac{\partial \Phi}{\partial a} = C_1, \quad \frac{\partial \Phi}{\partial b} = C_2, \quad \frac{\partial \Phi}{\partial c} = C_3. \quad . \quad . \quad (74)$$

These three equations give the locus of the agreement in phase, and again the analogy with Jacobi's theory is obvious.

Following this study of wave propagation, we pass on to seek the equations of propagation which we must adopt in wave mechanics for the associated waves of a particle.

CHAPTER V

THE EQUATIONS OF PROPAGATION OF THE WAVE ASSOCIATED WITH A PARTICLE

1. The Criterion for the Choice of the Equations of Propagation

IN the special case of the motion of a particle in the absence of a field of force it has been possible to establish a correspondence between waves and particles This correspondence finds expression in the statement that a particle of energy W and of momentum **p** must be associated with a wave travelling in the direction of motion, which is the direction of the vector **p**, and which has the frequency $\nu\left(=\frac{W}{h}\right)$ and wave-length $\lambda = \frac{h}{p}$ The motion proceeds as if empty space had an index of refraction for this wave of value $n = \sqrt{1 - \frac{\nu^2}{\nu_0^2}}$, where ν_0 denotes a constant characteristic of the particle and related to its proper mass m by the relation $\nu_0 = \frac{mc^2}{h}$. The velocity of the particle is equal to the velocity of the group corresponding to this law of dispersion.

Further, there has been revealed (Chap. III, § 5) a connection between the principle of least action and Fermat's principle, and this analogy between the old mechanics and geometrical optics has been confirmed by the fact that the motion of a wave group, when the order of approximation is that of geometrical optics, is expressible by equations strikingly analogous to those of Jacobi (Chap. IV).

We shall thus seek equations of propagation for the associated waves such that, to this order of approximation, the rays coincide with the trajectories of the old dynamics.

One essential point may be mentioned. The wave-length

λ and the period $T\left(=\frac{1}{\nu}\right)$ of the associated waves are proportional to Planck's constant h. Now we have seen in the last chapter that when λ and T become very small the principles of geometrical optics become exactly applicable. Thus whenever it is legitimate to consider h as a negligible quantity the old mechanics is sufficient. We must choose our wave equations in such a way that when h tends to zero they give us the equations of the old mechanics. This is a criterion for the choice of the equations.

2. The Wave Equation in the Absence of a Field of Force

We take first the simplest case of motion with no field of force It is agreed that we must adopt the equation :

$$\nabla^2\psi - \frac{1}{c^2}\frac{\partial^2\psi}{\partial t^2} = \frac{4\pi^2 m^2 c^2}{h^2}\psi. \quad . \quad . \quad . \quad (1)$$

Let us substitute the expression which represents a plane monochromatic wave. Since we have $\frac{\partial^2\psi}{\partial t^2} = 4\pi\nu^2\psi$ in this case, (1) becomes

$$\nabla^2\psi + \frac{4\pi^2\nu^2}{c^2}\left(1 - \frac{m^2c^4}{h^2\nu^2}\right)\psi = 0 \quad . \quad . \quad (2)$$

Since $mc^2 = h\nu_0$, by definition, we can also write (2) in the form :

$$\nabla^2\psi + \frac{4\pi^2\nu^2}{c^2}\left(1 - \frac{\nu_0^2}{\nu^2}\right)\psi = 0. \quad . \quad . \quad (3)$$

This goes back to the form (4) of the preceding chapter, if we write :

$$n = \sqrt{1 - \frac{\nu_0^2}{\nu^2}}. \quad . \quad . \quad (4)$$

This is what we ought to find in order to be in agreement with the former results which we have just recalled.

Let us write the simple sinusoidal wave in the form :

$$\psi(x, y, z, t) = a\cos 2\pi\left\{\nu t - \frac{n\nu}{c}(\alpha x + \beta y + \gamma z)\right\} = a\cos\frac{2\pi}{h}\phi, \quad (5)$$

in which $\frac{\phi}{h}$ denotes what Φ denoted in the preceding chapter, and from this point the term phase will be applied to ϕ.

Thus :

$$\phi = h\nu t - h\nu\frac{n}{c}(\alpha x + \beta y + \gamma z) \qquad . \quad . \quad (6)$$

and consequently :

$$\frac{\partial\phi}{\partial t} = h\nu, \quad \frac{\partial\phi}{\partial x} = -\frac{nh\nu}{c}\alpha, \quad \frac{\partial\phi}{\partial y} = -\frac{nh\nu}{c}\beta, \quad \frac{\partial\phi}{\partial z} = -\frac{nh\nu}{c}\gamma. \quad (7)$$

We must write :

$$h\nu = W, \quad \frac{nh\nu}{c} = \frac{h}{\lambda} = p, \quad . \quad . \quad . \quad (8)$$

so that we deduce :

$$W = \frac{\partial\phi}{\partial t}, \quad p_x = -\frac{\partial\phi}{\partial x}, \quad p_y = -\frac{\partial\phi}{\partial y}, \quad p_z = -\frac{\partial\phi}{\partial z}. \quad (9)$$

These are exactly the equations which Jacobi's function satisfies, and we are thus led to identify the phase with this function.

3. The Wave Equation in a Constant Field of Force

Let us take the slightly more complicated case of a constant field of force which corresponds to the case of permanent but heterogeneous refracting media. The field of force is characterised by a potential function $F(x, y, z)$. The law of dispersion, which, as we shall show, it is convenient to adopt, is :

$$n = \sqrt{\left(1 - \frac{F}{h\nu}\right)^2 - \frac{\nu_0^2}{\nu^2}} \qquad . \quad . \quad (10)$$

where $mc^2 = h\nu_0$ We obtain, of course, the law of dispersion given by (4) for a zero field of force when $F = 0$. The wave equation for monochromatic waves of frequency ν must then be written :

$$\nabla^2\psi + \frac{4\pi^2\nu^2}{c^2}\left\{\left(1 - \frac{F}{h\nu}\right)^2 - \frac{\nu_0^2}{\nu^2}\right\}\psi = 0. \qquad . \quad (11)$$

From what we know already, geometrical optics will apply if the function $F(x, y, z)$ varies slowly enough to be considered appreciably constant in a region containing many wave-lengths. We may then take as the solution :

$$\psi(x, y, z, t) = a \cos 2\pi\left(\nu t - \frac{\nu}{c}\int n dl\right), \qquad . \quad (12)$$

the integral being taken along a curve normal to a family of complete integrals of the equation :

$$\left(\frac{\partial\Phi_1}{\partial x}\right)^2 + \left(\frac{\partial\Phi_1}{\partial y}\right)^2 + \left(\frac{\partial\Phi_1}{\partial z}\right)^2 = \frac{n^2}{c^2}\nu^2, \quad . \quad (13)$$

the integrals depending upon two parameters, α and β, and n being a function of x, y and z.

In a wave group the locus of phase agreement is defined by the equations :

$$\frac{\partial\Phi_1}{\partial\alpha} = C_1, \quad \frac{\partial\Phi_1}{\partial\beta} = C_2$$

and motion on the locus by :

$$\frac{\partial\Phi}{\partial\nu} = t + C_3.$$

In order to arrive at the laws of the old dynamics, it will suffice to suppose that the phase :

$$h\Phi = \phi = h\nu t - \frac{h\nu}{c}\int n\,dl = h\nu t - \phi_1(x, y, z) \quad . \quad (14)$$

is to be identified with Jacobi's function :

$$\begin{aligned} S(x, y, z, t, W, \alpha, \beta) &= Wt - \int(p_x dx + p_y dy + p_z dz) \\ &= Wt - S_1(x, y, z, W, \alpha, \beta). \quad . \quad (15) \end{aligned}$$

This leads us to write :

$$\frac{\partial\phi}{\partial t} = \frac{\partial S}{\partial t} = W = h\nu,$$

$$-\frac{\partial\phi}{\partial x} = \frac{\partial S_1}{\partial x} = p_x = \frac{nh\nu}{c}\alpha, \quad . \quad . \quad (16)$$

with similar equations in y and z, whence :

$$p = \frac{nh\nu}{c} = \frac{h\nu}{V} = \frac{h}{\lambda}. \quad . \quad . \quad . \quad (17)$$

From this identification of S with ϕ and of S_1 with ϕ_1 we deduce several important theorems.

Theorem I.—The principle of least action of Maupertuis coincides with Fermat's principle.

We have, in fact,

$$\int dS_1 = \int(p_x dx + p_y dy + p_z dz) = \int d\phi_1$$
$$= \int \frac{nh\nu}{c}(\alpha dx + \beta dy + \gamma dz) = \frac{h\nu}{c}\int ndl, \quad (18)$$

and the condition of Maupertuis, $\delta S_1 = 0$, coincides with that of Fermat, $\delta\int ndl = 0$.

In other words, the rays of the associated wave are identical with the possible trajectories of the particle which correspond to a complete integral of Jacobi's equation.

Theorem II.—The equation of geometrical optics coincides with that of Jacobi.

In its relativistic form the latter is :

$$\frac{1}{c^2}\left(\frac{\partial S}{\partial t} - F\right)^2 - \left(\frac{\partial S}{\partial x}\right)^2 - \left(\frac{\partial S}{\partial y}\right)^2 - \left(\frac{\partial S}{\partial z}\right)^2 = m^2c^2 \quad (19)$$

and in the present case may be written :

$$\frac{1}{c^2}(h\nu - F)^2 - \left(\frac{\partial S_1}{\partial x}\right)^2 - \left(\frac{\partial S_1}{\partial y}\right)^2 - \left(\frac{\partial S_1}{\partial z}\right)^2 = \frac{h^2\nu_0^2}{c^2},$$

$$\left(\frac{\partial S_1}{\partial x}\right)^2 + \left(\frac{\partial S_1}{\partial y}\right)^2 + \left(\frac{\partial S_1}{\partial z}\right)^2$$
$$= \frac{h^2\nu^2}{c^2}\left\{\left(1 - \frac{F}{h\nu}\right)^2 - \frac{\nu_0^2}{\nu^2}\right\} = \frac{n^2h^2\nu^2}{c^2}. \quad . \quad (20)$$

If we replace Φ_1 by $\frac{\phi_1}{h} = \frac{S_1}{h}$ in equation (13) we obtain (20), and thus the theorem is proved.

Theorem III.—The equations of the trajectory and of motion which are given by the theory of Jacobi are identical with those of the locus and motion of points where there is agreement in phase in a wave group. This is a direct consequence of the relation $\phi = S$.

Theorem IV.—The velocity of the particle defined by the old dynamics is the same as the group velocity of the associated waves.

To show this directly we start from Jacobi's equation of motion :

$$\frac{\partial S_1}{\partial W} = t + C_3. \quad . \quad . \quad . \quad (21)$$

If dl is an element of the path described by the particle in time dt, we have

$$\frac{\partial^2 S_1}{\partial l \partial W} dl = dt, \qquad (22)$$

and since $\frac{\partial S_1}{\partial l} = p$, the speed of the particle is given by v, where

$$\frac{1}{v} = \left(\frac{dl}{dt}\right)^{-1} = \frac{\partial^2 S_1}{\partial l \partial W} = \frac{\partial p}{\partial W}. \qquad (23)$$

This may be written ·

$$\frac{1}{v} = \frac{\partial p}{\partial W} = \frac{\partial\left(\frac{nh\nu}{c}\right)}{\partial(h\nu)} = \frac{1}{c}\frac{\partial(n\nu)}{\partial \nu} = \frac{1}{U}, \qquad (24)$$

which is the result required to establish the theorem.

We have seen above that the relativistic form of the wave equation in a constant field of force is given by (11). In the case where Newtonian mechanics is sufficient we may write :

$$h\nu = mc^2 + E = mc^2 + \tfrac{1}{2}mv^2 + F(x, y, z), \qquad (25)$$

and the quotients $\frac{E}{h\nu}$ and $\frac{F}{h\nu}$ are very small in comparison with unity.

We may thus write approximately :

$$n = \sqrt{\left(1 - \frac{F}{h\nu}\right)^2 - \frac{\nu_0^2}{\nu^2}} = \sqrt{1 - \frac{2F}{h\nu} - \left(\frac{h\nu - E}{h\nu}\right)^2}$$

$$= \sqrt{\frac{2(E - F)}{h\nu}} = \sqrt{\frac{2(E - F)}{mc^2}} \qquad (26)$$

This is the law of dispersion which must be adopted when we approximate by using classical mechanics To this degree of approximation it is permissible to equate $n^2\nu^2$ to $\frac{2(E - F)mc^2}{h^2}$ and we obtain for the equation of a plane monochromatic wave of frequency $\nu = \frac{mc^2 + E}{h}$ in the constant field defined by $F(x, y, z)$ the non-relativistic form .

$$\nabla^2\psi + \frac{8\pi^2 m(E - F)}{h^2}\psi = 0. \qquad (27)$$

This is the now classical equation of Schrödinger.

4. The Wave Equation in Variable Fields of Force

We have just found a suitable form for the equation of propagation for monochromatic waves in constant fields of force. This form, as we have already said, must be considered as a degeneration of a more general one, in which the frequency does not occur, and which is suitable not only in the case of a superposition of monochromatic waves but also in the case of fields of force which are variable in time.

The idea which must guide us in seeking this general equation is that to the approximation of geometrical optics, to be precise when h is supposed infinitely small, the equation of geometrical optics must be identified with Jacobi's equation, so that the phase ϕ can be identified with Jacobi's function.

The general relativistic equation which satisfies this condition is the following :

$$\nabla^2\psi - \frac{1}{c^2}\frac{\partial^2\psi}{\partial t^2} + \frac{4\pi i}{hc^2}\mathrm{F}\frac{\partial\psi}{\partial t} - \frac{4\pi^2}{h^2}\left(m^2c^2 - \frac{\mathrm{F}^2}{c^2}\right)\psi = 0, \quad (28)$$

in which F is a function of x, y, z and t.

For $\mathrm{F} = 0$ we obtain again equation (1). If F depends only upon x, y and z, and not upon t, we can take a monochromatic solution of the form :

$$\psi(x, y, z, t) = a(x, y, z)\cos 2\pi\{\nu t - \Phi_1(x, y, z)\} \quad (29)$$

and by making use of the complex form $\psi = ae^{2\pi i(\nu t - \Phi_1)}$ we obtain .

$$\frac{\partial\psi}{\partial t} = 2\pi i\nu\psi, \quad \frac{\partial^2\psi}{\partial t^2} = -4\pi^2\nu^2\psi. \quad (30)$$

Equation (28) now takes the degenerate form

$$\nabla^2\psi + \frac{4\pi^2\nu^2}{c^2}\psi - \frac{8\pi^2\nu}{hc^2}\mathrm{F}\psi - \frac{4\pi^2}{h^2}\left(m^2c^2 - \frac{\mathrm{F}^2}{c^2}\right)\psi = 0, \quad (31)$$

which is identical with (11)

Let us consider the general case where F depends on the time or the case of the variable field. We shall show that if the function ψ, written in the complex form, satisfies equation (28) we can obtain Jacobi's equation in ϕ if we suppose h to be infinitely small. By substitution of $\psi = ae^{\frac{2\pi i}{h}\phi}$ in (28), and equating the real part to zero, we obtain :

$$\nabla^2 a - \frac{1}{c^2}\frac{\partial^2 a}{\partial t^2} - \frac{4\pi^2 a}{h^2}\left\{\sum\left(\frac{\partial\phi}{\partial x}\right)^2 - \frac{1}{c^2}\left(\frac{\partial\phi}{\partial t}\right)^2\right\}$$

$$- \frac{8\pi^2 F}{h^2 c^2} a \frac{\partial\phi}{\partial t} - \frac{4\pi^2}{h^2}\left(m^2c^2 - \frac{F^2}{c^2}\right)a = 0. \quad . \quad (32)$$

If h is supposed very small the terms containing $\frac{1}{h^2}$ are of much greater importance than the others and, after removing a common factor, we obtain :

$$\frac{1}{c^2}\left(\frac{\partial\phi}{\partial t} - F\right)^2 - \sum\left(\frac{\partial\phi}{\partial x}\right)^2 = m^2c^2, \quad . \quad . \quad (33)$$

and ϕ thus satisfies the relativistic general equation of Jacobi (Chap. II, 32).

Equation (33) can be considered as being the equation of geometrical optics for the associated waves. As we have seen, if $\phi(x, y, z, t, \alpha, \beta, \gamma)$ denotes a complete integral of this equation (33), the three relations :

$$\frac{\partial\phi}{\partial\alpha} = C_1, \quad \frac{\partial\phi}{\partial\beta} = C_2, \quad \frac{\partial\phi}{\partial\gamma} = C_3, \quad . \quad . \quad (34)$$

define the motion of states of phase agreement in a wave group and these three relations are nothing more than Jacobi's equations of motion. In this case also and in complete generality the motion of the particle, to the approximation of geometrical optics, can be regarded as that of a group of associated waves.

A very special characteristic of equation (28) is that it contains an imaginary coefficient and that, in order to satisfy it, the wave function must be taken in the complex form. In the equations of the classical wave theory the coefficients are real, and the real wave function, $\psi = a \cos 2\pi\Phi$, must satisfy the wave equation. The complex form of ψ is also a solution and the calculations are usually made by means of it, only, however, to return to the real part at the end. The use of the complex form in that case is merely a simple mathematical device In the present theory this is by no means the case ; the real wave function does not satisfy equation (28), and the complex function itself is the solution.

Just as in the case of constant fields of force we passed from the relativistic equation (11) to the non-relativistic equation of Schrödinger (27), so we can in the general case pass from the relativistic equation (28) to a non-relativistic form.

We have to remind ourselves that in the dynamics of the theory of relativity the energy is given by :

$$W = \frac{mc^2}{\sqrt{1-\beta^2}} + F(x, y, z, t) = mc^2 + T + F = mc^2 + E, \quad (35)$$

T being the kinetic and F the potential energy. E is the energy as defined in Newtonian dynamics, being equal to the relativistic energy diminished by the internal energy mc^2, and Newtonian dynamics is applicable when the ratio $\frac{E}{mc^2}$ is small. To carry this over into wave mechanics we write the wave function in the form :

$$\psi(x, y, z, t) = e^{\frac{2\pi i}{h}mc^2 t}\psi_r(x, y, z, t). \quad (36)$$

ψ_r is thus the expression obtained on removing the term $\frac{mc^2}{h}t$ from the phase of the complex wave, that is to say, by reducing the frequency from $\frac{W}{h}$ to $\frac{E}{h}$.

We shall call ψ_r the reduced wave function, and $\frac{E}{h}$ the reduced frequency. Substituting (36) in (28), we obtain :

$$\nabla^2\psi_r - \frac{1}{c^2}\left(\frac{\partial^2\psi_r}{\partial t^2} + \frac{4\pi i}{h}mc^2\frac{\partial\psi_r}{\partial t} - \frac{4\pi^2}{h^2}m^2c^4\psi_r\right)$$
$$+ \frac{4\pi i}{hc^2}F\left(\frac{\partial\psi_r}{\partial t} + \frac{2\pi i}{h}mc^2\psi_r\right) - \frac{4\pi^2}{h^2}\left(m^2c^2 - \frac{F^2}{c^2}\right)\psi_r = 0. \quad (37)$$

The term containing $F^2\psi_r$ is negligible in comparison with that containing $Fmc^2\psi_r$, a similar remark applies to $F\frac{\partial\psi_r}{\partial t}$ and $mc^2\frac{\partial\psi_r}{\partial t}$ and also to $\frac{\partial^2\psi_r}{\partial t^2}$ and $mc^2\,\frac{\partial\psi_r}{\partial t}$, because all the derivatives of ψ_r with respect to the time are small compared with mc^2. Thus :

$$\nabla^2\psi_r - \frac{8\pi^2}{h^2}mF\psi_r = \frac{4\pi i m}{h}\frac{\partial\psi_r}{\partial t}. \quad . \quad . \quad (38)$$

This is the non-relativistic equation [1] which the reduced wave function must satisfy.

[1] The non-relativistic wave equation is of the first order in t, while the relativity equation is of the second order in t. This is an important point of difference which Dirac has brought forward.

If the field does not depend on the time, we may write :

$$\psi_r = ae^{\frac{2\pi i}{h}(Et - \phi_1)} \quad . \quad . \quad . \quad (39)$$

where a and ϕ_1 are functions of x, y and z, and we readily return once more to Schrödinger's equation (27).

Equation (38) is often written without the suffix r, but it must always be remembered that it is the reduced wave function of which the frequency is diminished by $\frac{mc^2}{h}$ which is a solution of (38).

5. A Device for Finding Equation 38

We can find the non-relativistic wave-equation by making use of a device which is somewhat automatic and which has great importance in the comparison of Heisenberg's matrix theory with wave mechanics. We know that Jacobi's equation in Newtonian mechanics is :

$$H\left(q, t, -\frac{\partial S}{\partial q}\right) - \frac{\partial S}{\partial t} = 0, \quad . \quad . \quad (40)$$

(Chap. II, 9), where $H\left(q, t, -\frac{\partial S}{\partial q}\right)$ denotes what the energy H becomes when expressed in terms of the co-ordinates q, of the time t and of the momenta p when the last are replaced by $-\frac{\partial S}{\partial q}$. If we take the first term of (40) and replace $\frac{\partial S}{\partial q}$ by the symbol $\frac{h}{2\pi i}\frac{\partial}{\partial q}$, and $\frac{\partial S}{\partial t}$ by $\frac{h}{2\pi i}\frac{\partial}{\partial t}$, we obtain an operator.

Now apply this operator to the reduced function ψ and equate to zero ; if the q's are rectangular cartesian co-ordinates we obtain equation (38). We have, in fact, in this case :

$$T = \tfrac{1}{2}m(\dot{x}^2 + \dot{y}^2 + \dot{z}^2), \quad . \quad . \quad . \quad (41)$$

so that :

$$H(q, p, t) = \frac{1}{2m}(p_x^2 + p_y^2 + p_z^2) + F(x, y, z, t), \quad . \quad (42)$$

and Jacobi's equation is :

$$\frac{1}{2m}\left\{\left(\frac{\partial S}{\partial x}\right)^2 + \left(\frac{\partial S}{\partial y}\right)^2 + \left(\frac{\partial S}{\partial z}\right)^2\right\} + F - \frac{\partial S}{\partial t} = 0. \quad . \quad (43)$$

The operator obtained by the method described is :

$$-\frac{h^2}{8\pi^2 m}\left(\frac{\partial^2}{\partial x^2}+\frac{\partial^2}{\partial y^2}+\frac{\partial^2}{\partial z^2}\right)+\mathrm{F}-\frac{h}{2\pi i}\frac{\partial}{\partial t} \quad . \quad (44)$$

and we arrive at the wave equation :

$$\frac{1}{m}\nabla^2\psi-\frac{8\pi^2}{h^2}\mathrm{F}\psi=\frac{4\pi i}{h}\frac{\partial\psi}{\partial t} \quad . \quad . \quad . \quad (45)$$

which is identical with (38). It may be easily verified that the same process applied to non-rectangular co-ordinates gives an incorrect wave equation.

CHAPTER VI

CLASSICAL MECHANICS AND WAVE MECHANICS

1. The Meaning of Amplitude in Classical Mechanics

THE old systems of mechanics correspond, as we now know, to the case where the propagation of the ψ-waves follows the laws of geometrical optics. The phase function ϕ can then be identified with Jacobi's function. But we have now to enquire what is the meaning to be attributed to the amplitude a if we wish provisionally to preserve the conception of particles localised in space.

We shall be content for the present with the study of the non-relativistic equations. Of course, these considerations will not be applicable to particles in very rapid motion, for example to light corpuscles, and when we consider the case of photons we shall have to resume our discussion.

Let us begin with the general non-relativistic equation

$$\nabla^2\psi - \frac{8\pi^2 m}{h^2}F\psi = \frac{4\pi i m}{h}\frac{\partial\psi}{\partial t} \quad . \quad . \quad (1)$$

and substitute :

$$\psi = ae^{\frac{2\pi i}{h}\phi}, \quad . \quad . \quad . \quad . \quad (2)$$

a and ϕ being two real functions, the modulus and argument of the complex quantity ψ. We obtain by separating the real and imaginary parts :

$$-\nabla^2 a + \frac{4\pi^2}{h^2}a\sum\left(\frac{\partial\phi}{\partial x}\right)^2 + \frac{8\pi^2 m}{h^2}Fa = \frac{8\pi^2 m}{h^2}a\frac{\partial\phi}{\partial t}, \quad . \quad (3)$$

$$\frac{4\pi i}{h}\sum\frac{\partial a}{\partial x}\frac{\partial\phi}{\partial x} + \frac{2\pi i}{h}\nabla a^2\phi = \frac{4\pi i}{h}m\frac{\partial a}{\partial t}. \quad . \quad (4)$$

It follows from the discussions of Chapter IV $\left(\text{where } \Phi = \frac{\phi}{h}\right)$ that if geometrical optics is applicable, the term $\nabla^2 a$ is negligible with respect to $\frac{4\pi^2}{h^2} a \sum \left(\frac{\partial \phi}{\partial x}\right)^2$. We can therefore write our equations (3) and (4) in the form :

$$\frac{1}{2m} \sum \left(\frac{\partial \phi}{\partial x}\right)^2 + F(x, y, z, t) = \frac{\partial \phi}{\partial t} \quad . \quad . \quad (5)$$

and

$$\sum \frac{\partial a}{\partial x} \frac{\partial \phi}{\partial x} + \frac{1}{2} a \nabla^2 \phi = m \frac{\partial a}{\partial t}. \quad . \quad . \quad (6)$$

Equation (5) shows that ϕ is identical with Jacobi's function, a result already known, and equation (6) will show us the meaning of a

Let $S(x, y, z, t, \alpha, \beta, \gamma)$ be a complete integral of Jacobi's equation where α, β and γ are three constants. According to Jacobi's theory the equations of motion are :

$$\frac{\partial S}{\partial \alpha} = C_1, \quad \frac{\partial S}{\partial \beta} = C_2, \quad \frac{\partial S}{\partial \gamma} = C_3. \quad . \quad . \quad (7)$$

There is thus an infinite number of possible modes of motion of the particle which correspond to the same function of Jacobi, that is to say, correspond to the same value of the constants α, β, γ, but with a different choice of the constants C_1, C_2, C_3. We shall say that these modes belong to the same class.

Instead of picturing a single particle describing a path, let us imagine an assembly of identical particles in motion in modes belonging to the same class. We know that the momenta p_x, p_y, p_z are deduced from S by the equations :

$$p_x = -\frac{\partial S}{\partial x}, \quad p_y = -\frac{\partial S}{\partial y}, \quad p_z = -\frac{\partial S}{\partial z}, \quad . \quad (8)$$

or vectorially :

$$\mathbf{p} = -\text{grad } S. \quad . \quad . \quad . \quad (9)$$

In Newtonian mechanics $\mathbf{p} = m\mathbf{v}$, hence :

$$\mathbf{v} = -\frac{1}{m} \text{grad } S. \quad . \quad . \quad . \quad (10)$$

Thus the motion of the cloud of particles is known completely if S is known. Since we may now identify ϕ with S, equation (6) is equivalent to :

$$\frac{\partial a}{\partial t} + \sum v_x \frac{\partial a}{\partial x} + \frac{1}{2} a \operatorname{div} \mathbf{v} = 0. \quad . \quad . \quad (11)$$

By multiplication by $2a$ we find at once :

$$\frac{\partial a^2}{\partial t} + \operatorname{div}(a^2 \mathbf{v}) = 0. \quad . \quad . \quad . \quad (12)$$

Moreover, the motion of the cloud of particles must satisfy the equation of continuity, which is the expression of the fact that the increase in number of particles in unit time in a region of space is equal to the difference between the number entering and leaving in that time.

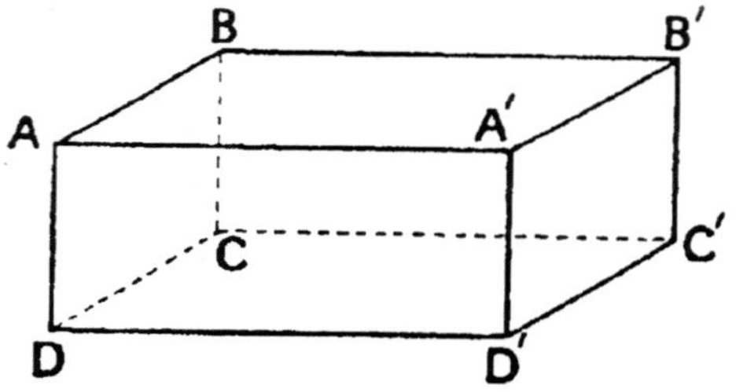

FIG. 2.

Let ABCD A'B'C'D' be a small parallelepiped with faces perpendicular to the axes of co-ordinates and with infinitesimal sides of lengths dx, dy, dz. Let ρ, v_x, v_y, v_z denote the density and velocity components of the cloud at the centre of the parallelepiped. The flux of particles in the interval dt across ABCD is $\left\{\rho v_x - \frac{1}{2}\frac{\partial}{\partial x}(\rho v_x)\,dx\right\}dt\,dy\,dz$, and across A'B'C'D' in the same time the flux is $\left\{\rho v_x + \frac{1}{2}\frac{\partial}{\partial x}(\rho v_x)dx\right\}dt\,dy\,dz$. Thus the excess of those entering over those leaving in this direction is $-\frac{\partial}{\partial x}(\rho v_x)dt\,dx\,dy\,dz$, and a similar calculation applied to the other pairs of faces shows that the total excess is

$$-\operatorname{div}(\rho \mathbf{v})\,dt\,dx\,dy\,dz.$$

This must be equal to the increase during the time dt in the number $\rho\, dx\, dy\, dz$ of particles present in the element of volume. This increase is $\frac{\partial \rho}{\partial t} dt\, dx\, dy\, dz$, so that we obtain the equation of continuity :

$$\frac{\partial \rho}{\partial t} + \text{div}\,(\rho \mathbf{v}) = 0. \quad . \quad . \quad . \quad (13)$$

From a comparison of this equation with (12) we are led to write :

$$\rho = \text{K}a^2, \quad . \quad . \quad . \quad . \quad (14)$$

where K is a constant of proportionality which may be put equal to unity, since a may be multiplied by an arbitrary constant. We can thus say that the square of the amplitude of the ψ-wave or its intensity must be considered as measuring at each instant and at each point the density of the cloud of particles.

2. The Probability of Occurrence

The cloud of particles imagined in the preceding paragraph helps particularly in the visualisation of the assembly of possible modes of motion of the same class for a single particle. The density of this cloud may be considered as representing the probability that a particle, of which the mode of motion belongs to the class considered but of which the actual position is unknown, occupies a particular point at a particular time. Thus a restatement of the result obtained at the end of the last paragraph is that the intensity of the ψ-wave measures at each point at each instant the probability that the associated particle will occupy the point at the particular instant. This is the proposition which we described in the introduction as the principle of interference. We see that when the ψ-wave is propagated according to the laws of geometrical optics, the exactness of the principle is automatically guaranteed by the fact that under these conditions the laws of the old systems of mechanics are applicable to the motion of the particle.

The cloud of particles associated with one and the same wave appears therefore to be interpretable as a probability. We can consider this cloud as forming a fictitious fluid, the probability fluid, of which the density, equal to a^2 by (14), gives at all points and times the probability of occurrence of the particle associated with the ψ-wave considered. The infinitely small portions of this fluid, the probability elements as we shall describe them, describe paths which coincide with possible paths of the particle of which the exact position is unknown. All this theory is very clear in the special case we are considering where geometrical optics is applicable for the propagation of the ψ-wave. We shall see that the difficulties begin when we leave the domain where geometrical optics applies.

We must underline one important point. The phase function is determined quite independently of the amplitude, and from this it follows by the equations of Jacobi's theory that the motion of the particle in its path is quite independent of the function a. This is necessary in order that we may agree with the old mechanics in considering the motion of the particle as being completely determined by the six initial conditions of position and velocity (i e. the six constants of Jacobi's theory). Were the determination of ϕ not independent of that of a, the form of ϕ would depend on the values of that function at the different points of space at the initial instant, and this would mean that the motion of the particle would depend not only upon the initial conditions but also on the probability that the initial co-ordinates had this or that set of values. We shall see that it is this paradoxical circumstance which presents itself when we try to extend the ideas of the old mechanics to the domain proper of the new mechanics.

Let us consider closely the way in which the function $a(x, y, z, t)$ must be determined when we assume that Jacobi's function $S(x, y, z, t, \alpha, \beta, \gamma)$, which is a complete integral of (5), is known. We must find a function satisfying (6) and such that at the initial instant t_0, $a(x, y, z, t_0)$ gives the probability of occurrence of the particle. If, for example, we have carried out an experiment at the instant t_0 to determine the position of the particle, the result is always affected by a certain possible error, and must be expressed by saying that the probability that the particle was at the point (x, y, z) at time t_0 is given by a function $f(x, y, z)$—the region of space where this function has a value appreciably different from zero being the smaller the more exact the experiment—we shall have therefore to impose as an initial condition which the integral, a, of (6) must satisfy, the relation :

$$a^2(x, y, z, t_0) = f(x, y, z). \qquad (15)$$

The meaning of f implies :

$$\int f dv = 1, \qquad (16)$$

where the integral is taken over all space so that the function a always satisfies the condition :

$$\int a^2(x, y, z, t)dv = 1, \qquad (17)$$

since the left-hand side of (17) measures the total probability that the particle occupies a point somewhere in space at time t and this total probability, being a certainty, is evidently unity.

3. Concrete Examples

We give two examples to make these points clear. Let us take first the case where there is no field of force. The plane monochromatic wave is then a solution of the wave-equation. Its amplitude is constant, which means that if we consider an infinite number of particles forming a homogeneous unlimited cloud, all moving with the same velocity, the density will undergo no change with the motion.

More instructive is the case of the motion of an unlimited cloud of particles with the same energy all moving in the direction of a uniform field of force acting upon them. We can describe all the phenomena by a single variable x.

If we resume the notation of Chapter II, § 6, we have :

$$F(x) = -kx \qquad (18)$$

and the abscissa of each particle is given by :

$$x = x_0 + v_0 t + \frac{1}{2}\frac{k}{m}t^2, \qquad (19)$$

x_0 being the abscissa and v_0 the velocity of this particle at time $t = 0$. We have found that the complete integral of Jacobi's equation where W plays the part of an arbitrary constant is :

$$S(x, t, W) = Wt - \frac{1}{3mk}\{2m(kx + W)\}^{\frac{3}{2}}. \qquad (20)$$

Moreover, equation (6), in which we may replace ϕ by S, gives us :

$$\frac{\partial a}{\partial x}\frac{\partial S}{\partial x} + \frac{1}{2}a\frac{\partial^2 S}{\partial x^2} = m\frac{\partial a}{\partial t} \quad . \quad . \quad . \quad (21)$$

As we are determining the motion of an indefinite cloud of particles, we may suppose the motion permanent in such a way that a is independent of the time. Then (21) will become simpler and we have :

$$\frac{\partial a}{\partial x}\frac{\partial S}{\partial x} + \frac{1}{2}a\frac{\partial^2 S}{\partial x^2} = 0 \quad . \quad . \quad (22)$$

Now, by (20) :

$$\frac{\partial S}{\partial x} = -\sqrt{2m(kx + W)}, \quad \frac{\partial^2 S}{\partial x^2} = \frac{-mk}{\sqrt{2m(kx + W)}}, \quad (23)$$

thus the amplitude a must satisfy the equation .

$$\frac{1}{a}\frac{da}{dx} = -\frac{k}{4(kx + W)} \quad . \quad . \quad (24)$$

of which the integral is

$$a = C(kx + w)^{-\frac{1}{4}} \quad . \quad . \quad (25)$$

where C is a constant.

By (14) the density of the cloud is therefore :

$$\rho = a^2 = \frac{C}{\sqrt{kx + W}} = \rho_0\frac{\sqrt{kx_0 + W}}{\sqrt{kx + W}}, \quad . \quad (26)$$

where ρ_0 is the value of ρ for a certain value x_0 of x.

The density of the cloud thus diminishes in the direction of the field. Since we are considering a case where wave mechanics and the old mechanics are identical, we ought to be able to find (26) by means of the classical equations of motion. We proceed to show that this is possible.

Let us fix our attention upon a certain abscissa x_0 and upon the particles to be found in the plane x_0 at the instant $t = 0$. These particles begin with a velocity v_0, and at time t they will have reached the plane with abscissa $x = x_0 + v_0 t + \frac{1}{2}\frac{k}{m}t^2$, by (19). The particles lying in the plane $(x_0 - \delta x_0)$ had a velocity

$v_0 - \delta v_0$ at $t = 0$, and at time t they will have reached the plane with abscissa .

$$x' = (x_0 - \delta x_0) + (v_0 - \delta v_0)t + \frac{1}{2}\frac{k}{m}t^2. \quad . \quad (27)$$

Thus the particles which at zero time occupied a cylinder of unit cross-section bounded by the planes x_0 and $x_0 - \delta x_0$ will occupy at t a cylinder of the same cross-section bounded by the planes x and x'. If N is the number of corpuscles within these limits, the density at x_0 is

$$\rho_0 = \frac{\mathrm{N}}{\delta x_0} \quad . \quad . \quad (28)$$

and at x :

$$\rho = \frac{\mathrm{N}}{x - x'} = \frac{\mathrm{N}}{\delta x_0 + v_0 t} = \frac{\mathrm{N}}{\delta x_0} \frac{1}{1 + \frac{\delta v_0}{\delta x_0}t} = \frac{\rho_0}{1 + \frac{\delta v_0}{\delta x_0}t}. \quad (29)$$

But since by hypothesis all the particles of the cloud have the same energy W, the velocity and abscissa of each particle are related by the equation :

$$\tfrac{1}{2}mv^2 - kx = \mathrm{W} \quad . \quad . \quad . \quad (30)$$

or

$$v = \sqrt{\frac{2(\mathrm{W} + kx)}{m}}. \quad . \quad . \quad . \quad (31)$$

Since δv_0 is the variation which the velocity undergoes for a change of δx_0 in the abscissa, we have by (31) ·

$$\delta v_0 = \frac{k\delta x_0}{\sqrt{2m(\mathrm{W} + kx_0)}} \quad . \quad . \quad . \quad (32)$$

and (29) becomes :

$$\rho = \frac{\rho_0}{1 + \frac{kt}{\sqrt{2m(kx_0 + \mathrm{W})}}} = \rho_0 \frac{\sqrt{kx_0 + \mathrm{W}}}{\sqrt{kx_0 + \mathrm{W}} + \frac{kt}{\sqrt{2m}}}. \quad (33)$$

We have also :

$$v = v_0 + \frac{k}{m}t \quad . \quad . \quad . \quad (34)$$

and by (31) ·

$$\sqrt{kx + \mathrm{W}} = \sqrt{kx_0 + \mathrm{W}} + \frac{kt}{\sqrt{2m}}, \quad . \quad . \quad (35)$$

so that we obtain finally for ρ the expression :

$$\rho = \rho_0 \frac{\sqrt{kx_0 + W}}{\sqrt{kx + W}}, \quad . \quad . \quad . \quad (36)$$

and this is the formula (26) obtained from the amplitude of the associated wave.

4. Summary of the Chapter

We have thus established a parallelism between the old mechanics and the propagation of the ψ-waves when this proceeds according to the laws of geometrical optics.

Jacobi's function then becomes identical with the phase function of the ψ-waves, and if we preserve the classical concept of particles describing well-defined paths with definite velocities, we may imagine a cloud of particles describing all the paths which correspond to one and the same function of Jacobi, in which case the density of the cloud can always be measured by the intensity of the associated wave. We may also imagine a probability fluid the elements of which describe the paths which correspond to a given form of Jacobi's function, and we may say that the density of this fluid measures at each point of space and time the probability of occurrence of a single particle. Our information about this particle is only that it describes one of the paths, but we do not know which.

All these conceptions are in this case clear and quite in harmony with classical ideas, but is it possible to extend them when the conditions of geometrical optics do not prevail ? We shall see that we must at all cost hold to the view that the intensity of the ψ-wave measures the probability of occurrence of the particle, even if our effort makes us sacrifice the traditional idea which gives to the particles a position, a velocity and a well-defined path.

CHAPTER VII

THE PRINCIPLE OF INTERFERENCE AND THE DIFFRACTION OF ELECTRONS BY CRYSTALS

1. The Principle of Interference

THE essential principle which is used in the theory of light to anticipate the results of an experiment in interference or diffraction is that the square of the amplitude, or the intensity, is a measure of the quantity of luminous energy which is present on the average at each point of space. Further, the optical experiments on interference have always given the same result however feeble the intensity of the light used. Thus if we admit the existence of particles of luminous energy, or photons, it is necessary to suppose that for each photon the probability of occurrence is proportional at each point to the intensity of the luminous wave associated with them, this is what we describe as the principle of interference. As we have said in the introduction, it is quite natural in wave mechanics to try to take over this principle from the case of light to that of material particles, that is, to admit that the intensity of the ψ-wave always measures the probability of occurrence of the particle at a particular point of space and time, even though the principles of geometrical optics may not be applicable to the propagation of this wave. Let $P(x, y, z, t)dv$ denote the probability that the particle lies at time t within the element of volume dv, and let (x, y, z) denote the co-ordinates of the centre of this element. By writing :

$$\psi(x, y, z, t) = a(x, y, z, t)e^{\frac{2\pi i}{h}\phi(x, y, z, t)}, \quad . \quad . \quad (1)$$

we have :

$$P = Ka^2 = K\psi\bar{\psi}, \quad . \quad . \quad . \quad (2)$$

$\bar{\psi}$ denoting the complex conjugate of ψ. By a convenient choice of the arbitrary constant factor of a we may make $K = 1$.

The relation (2) is the expression of the principle of interference.

All experiments which have been carried out with particles under conditions where the propagation of the associated waves proceeds according to the laws of geometrical optics verify of necessity the principle of interference, as follows from the preceding chapter. To obtain experimental proof of the general value of the principle it is therefore necessary to turn to phenomena where the associated wave propagation proceeds no longer according to these laws. This is exactly what takes place in experiments on diffraction of electrons by crystals. These experiments may be considered as supplying at one and the same time proof of the necessity of introducing associated waves and proof of the exactness of the principle of interference in its application to material particles.

2. The Diffraction of Electrons

Davisson and Germer have the honour of being the first to obtain diffraction of electrons by crystals. They directed a beam of electrons, all having the same velocity, normally on the face of a nickel crystal, this face of incidence being one of the faces of the regular octahedron of the cubical system of nickel. The electrons first used by Davisson and Germer were very slow ones of 50 to 200 volts; later these American physicists extended their researches to electrons of several hundred volts. The results obtained showed very clearly that there was a concentration of electrons scattered in the directions in which the associated wave is expected to present a maximum as a result of the agreement in phase between the waves diffracted by the different crystal centres. The phenomenon is thus exactly comparable with that of Laue for X-rays. The numerical values have, moreover, indicated clearly that a wavelength of magnitude

$$\lambda = \frac{h}{mv} \qquad \qquad (3)$$

must be attributed to the associated wave, as was indicated by the general theory of Chapter III. Nevertheless, certain differences were found between the results of the experiment and the deductions from the theory of Bragg and Laue obtained by applying (3). It seems possible to explain these differences by taking into account the possibility that within the crystal the index of refraction for the electron waves differs appreciably from that in empty space.

Experiments of the same kind have been very brilliantly repeated by Professor G P. Thomson in a different way. He made use of a method exactly analogous to that of Debye and Sherrer for X-rays by using electrons of great velocities, obtained by subjecting them to potentials of some thousands of volts. Under these circumstances the complications due to the refractive index of the crystals disappear. We have, in fact, found that in a field in which the potential function is $F(x, y, z)$ the refractive index of the associated wave is

$$n = \sqrt{\frac{2(E - F)}{mc^2}} \qquad (4)$$

Outside the field $F = 0$ and the index is

$$n_0 = \sqrt{\frac{2E}{mc^2}}. \qquad (5)$$

The refractive index of the crystal with respect to empty space for the associated waves of an electron with energy E is thus :

$$\frac{n}{n_0} = \sqrt{1 - \frac{F}{E}}, \qquad (6)$$

F being the potential energy of the electron at the point (x, y, z), due to its interaction with the centres of the crystalline medium. Since F does not depend upon E it is evident that $\frac{n}{n_0}$ approaches the value unity as E increases indefinitely.

In the experiments of Davisson and Germer the refractive index $\frac{n}{n_0}$ could have differed from unity by nearly $\frac{1}{10}$; for the electrons in Thomson's experiment, which were 50 to 100 times faster than those in the former, the difference between $\frac{n}{n_0}$ and unity was negligible. We shall see in detail further on that the results were quite in agreement with the theory of Bragg and Laue and with formula (3).

Other very remarkable experiments on the diffraction of electrons have been made in Germany by Rupp, who caused slow electrons to pass through metal films. Here again the theory was verified, but with a slight systematic deviation which was attributed to the refractive index. Quite recently, Rupp, making use of the method so successfully applied by Thibaud for X-rays, was able to diffract a beam of electrons at grazing incidence on an ordinary optical grating. The formula (3) was again verified with great exactness, and the wave-length of the associated electron wave has thus been measured directly by a ruled grating

In the present work it is impossible to examine in detail all the experimental results, which are already numerous We shall limit ourselves to the study of Thomson's experiments which are free from the difficulty with regard to the refractive index. For the other experiments the reader is referred to the original memoirs. The essential point for us is that experiment has provided a wonderful confirmation both of the existence of associated electron waves and of the formula for the wave-length in terms of the velocity. It has also shown the validity of the principle of interference, even in its application to material particles.

3. Preliminaries to the Study of G. P. Thomson's Experiments

The method of G. P. Thomson is to send an approximately homogeneous beam of electrons across a very thin metal film We regard such a film nowadays as made up of very small crystals joined together. In order to see to what phenomenon the scattering of waves by these crystals must give rise we must first recall some of the notions of crystallography.

Since the work of Bravais we regard all crystals as formed of material centres arranged according to regular laws in the form of a lattice. The simplest type of lattice is that in which any displacement of the form $n_1\mathbf{a} + n_2\mathbf{b} + n_3\mathbf{c}$ causes one crystalline centre to be carried over to another, **a**, **b**, **c** being three vectors not all in the same plane and n_1, n_2, n_3 being any three integers. The centres or nuclei thus form the corners of an infinite number of parallelepipeds situated side by side. If we consider two nuclei, A and B, of a simple lattice, the displacement which makes one pass into the others is thus of the form $n(h\mathbf{a} + j\mathbf{b} + k\mathbf{c})$, where n is an integer, while h, j, k are three integers with no common factor. The straight line AB thus carries an infinite number of centres which may be derived from one another by means of the displacement $h\mathbf{a} + j\mathbf{b} + k\mathbf{c}$. It follows that any plane containing three nuclei not in a straight line contains an infinite number of nuclei at the corners of adjacent parallelograms ; such a plane is called reticular. If a reticular plane is subject to a displacement $n_1\mathbf{a} + n_2\mathbf{b} + n_3\mathbf{c}$ we obtain another parallel reticular plane, and thus the reticular planes form a system of parallel planes. In order to describe a family of reticular planes we will take three co-ordinate axes passing through a nucleus of the lattice and parallel respectively to the three vectors $\mathbf{a}$, $\mathbf{b}$ and $\mathbf{c}$. We will then consider that plane of the family closest to the origin which cuts the three axes in three nuclei situated on the positive sides. This plane cuts the x-axis at the point m_1a. the y-axis at m_2b and the z-axis at m_3c. The indices of the family of reticular planes considered are the smallest whole numbers (h_1, h_2, h_3) which are proportional to the reciprocals of (m_1, m_2, m_3).

The plane which serves to define the numbers (m_1, m_2, m_3) is represented by the equation :

$$\frac{x}{m_1a} + \frac{y}{m_2b} + \frac{z}{m_3c} = 1. \qquad (7)$$

Let k denote the lowest common multiple of m_1, m_2 and m_3, then :

$$h_1 = \frac{k}{m_1}, \quad h_2 = \frac{k}{m_2}, \quad h_3 = \frac{k}{m_3}, \qquad (8)$$

and equation (7) may be written :

$$h_1\frac{x}{a} + h_2\frac{y}{b} + h_3\frac{z}{c} = k. \qquad (9)$$

All the reticular planes of the same family have therefore an equation of the form :

$$h_1\frac{x}{a} + h_2\frac{y}{b} + h_3\frac{z}{c} = \text{constant}. \qquad (10)$$

Now it is easy to see that a plane of the family considered passes through every nucleus of the lattice. Suppose that P is a plane passing through a nucleus A, and let B be another nucleus not lying in P. We pass from A to B by a displacement $n_1\mathbf{a} + n_2\mathbf{b} + n_3\mathbf{c}$, and this displacement transforms P into a parallel plane P′ passing through B. Every nucleus situated in P is transformed to one situated in P′. The plane P′, which contains an infinite number of nuclei, is a reticular plane of the same family as P, and it passes through the nucleus B which is chosen arbitrarily.

With the notation just used we proceed to calculate the distance between parallel planes P and P′, but we shall make the restriction that the vectors **a**, **b**, **c** are mutually perpendicular, since this is the only case to which we shall have to apply our formulæ. Let A be the origin of co-ordinates so that the plane P has for its equation :

$$h_1\frac{x}{a} + h_2\frac{y}{b} + h_3\frac{z}{c} = 0 \quad . \quad . \quad . \quad (11)$$

where (h_1, h_2, h_3) are the indices of the family of planes of which P is a member. The co-ordinates of B are (n_1a, n_2b, n_3c), and since the co-ordinates are rectangular the distance from B to the plane P is given by the formula of analytical geometry :

$$d = \frac{h_1n_1 + h_2n_2 + h_3n_3}{\sqrt{\left(\frac{h_1}{a}\right)^2 + \left(\frac{h_2}{b}\right)^2 + \left(\frac{h_3}{c}\right)^2}}. \quad . \quad . \quad (12)$$

B may be any nucleus whatever, that is to say, we may choose for (n_1, n_2, n_3) any whole numbers, positive or negative, and the numerator of (12) may consequently have any integral value. Thus we conclude that the reticular planes of the family (h_1, h_2, h_3) are equidistant from one another with a separation

$$d_{h_1h_2h_3} = \frac{1}{\sqrt{\left(\frac{h_1}{a}\right)^2 + \left(\frac{h_2}{b}\right)^2 + \left(\frac{h_3}{c}\right)^2}}. \quad . \quad (13)$$

In the case of a cubic lattice $a = b = c$ and :

$$d_{h_1h_2h_3} = \frac{a}{\sqrt{h_1^2 + h_2^2 + h_3^2}}. \quad . \quad . \quad (14)$$

The simple cubic lattice is formed by nuclei situated at the corners of an infinite number of cubes in juxtaposition. It is defined by three vectors (**a**, **b**, **c**) mutually perpendicular and of the same length a. The most important families of reticular planes are :

(100) cube faces.
(111) faces of octahedra.
(110) faces of dodecahedra.

The corresponding equidistances are :

$$d_{100} = a, \quad d_{111} = \frac{a}{\sqrt{3}}, \quad d_{110} = \frac{a}{\sqrt{2}}.$$

But it often happens that actual cubic lattices have a more complicated structure. It may happen, for example, that each elementary cube carries not only nuclei at the corners, but also a nucleus at its centre and we then have a lattice of centred cubes.

It is just as if we had two simple cubic lattices displaced from one another by $\frac{1}{2}(\mathbf{a} + \mathbf{b} + \mathbf{c})$. The most general displacement which then makes one nucleus pass into another is $\left(n_1 + \frac{\epsilon_1}{2}\right)\mathbf{a} + \left(n_2 + \frac{\epsilon_2}{2}\right)\mathbf{b} + \left(n_3 + \frac{\epsilon_3}{2}\right)\mathbf{c}$, where (n_1, n_2, n_3) are integers and $(\epsilon_1, \epsilon_2, \epsilon_3)$ are equal to 0 or 1. If we repeat the argument above in this case we find that the separation of the planes of a family (h_1, h_2, h_3) is :

$$\left.\begin{aligned} d_{h_1h_2h_3} &= \frac{a}{\sqrt{h_1^2 + h_2^2 + h_3^2}} \text{ if } (h_1 + h_2 + h_3) \text{ is even} \\ \text{and} \quad d_{h_1h_2h_3} &= \frac{1}{2}\frac{a}{\sqrt{h_1^2 + h_2^2 + h_3^2}} \text{ if } (h_1 + h_2 + h_3) \text{ is odd.} \end{aligned}\right\} \quad (15)$$

Finally, and this is the case in Thomson's experiments, we may have a cubic lattice in which each elementary cube carries a nucleus at the centre of each of its six faces ; this is a face-centred lattice. The most general displacement which carries one nucleus into another is now

$$\left(n_1 + \frac{\epsilon_1}{2}\right)\mathbf{a} + \left(n_2 + \frac{\epsilon_2}{2}\right)\mathbf{b} + \left(n_3 + \frac{\epsilon_3}{2}\right)\mathbf{c},$$

where the n's have the same significance as before, but the ϵ's are either all zero or two have the values unity and the third is zero. The distance from a nucleus B to a reticular plane passing through A is:

$$d = \frac{\left(n_1 + \frac{\epsilon_1}{2}\right)h_1 + \left(n_2 + \frac{\epsilon_2}{2}\right)h_2 + \left(n_3 + \frac{\epsilon_3}{2}\right)h_3}{\sqrt{h_1^2 + h_2^2 + h_3^2}}. \quad . \quad (16)$$

If the h's are all odd or all even, we have:

$$d_{h_1h_2h_3} = \frac{a}{\sqrt{h_1^2 + h_2^2 + h_3^2}}, \quad . \quad . \quad (17)$$

while if odd and even values of the h's occur, we have

$$d_{h_1h_2h_3} = \frac{1}{2} \cdot \frac{a}{\sqrt{h_1^2 + h_2^2 + h_3^2}} = \frac{a}{\sqrt{(2h_1)^2 + (2h_2)^2 + (2h_3)^2}}. \quad (18)$$

Thus we may say that (17) applies in the latter case provided the indices are doubled.

4. Experiments of G. P. Thomson

Let us return to G. P. Thomson's experiments and suppose that a homogeneous beam of cathode rays in its passage through a thin metal film encounters in one of the small crystals of which the film is composed a plane with indices (h_1, h_2, h_3) at an angle of incidence θ, where θ denotes the complement of the angle of incidence usually considered in optics. The wave associated with the incident electrons will undergo a strong scattering in the direction of regular reflection if there is agreement in phase amongst the elementary waves scattered by the nuclei of the different reticular planes of indices (h_1, h_2, h_3).

In the first place, the waves scattered by two centres A and B lying in the same reticular plane are always in phase in the direction of regular reflection, since the optical paths A′B and AB′ are equal, both having the value AB cos θ (Fig. 3).

If, further, the waves scattered by two centres A and C, situated as in the figure, are in phase, the waves scattered by all the nuclei of the crystal will be in phase and we shall have in the direction of regular reflection a large maximum of intensity. The condition for this is that the optical paths of the ray scattered by A and of that scattered by C differ by an integral multiple of the wave-length. This gives:

$$DC + CD' = n\lambda \ (n = \text{an integer}),$$

i.e.

$$2d_{h_1h_2h_3} \sin \theta = n\lambda. \quad . \quad . \quad . \quad (19)$$

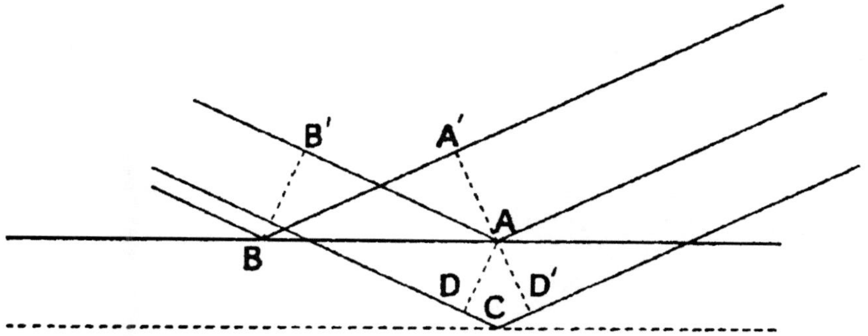

FIG. 3.

This is the well-known relation of Bragg for X-rays. His demonstration assumes that the difference between the idea of refraction for the crystal and for empty space may be neglected,

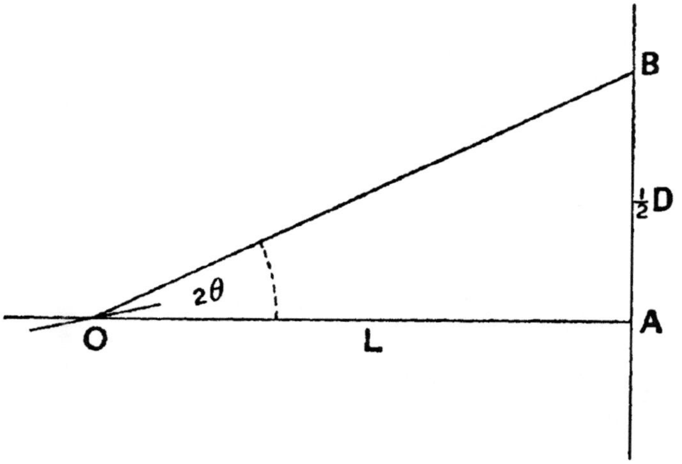

OA = L; AB = ½D.

FIG. 4.

and we have seen that this is a legitimate assumption for the case of Thomson's experiments.

Let L be the distance from the metal film to the photographic plate on which the electrons are received. We expect to obtain for each reflection on a small crystal a small spot at a distance $\frac{D}{2}$ from the direction of the cathode beam, where $\frac{D}{2} = L \tan 2\theta$, if the principle of interference holds for the electrons, that is to say, if the square of the amplitude of the wave measures the probability of occurrence of electrons at each point.

The wave-length λ of the wave associated with the incident electrons is the magnitude which controls this phenomenon. From the general formulæ :

$$\lambda = \frac{h}{p} = \frac{h}{mv}\sqrt{1-\beta^2}. \quad (20)$$

The velocity of the electrons is determined by the potential difference P applied to put them in motion. We have :

$$\frac{mc^2}{\sqrt{1-\beta^2}} - mc^2 = eP, \quad (21)$$

whence

$$\frac{1}{1-\beta^2} - 1 = \frac{\beta^2}{1-\beta^2} = \frac{2eP}{mc^2} + \frac{e^2P^2}{m^2c^4} \quad (22)$$

and

$$\frac{\sqrt{1-\beta^2}}{\beta c} = \frac{1}{\sqrt{\frac{2eP}{m} + \frac{e^2P^2}{m^2c^2}}}, \quad (23)$$

whence finally :

$$\lambda = \frac{h}{\sqrt{2meP\left(1 + \frac{eP}{2mc^2}\right)}}. \quad (24)$$

The term $\frac{eP}{2mc^2}$ is always small, so that it is sufficient to write :

$$\lambda = \frac{h}{\sqrt{2meP}}\left(1 - \frac{eP}{4mc^2}\right), \quad (25)$$

and in this formula the value of e is $-4{\cdot}77 \times 10^{-10}$ e.s.u.

If P be expressed in volts (25) must be replaced by :

$$\lambda = h\sqrt{\frac{150}{meP}}\left(1 - \frac{eP}{1200mc^2}\right). \quad (26)$$

In Thomson's experiments the correction term was never greater than 3 per cent., so that we may write as an approximate formula :

$$\lambda = h\sqrt{\frac{150}{me\text{P}}}, \quad . \quad . \quad . \quad (27)$$

which can be obtained directly from the non-relativistic relations

$$\lambda = \frac{h}{mv} \quad \text{and} \quad \frac{1}{2}mv^2 = e\text{P}$$

By applying the foregoing relations we find for 25,000 volt electrons the value $0{\cdot}75 \times 10^{-9}$ cms for the wave-length, which shows that the electronic waves correspond to very hard X-rays. As the ordinary crystal lattices have plane separations of the order of 10^{-8} cms., the angles θ will be very small, and it will be sufficient to replace $\sin\theta$ and $\tan 2\theta$ in the formulæ by θ and 2θ respectively. We have, therefore, approximately .

$$2d\theta = n\lambda \text{ and } \frac{\text{D}}{2} = \text{L} \quad 2\theta,$$

whence

$$\text{D} = \frac{2n\lambda\text{L}}{d_{h_1h_2h_3}}. \quad . \quad . \quad . \quad . \quad (28)$$

If the microcrystals of the film are oriented by chance, we shall obtain on the photographic plate not a spot but an infinite number of spots describing a continuous ring, of diameter D, about the line of incidence of the beam If the metal film contains microcrystals presenting any degree of specialised orientation, we shall have more complicated appearances, certain rings being absent others interrupted. This has been observed. It must be noted that the films should be very thin in order that the electron beam should not be too much absorbed nor subject to multiple scattering.

The first experiments carried out by Thomson as a test were made on aluminium and gold. One of the first things to be verified is that for a given ring, i.e one produced by a particular family of reticular planes, the ratio $\frac{\text{D}}{\lambda}$ is constant. In other words, if the tension P is progressively increased, the ring system will contract and if the contraction of a ring be followed, the relation

$$\frac{D}{\lambda} = \text{constant},$$

or

$$D\sqrt{P}\left(1 + \frac{eP}{1200\, mc^2}\right) = \text{constant} \quad . \qquad (29)$$

must be verified.

The following are tables of values given by Thomson :—

Aluminium

P (volts)	D (cms)	$D\sqrt{P}\left(1+\frac{1}{1200}\frac{eP}{mc^2}\right)$
64,000	1·47	384
57,600	1 62	398
45,000	1 78	388
34,500	2·00	378

Gold

58,000	1·50	371
55,000	1·58	381
44,000	1·75	376
33,700	2 00	374

Platinum

45,000	1·85	402
40,000	1 96	400
34,500	2 23	421
25,500	2 46	398

Aluminium (with another value of L)

34,500	1·64	310
27,500	1 84	310
26,200	1·86	305
21,800	2 09	312

Platinum (with another value of L)

29,000	1·84	319
24,000	1 98	311

The variation of wave-length with the potential P and consequently with the velocity of the electrons is thus well verified.

For a particular potential, D and D′ corresponding to the reflections on reticular planes with indices (h_1, h_2, h_3) and (h_1', h_2', h_3') are in the ratio :

$$\frac{D'}{D} = \frac{d_{h_1h_2h_3}}{d_{h_1'h_2'h_3'}} . \qquad (30)$$

Since the metals used crystallise in the face-centred cubic system, we have :

$$d_{h_1h_2h_3} = \frac{a}{\sqrt{h_1^2 + h_2^2 + h_3^2}}, \quad . \quad . \quad (31)$$

a being the edge of the cube and the indices being doubled if they are not all odd or all even. Thus with this convention :

$$\frac{D'}{D} = \frac{\sqrt{h_1^2 + h_2^2 + h_3^2}}{\sqrt{h_1'^2 + h_2'^2 + h_3'^2}} \quad . \quad . \quad (32)$$

In a series of experiments on aluminium, Thomson obtained rings with diameters proportional to :

$$\begin{array}{lllll}
\sqrt{4}, & \sqrt{8\cdot00}, & \sqrt{10\cdot9}, & \sqrt{16\cdot5}, & \sqrt{27}, \\
\sqrt{4}, & \sqrt{7\cdot65}, & \sqrt{10\cdot6}, & \sqrt{14\cdot8}, & \\
\sqrt{4}, & \sqrt{8\cdot05}, & \sqrt{11\cdot05}, & \sqrt{15\cdot8}, & \sqrt{28}, \\
\sqrt{4} & \sqrt{7\cdot93}, & \sqrt{11\cdot4}, & \sqrt{16}, & \\
\sqrt{4}, & \sqrt{7\cdot95}, & \sqrt{10\cdot8}, & \sqrt{15\cdot8}, & \sqrt{26\cdot6}, \\
\sqrt{4}, & \sqrt{8\cdot00}, & \sqrt{10\cdot9}, & \sqrt{15\cdot4}, & \sqrt{27\cdot4}
\end{array}$$

This series is a good approximation to the series :

$$\sqrt{4}, \quad \sqrt{8}, \quad \sqrt{11}, \quad \sqrt{16}, \quad \sqrt{27},$$

which corresponds to the reticular planes :

200, 220, 311, 400, 511

In the same way the following series has been found for platinum :

$$\begin{array}{llllllll}
\sqrt{3}, & \sqrt{4\cdot00}, & \sqrt{7\cdot95}, & \sqrt{11\cdot1}, & \sqrt{16\cdot2}, & \sqrt{18\cdot8}, & \sqrt{23\cdot2}. & \sqrt{26\cdot8}, \\
\sqrt{3}, & \sqrt{4\cdot05}, & \sqrt{8\cdot05}, & \sqrt{11\cdot4}, & \sqrt{15\cdot2}, & \sqrt{18\cdot4}, & \sqrt{22\cdot5}, & \sqrt{26\cdot3}, \\
\sqrt{3}, & \sqrt{3\cdot98}, & \sqrt{7\cdot95}, & \sqrt{10\cdot8}, & \sqrt{15\cdot2}, & \sqrt{18\cdot3}, & \sqrt{23\cdot8}, & \sqrt{26\cdot4},
\end{array}$$

and these correspond to the series :

$$\sqrt{3}, \quad \sqrt{4}, \quad \sqrt{8}, \quad \sqrt{11}, \quad \sqrt{16}, \quad \sqrt{19}, \quad \sqrt{24}, \quad \sqrt{27},$$

associated with the reticular planes :

111, 200, 220, 311, 400, 331, 422, 333.

We have similarly two series for gold :

$$\begin{array}{lllll}
\sqrt{3}, & \sqrt{4\cdot2}, & \sqrt{7\cdot9}, & \sqrt{11\cdot5}, & \sqrt{19\cdot9}, \\
\sqrt{3}, & \sqrt{4\cdot08}, & \sqrt{8}, & \sqrt{11\cdot1}, & \sqrt{19\cdot9},
\end{array}$$

which are very close to the series .

$$\sqrt{3}, \quad \sqrt{4}, \quad \sqrt{8}, \quad \sqrt{11}, \quad \sqrt{20},$$

corresponding to the planes :

111, 200, 220, 311, 420.

Having in this way found the indices of the reflecting planes, we can calculate the edges of the cubes and compare the results with the values found in X-ray experiments. The results are :

	Al	Au.	Pt.
For cathode rays, $a =$	4·035Å,	4·20Å,	3·89Å.
For X-rays, $a =$	4·063Å,	4·06Å,	3·91Å.

Thomson also verified, in a very interesting way, that the production of impressions on the photographic plate was by electrons scattered by the film and not by secondary X-rays. This was done by establishing a magnetic field between the film and the plate and observing the displacement of the ring pattern as a whole by the action of the field. He was, in this way, able to verify that the velocity of the scattered electrons was equal to that of those incident.

The first of Thomson's experiments were carried out with a celluloid film, and gave definite results but rather qualitative in character. One of his pupils, Mr. Reid, has since resumed these experiments and found a good agreement with theory by assuming the existence of two plane separations of 3·67Å and 4·35Å, while the distances measured by Müller for the fatty acids are 3·67Å and 4·08Å. Finally, another collaborator of Thomson's, Mr. Ironside, has also obtained a confirmation of the theory for films of copper, silver and tin, metals which crystallise also in face-centred cubes. The following are examples of the values of the sides of the elementary cubes which he has obtained compared with those obtained with X-rays :

	Ag.	Cu	Sn.
For cathode rays, $a =$	4·11Å,	3·66Å,	2·86Å
For X-rays. $a =$	4·08Å,	3·60Å,	2·91Å.

CHAPTER VIII

THE PRINCIPLE OF INTERFERENCE AND THE SCATTERING OF CHARGED PARTICLES BY A FIXED CENTRE

1. The Scattering of Charged Particles According to Classical Mechanics

WE pass on to another example of the value of the principle of interference in its application to material particles ; we shall in fact show that the principle of interference applied to electrified particles gives Rutherford's law for the scattering of these particles in their passage through matter, a law which has been verified by experiment (Rutherford and Chadwick) We will begin with the classical method by which Rutherford established the law, then by means of a calculation by Wentzel we will show that we arrive at the same result by using the ideas of wave mechanics and the principle of interference.

Let e and m denote the charge and mass of the incident particles, e_1 the charge of the scattering centre, supposed fixed, close to which the incident particles pass in traversing the matter. We shall suppose, in accordance with the conditions of the experiment, that in the beginning the charged particles all move with the same velocity $\mathbf{v}$ in a certain direction. We will take the position of the fixed centre as origin and the direction of the initial motion as the axis of x (Fig. 5).

Once out of the region where the action of the centre is appreciable, each particle will again move in a straight line with a uniform velocity $\mathbf{v}$ but in a direction which makes a certain angle with the original direction of motion The principle of conservation of moment of momentum about O gives :

$$mvb = -mr^2\frac{d\theta}{dt}, \qquad (1)$$

(r, θ) being the polar co-ordinates of the particle at time t and b the initial distance from the polar axis.

Again, taking account of Coulomb's law, the equation of motion along Oy perpendicular to Ox is :

$$m\frac{dv_y}{dt} = \frac{ee_1}{r^2}\sin\theta = -\frac{ee_1}{bv}\sin\theta \cdot \frac{d\theta}{dt} \quad . \quad . \quad (2)$$

Integrating :

$$mv\sin\alpha = \frac{ee_1}{vb}(1 + \cos\alpha), \quad . \quad . \quad . \quad (3)$$

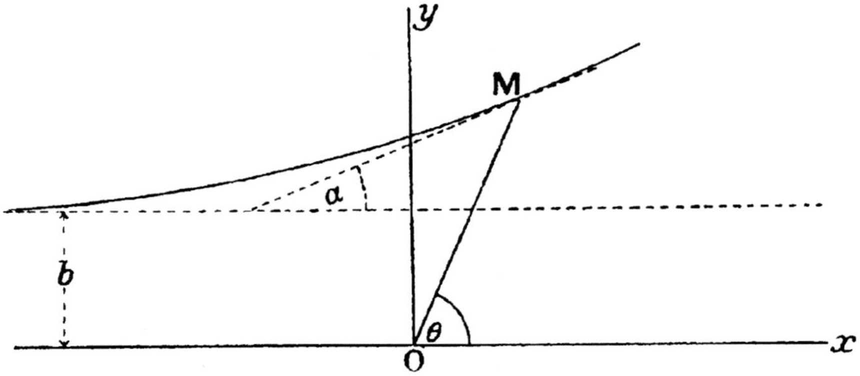

FIG. 5.

where the limits are for θ, π to α, and for v_y, 0 to $v\sin\alpha$.

From (3) we find .

$$b = \frac{ee_1}{mv^2\sin\alpha}(1 + \cos\alpha) = \frac{ee_1}{mv^2}\cot\frac{\alpha}{2}. \quad . \quad (4)$$

Now the probability that the distance between the initial trajectory and the x-axis should lie between b and $b + db$ is clearly $2\pi bdb$ multiplied by a constant It is also equal to the probability $P(\alpha)d\alpha$ that the final angle made with x-axis should lie within the range α to $(\alpha + d\alpha)$, which corresponds according to (4) to the range b to $b + db$. Taking account of the fact that α and b vary in opposite senses, we have :

$$P(\alpha)d\alpha = -A2\pi bdb = -B\frac{db^2}{d\alpha}d\alpha = -B\frac{e^2e_1{}^2}{m^2v^4}\frac{d}{d\alpha}\left(\cot^2\frac{\alpha}{2}\right)d\alpha, \quad . \quad . \quad . \quad (5)$$

where A is a constant and $B = \pi A$.

The number of particles undergoing a deviation included between α_1 and α_2 is proportional to $\left(\cot^2\frac{\alpha_1}{2} - \cot^2\frac{\alpha_2}{2}\right)$, which is Rutherford's law. There is, however, a difficulty, for if we integrate (5) from 0 to α_0 we see that the number of particles undergoing a deviation less than α_0 is infinitely great. This may appear to be an objection to the result of the calculation, but it is not so, for we have in fact implicitly supposed the incident beam of particles unlimited laterally, and if this is so there would be an infinite number of particles passing far enough from the centre to undergo no appreciable deviation. But in practice the beams of particles are always limited laterally, so that the calculation no longer applies to large values of b, that is to say, to small values of α, and it is precisely for these small values of α that $\int P(\alpha)d\alpha$ diverges.

2. The Calculation by means of Wave Mechanics

Let us now take the point of view of the new mechanics We must associate with the incident particles the wave :

$$\psi_0(x, t) = a_0 e^{\frac{2\pi i}{h}(Wt - mvx)}, \qquad (6)$$

where a_0 is a constant and where W has the value :

$$W = mc^2 + \tfrac{1}{2}mv^2 = mc^2 + E, \qquad (7)$$

the second term being very small relatively to the first if we restrict ourselves to the Newtonian approximation as in the preceding paragraph. The wave-length has the value :

$$\lambda = \frac{h}{mv}, \qquad (8)$$

and under the usual experimental conditions it is always very small and of the order of that of X-rays.

In the neighbourhood of the scattering centre, O, a field of force with a potential function $F(r)$ exists, and the wave-equation is :

$$\nabla^2\psi + \frac{8\pi^2 m}{h^2}(E - F)\psi = 0. \qquad (9)$$

When the ψ-waves enter this region we have a condition similar to that which occurs when a light wave enters a non-homogeneous refracting medium ; a scattered wave is superposed upon the incident wave ψ_0

We suppose that the scattering does not appreciably enfeeble the incident wave, whence :

$$\psi = \psi_0 + \psi_1, \quad \psi_1 \ll \psi_0 \qquad (10)$$

Since ψ_0 satisfies the equation :

$$\nabla^2\psi_0 + \frac{8\pi^2 m}{h^2}E\psi_0 = 0 \qquad (11)$$

the scattered wave is an approximate solution of the equation :

$$\nabla^2\psi_1 + \frac{8\pi^2 m}{h^2}E\psi_1 = \frac{8\pi^2 m}{h^2}F\psi_0. \qquad (12)$$

a result which follows from (9) and (10). Now, since the frequency $\frac{W}{h}$ is approximately equal to $\frac{mc^2}{h}$ for the incident as for the scattered wave, we have

$$\frac{\partial^2\psi_1}{\partial t^2} = -\frac{4\pi^2 m^2 c^4}{h^2}\psi_1 \text{ or } \frac{8\pi^2 m}{h^2}\psi_1 = -\frac{2}{mc^4}\frac{\partial^2\psi_1}{\partial t^2}, \qquad (13)$$

and substituting (13) in (12),

$$\nabla^2\psi_1 - \frac{2E}{mc^4}\frac{\partial^2\psi_1}{\partial t^2} = \frac{8\pi^2 m}{h^2}F\psi_0 \qquad (14)$$

Since $2E = mv^2$, we have .

$$\nabla^2\psi_1 - \frac{1}{V^2}\frac{\partial^2\psi_1}{\partial t^2} = \frac{8\pi^2 m}{h^2}F\psi_0. \qquad (15)$$

where

$$V = \frac{c^2}{v}. \qquad (16)$$

$\psi_0(x, t)$ and $F(r)$ being given in this problem, the equation (15) is of the form :

$$\nabla^2\psi_1 - \frac{1}{V^2}\frac{\partial^2\psi_1}{\partial t^2} = \sigma(x, y, z, t), \qquad (17)$$

where

$$\sigma(x, y, z, t) = \frac{8\pi^2 m}{h^2}F(r)\psi_0(x, t) \qquad (18)$$

The solution of (17) is given by Kirchhoff's well-known formula of retarded potentials :

$$\psi_1 = -\frac{1}{4\pi}\iiint\left[\frac{\sigma}{\rho}\right]_{t-\frac{\rho}{V}} d\tau, \qquad . \quad . \quad (19)$$

$d\tau$ being an element of volume surrounding a point M of the region of integration, and ρ denoting the distance PM, where P is the point for which ψ_1 is calculated at a time t. The suffix $\left(t - \frac{\rho}{V}\right)$ denotes that $\frac{\sigma}{\rho}$ has its value, not at the instant t, but at the instant $\left(t - \frac{\rho}{V}\right)$. In this case we must write :

$$[F\psi_0]_{t-\frac{r}{V}} = F(r)a_0 e^{2\pi i\left(\frac{Wt}{h} - \frac{x+\rho}{\lambda}\right)}, \qquad . \quad (20)$$

and therefore from (18) and (19) :

$$\psi_1 = -\frac{2\pi m}{h^2} a_0 e^{\frac{2\pi i}{h}Wt} \iiint \frac{F}{\rho} e^{-\frac{2\pi i}{\lambda}(x+\rho)} d\tau. \qquad (21)$$

A difficulty arises here, for it would be natural to write ·

$$F(r) = \frac{ee_1}{r} \quad . \quad . \quad . \quad . \quad (22)$$

since the action of the scattering centre on the incident particles follows Coulomb's law If, however, we use this relation, the integral of (21) will be divergent, as we shall see from our calculation. To avoid this difficulty, Wentzel has written ·

$$F(r) = \frac{ee_1}{r} e^{-kr}, \quad . \quad . \quad . \quad . \quad (23)$$

k having the property that $k\lambda \ll 1$. In a region surrounding the centre O and of dimensions large compared with the wave-length, the expression (23) is approximately identical with that of Coulomb. But in regions far removed from O the exponential factor is appreciable and the rapid decrease in F with increase in r prevents infinite scattering. We believe that it is possible to interpret Wentzel's device in the following way. By representing the incident wave as plane and monochromatic we thereby assume the incident beam to be actually unlimited, and this cannot correspond to anything occurring in practice.

The incident beam is necessarily limited laterally, and it would have to be represented by a train of waves of finite dimensions. If we wish to simplify the calculation by representing the incident beam by a monochromatic wave, we must of necessity correct the error thereby introduced, and this is done by introducing Wentzel's exponential factor to annul the influence of the distant portions of the monochromatic wave, these portions having in fact no real existence.

Let us accept Wentzel's hypothesis and calculate the scattered wave at a point P very distant from O (Fig. 6).

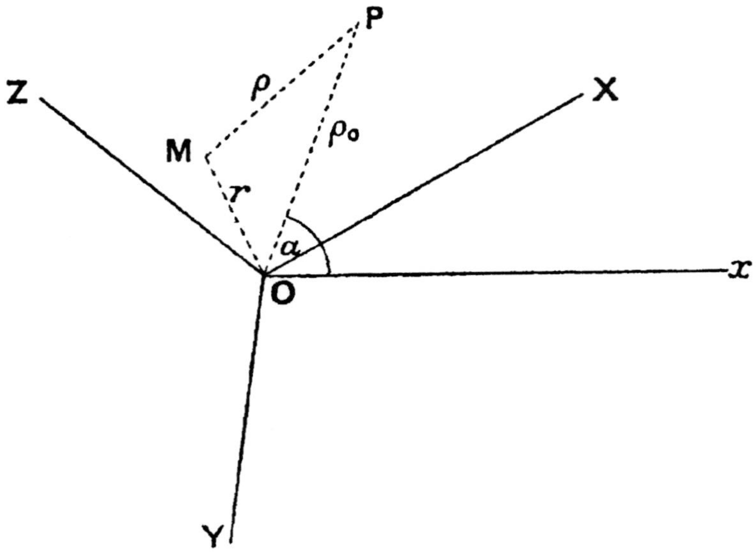

FIG. 6.

On account of the factor e^{-kr} the integration (21) concerns only the immediate neighbourhood of O; we may thus replace ρ by OP $= \rho_0$ in the slowly varying factor $\frac{1}{\rho}$, and in the exponential factor write:

$$\rho = \rho_0 - r \cos \widehat{POM}. \quad \quad (24)$$

The equation (21) now becomes:

$$\psi_1 = -\frac{2\pi m}{h^2} \cdot ee_1 \frac{a_0}{\rho_0} e^{2\pi i\left(\frac{W}{h}t - \frac{\rho_0}{\lambda}\right)} \iiint \frac{e^{-kr + \frac{2\pi i}{\lambda}(r \cos \widehat{MOP} - x)}}{r} d\tau. \quad \quad (25)$$

Choose a system of rectangular co-ordinates (X, Y, Z) such that the plane XOZ coincides with the plane xOP and let OX and OZ be the internal and external bisectors respectively of the angle $x\hat{O}P = \alpha$. Let OY be perpendicular to the plane xOP. The polar co-ordinates of M are (r, θ, ϕ), with OZ as the polar axis. In the system (X, Y, Z) the direction cosines of Ox, OM, OP are given by the following table ·

	OX.	OY.	OZ.
Ox . .	$\cos\frac{\alpha}{2}$	O	$-\sin\frac{\alpha}{2}$
OM . .	$\sin\theta\cos\phi$	$\sin\theta\sin\phi$	$\cos\theta$
OP . .	$\cos\frac{\alpha}{2}$	O	$\sin\frac{\alpha}{2}$

Thus :

$$\left.\begin{aligned} \cos P\hat{O}M &= \sin\theta\cos\phi\cos\frac{\alpha}{2} + \cos\theta\sin\frac{\alpha}{2} \\ x = r\cos M\hat{O}x &= r\left(\sin\theta\cos\phi\cos\frac{\alpha}{2} - \cos\theta\sin\frac{\alpha}{2}\right) \\ r\cos M\hat{O}P - x &= 2r\cos\theta\sin\frac{\alpha}{2} \end{aligned}\right\} \qquad (26)$$

The integral in (25) becomes, therefore,

$$\int_0^{2\pi} d\phi \int_0^{\pi} \sin\theta\, d\theta \int_0^{\infty} e^{-kr + \frac{4\pi i}{\lambda} r\cos\theta\sin\frac{\alpha}{2}} r\,dr. \qquad . \quad (27)$$

The integration with respect to ϕ gives 2π. On integrating by parts with respect to r, noting that the real part of the exponent is negative, we find for the integral in r the value :

$$\frac{1}{\left(-k + \frac{4\pi i}{\lambda}\sin\frac{\alpha}{2}\cos\theta\right)^2}, \qquad . \quad (28)$$

or approximately :

$$-\frac{1}{\frac{16\pi^2}{\lambda^2}\sin^2\frac{\alpha}{2}\cos^2\theta}, \qquad . \quad . \quad (29)$$

on account of the order of magnitude of k.

We have also :

$$\int_0^\pi \frac{\sin\theta d\theta}{\cos^2\theta} = \left(\frac{1}{\cos\theta}\right)_0^\pi = -2, \quad . \quad . \quad (30)$$

so that finally the value of (27) is :

$$\frac{\lambda^2}{4\pi\sin^2\frac{\alpha}{2}} \quad . \quad (31)$$

Substituting (31) in (25) we have :

$$\psi_1 = -\frac{\lambda^2 mee_1}{2h^2}\frac{a_0}{\rho_0\sin^2\frac{\alpha}{2}}e^{2\pi i\left(\frac{W}{h}t-\frac{\rho_0}{\lambda}\right)}, \quad . \quad . \quad (32)$$

and since $\frac{m\lambda^2}{h^2} = \frac{1}{mv^2}$, the square of the amplitude at P of the scattered wave has the value :

$$a_1^2 = \frac{e^2e_1^2}{4m^2v^2}\frac{a_0^2}{\rho_0^2\sin^4\frac{\alpha}{2}}. \quad . \quad . \quad (33)$$

Let us consider the sphere with centre O and radius ρ_0. The number of scattered particles traversing the spherical zone corresponding to the angular interval α to $(\alpha + d\alpha)$ per unit time must be .

$$\frac{e^2e_1^2}{4m^2v^4}\frac{a_0^2}{\rho_0^2\sin^4\frac{\alpha}{2}} v\,2\pi\rho_0^2\sin\alpha\,d\alpha = \frac{\pi e^2e_1^2}{2m^2v^4}\cdot\frac{a_0^2}{\sin^4\frac{\alpha}{2}}v\sin\alpha\,d\alpha \quad (34)$$

since a_1^2 measures the density of the cloud of scattered particles. Moreover, the number of particles crossing a wave front, $x =$ constant, per unit time situated far away on the left of the centre O is clearly proportional to a_0^2v. The probability of a deviation between α and $(\alpha + d\alpha)$ is therefore :

$$P(\alpha)\,d\alpha = A\frac{e^2e_1^2}{m^2v^4}\cdot\frac{1}{\sin^4\frac{\alpha}{2}}\cdot 2\sin\frac{\alpha}{2}\cos\frac{\alpha}{2}\,d\alpha$$

$$= -A\frac{e^2e_1^2}{m^2v^4}\cdot\frac{d}{d\alpha}\left(\cot^2\frac{\alpha}{2}\right)d\alpha \quad . \quad . \quad (35)$$

where A is a constant.

We thus determine again Rutherford's formula, and as it has been verified by experiment we have here another example where the principle of interference applied to material particles gives a result in agreement with observation.

Our method of procedure has introduced approximations, but Gordon has shown that Rutherford's formula may be obtained rigorously without approximation in the determination of the wave-scattering

CHAPTER IX

THE MOTION OF THE PROBABILITY WAVE IN THE NEW MECHANICS

1. The Probability Cloud

WE saw in Chapter VI that in the limiting case, where the approximations of geometrical optics were applicable to the propagation of the associated wave, that is to say, in the limiting case of the old mechanics, it was possible to imagine a probability fluid moving in space so that its density was a measure at each point of space and time of the probability of occurrence of the particle.

We shall see that this is also valid in complete generality in the new mechanics if we accept the principle of interference which is confirmed by the diffraction of electrons by crystals.

We shall develop these ideas by the application of the non-relativistic equations.

We begin therefore with the wave equation :

$$\nabla^2\psi - \frac{8\pi^2 m}{h^2}\mathrm{F}\psi = \frac{4\pi i m}{h}\frac{\partial\psi}{\partial t}, \qquad (1)$$

and we substitute :

$$\psi(x, y, z, t) = a(x, y, z, t)e^{\frac{2\pi i}{h}\phi}, \qquad (2)$$

where ϕ also is a function of x, y, z, t, and a and ϕ are real functions.

In this way we obtain, as we have already seen (Chap. VI (3) and (4)) two equations which may be written thus :

$$\frac{1}{2m}\sum\left(\frac{\partial\phi}{\partial x}\right)^2 + \mathrm{F}(x, y, z, t) - \frac{h^2}{8\pi^2 m}\frac{\nabla^2 a}{a} = \frac{\partial\phi}{\partial t}, \qquad (3)$$

$$\sum\frac{\partial a}{\partial x}\frac{\partial\phi}{\partial x} + \frac{1}{2}a\nabla^2\phi = m\frac{\partial a}{\partial t}. \qquad (4)$$

In the present case a and ϕ can only be determined simultaneously, a circumstance in which it differs from that occurring in the approximation of geometrical optics. All the equations being of the first order in the time, the function $\psi(x, y, z, t)$ will be determined if we know its form $\psi(x, y, z, 0)$ at the origin of time. Let us suppose that we have in this way determined the function $\psi(x, y, z, t)$ and consequently the functions a and ϕ. Let us imagine a probability fluid of which the molecules or, perhaps preferably, the elements possess the mass m of the particle studied. Equation (4) shows, as in Chapter VI, that by attributing to the elements the velocity defined by :

$$\mathbf{v} = -\frac{1}{m}\,\text{grad}\,\phi, \qquad . \quad . \quad (5)$$

the density ρ of the probability cloud will always remain proportional to $a^2(x, y, z, t)$ if it was equal to $a^2(x, y, z, 0)$ initially. By (5) we can write (4)

$$\frac{\partial a^2}{\partial t} + \text{div}\,(a^2\mathbf{v}) = 0 \qquad . \quad (6)$$

and this expresses the condition of continuity if we write $\rho = Ka^2$. The constant K will be determined by the condition that $\iiint Ka^2 dv$ extended throughout the probability cloud is equal to unity, and since a by its definition may have a constant factor, we may include K in a^2 and say that the cloud density is equal to the square of the amplitude of the ψ-wave.

We can consider (3) as Jacobi's equation for the motion of the probability elements, their potential energy being $F + F_1$ where :

$$F_1(x, y, z, t) = -\frac{h^2}{8\pi^2 m}\frac{\nabla^2 a}{a}. \qquad . \quad (7)$$

This potential energy depends on the cloud density, and we can say that in order to obtain the motion of the probability elements, it is necessary to add the supplementary potential (7) to the ordinary potential F. Since F_1 depends upon h and is negligible when h is regarded as an infinitely small quantity, we may describe it as the quantum potential.

2. Equations of Motion of the Probability Elements

If we regard equation (3) as the Jacobi equation for the probability elements we are naturally led to introduce a Lagrangian function depending upon their co-ordinates, velocities and the time. This function will be

$$L(x, y, z, v_x, v_y, v_z, t) = \tfrac{1}{2}m(v_x^2 + v_y^2 + v_z^2) - F - F_1 \qquad (8)$$

The quantities

$$\frac{\partial L}{\partial v_x} = mv_x, \quad \frac{\partial L}{\partial v_y} = mv_y, \quad \frac{\partial L}{\partial v_z} = mv_z \quad . \qquad (9)$$

may be called the components of the momentum of the probability elements. The quantity

$$W = \sum \frac{\partial L}{\partial q_n} q_n - L = \frac{1}{2}mv^2 + F + F_1 \quad . \qquad (10)$$

may be described as the energy of the elements.

By (5) we shall have ·

$$p_x = mv_x = -\frac{\partial \phi}{\partial x}, \text{ etc.} \quad . \qquad (11)$$

The elements describe a path in space according to a certain law and their motion is described by equations like those of Lagrange. We have:

$$\frac{dp_x}{dt} = \frac{\partial p_x}{\partial x}v_x + \frac{\partial p_x}{\partial y}v_y + \frac{\partial p_x}{\partial z}v_z + \frac{\partial p_x}{\partial t} = \frac{1}{m}\sum p_x \frac{\partial p_x}{\partial x} + \frac{\partial p_x}{\partial t}. \qquad (12)$$

or by (11).

$$\left.\begin{aligned} \frac{dp_x}{dt} &= \frac{1}{m}\sum \frac{\partial \phi}{\partial x}\frac{\partial^2 \phi}{\partial x^2} - \frac{\partial^2 \phi}{\partial x \partial t} \\ &= \frac{\partial}{\partial x}\left\{\frac{1}{2m}\sum\left(\frac{\partial \phi}{\partial x}\right)^2 - \frac{\partial \phi}{\partial t}\right\} \end{aligned}\right\} \qquad (13)$$

Since ϕ is a solution of (3),

$$\frac{dp_x}{dt} = -\frac{\partial F}{\partial x} - \frac{\partial F_1}{\partial x} = \frac{\partial L}{\partial x}, \quad . \quad . \qquad (14)$$

and similarly:

$$\frac{dp_y}{dt} = -\frac{\partial F}{\partial y} - \frac{\partial F_1}{\partial y} = \frac{\partial L}{\partial y}, \quad . \quad . \qquad (15)$$

$$\frac{dp_z}{dt} = -\frac{\partial F}{\partial z} - \frac{\partial F_1}{\partial z} = \frac{\partial L}{\partial z} \quad . \quad . \qquad (16)$$

The terms $\left(\frac{\partial F}{\partial x}, \frac{\partial F}{\partial y}, \frac{\partial F}{\partial z}\right)$ are the force components in the classical sense, while $\left(\frac{\partial F_1}{\partial x}, \frac{\partial F_1}{\partial y}, \frac{\partial F_1}{\partial z}\right)$ are derived from the quantum potential F_1 in a way similar to the derivation of the former from the classical potential F, and may be described as the components of the quantum force This force depends on the density of the probability fluid, and is characteristic of the new mechanics When it can be neglected we return to the old dynamics and the motions of the probability elements are the various classical motions possible for the particle.

When it is not permissible to neglect the quantum force, the motion of the elements is very different from that of particles in the old dynamics. In particular we shall no longer find the general theorems of conservation of energy and momentum associated with them.

For example, if we consider the case of zero field ($F = 0$), it does not follow that p_x, p_y, p_z are constants on account of the occurrence of the quantum force in equations (14)-(16).

Whenever the ψ-wave is not plane and monochromatic, for example if there is a superposition of plane waves with interference, the amplitude is not constant, and although there is no field in the old sense of the word, there will be, nevertheless, a variation of the components of momenta as defined by (11) There is thus no longer conservation of momentum. Further, by (9), (10), and (14)-(16) there is no longer conservation of energy, for :

$$\frac{dW}{dt} - \sum\left(p_x\frac{d^2x}{dt^2} + \frac{dp_x}{dt} \cdot \frac{dx}{dt}\right) - \sum\frac{\partial L}{\partial x}\frac{dx}{dt} - \sum\frac{\partial L}{\partial v_x}\frac{dv_x}{dt} - \frac{\partial L}{\partial t}$$
$$= -\frac{\partial L}{\partial t} = \frac{\partial F}{\partial t} + \frac{\partial F_1}{\partial t}. \qquad (17)$$

It will not be sufficient to have $\frac{\partial F}{\partial t} = 0$, as occurs in a constant field, in order that there may be conservation of energy ; it will be necessary also for the amplitude of the ψ-wave to be independent of the time and this is not the case when ψ is a superposition of plane monochromatic waves. The probability motion does not proceed in general, even in the absence of an external field, with conservation of energy and momentum, and the cause of this is the existence of the quantum force.

3. The Theorem of Ehrenfest

It is possible to eliminate the quantum force by means of an integration extended to the assembly of probability elements, and in so doing to arrive at an important theorem due to Ehrenfest. Multiply equations (14) to (16) by $a^2\,dx\,dy\,dz$ and integrate throughout space under the assumption that we are concerned with a limited wave train, the amplitude of which is consequently zero at infinity. We obtain:

$$\iiint a^2\frac{dp_x}{dt}dx\,dy\,dz = -\iiint a^2\frac{\partial F}{\partial x}dx\,dy\,dz - \iiint a^2\frac{\partial F_1}{\partial x}dx\,dy\,dz$$

$$= -\iiint a^2\frac{\partial F}{\partial x}dx\,dy\,dz + \iiint\frac{h^2}{8\pi^2 m}a^2\frac{\partial}{\partial x}\left(\frac{\nabla^2 a}{a}\right)dx\,dy\,dz, \quad (18)$$

and two similar equations in y and z, where the integration is extended over all values of the variables.

We shall show that the integral

$$\iiint a^2\frac{\partial}{\partial x}\left(\frac{\nabla^2 a}{a}\right)dx\,dy\,dz$$

and the two similar to it vanish. To show this we must remember one of the forms of Green's theorem that if U and V are two continuous uniform functions of (x, y, z) within a domain D bounded by a closed surface S, we have:

$$\iiint_D (U\nabla^2 V - V\nabla^2 U)dv = \iint_S \left(U\frac{\partial V}{\partial n} - V\frac{\partial U}{\partial n}\right)dS. \quad (19)$$

where n denotes the variable along the normal to S reckoned positive towards the exterior. Let us write:

$$U = a, \quad V = \frac{\partial a}{\partial x}. \quad . \quad . \quad . \quad (20)$$

These functions are by hypothesis both zero at infinity, and if we take, as the domain D, the interior of a sphere whose radius tends to infinity, the right-hand side vanishes We obtain, therefore :

$$\iiint a\nabla^2\left(\frac{\partial a}{\partial x}\right)dv = \iiint \frac{\partial a}{\partial x}\nabla^2 a dv, \quad . \quad . \quad (21)$$

where the integrals are taken over the infinite domain D

But the integral

$$\iiint a^2 \frac{\partial}{\partial x}\left(\frac{\nabla^2 a}{a}\right)dv$$

may be written

$$\iiint \left(a\frac{\partial}{\partial x}(\nabla^2 a) - \frac{\partial a}{\partial x}\nabla^2 a\right)dv,$$

and this vanishes by (21). Equation (14) thus leads to ·

$$\iiint a^2\frac{dp_x}{dt}dv = m\iiint a^2\frac{d^2x}{dt^2}dv = -\iiint a^2\frac{\partial F}{\partial x}dv = \iiint a^2 f_x dv. \quad . \quad . \quad . \quad (22)$$

We can take the cloud density equal to a^2 provided that we choose the arbitrary constant factor of a so that : $\iiint a^2 dv = 1$. The integrals (22) are thus the average values in the probability cloud of the quantities $\frac{dp_x}{dt}, \frac{d^2x}{dt^2}, -\frac{\partial F}{\partial x}$ and f_x.

We obtain from (22) and the two similar equations which may be derived from (15) and (16) the relations

$$\overline{\frac{dp_x}{dt}} = m\overline{\gamma_x} = \overline{f_x} \text{ and two similar ones in } y \text{ and } z, \quad (23)$$

where the bars denote average quantities.

This is Ehrenfest's theorem, of which we shall have later an interesting application.[1]

[1] If we write $\bar{x} = \iiint a^2 x dv$, we can easily show that $\frac{d^2\bar{x}}{dt^2} = \overline{\frac{d^2x}{dt^2}}$, with similar equations in y and z ; (23) may be written :

$$m\frac{d^2\bar{x}}{dt^2} = \overline{f_x}, \text{ etc.}$$

We can state Ehrenfest's theorem by saying that the centre of gravity of the probability cloud moves like a particle of mass m in classical mechanics under the force with components $(\overline{f_x}, \overline{f_y}, \overline{f_z})$

If the classical force is zero we have :

$$\frac{\overline{dp_x}}{dt} = 0, \quad \frac{\overline{dp_y}}{dt} = 0, \quad \frac{\overline{dp_z}}{dt} = 0, \quad . \quad . \quad (24)$$

and we find in this case a theorem analogous to that of conservation of momentum of the classical theory. This is due to the fact that we have eliminated the quantum force by means of an integration throughout the whole of the cloud

In the same way, we can obtain a theorem analogous to that of conservation of energy. From (17) we have :

$$\frac{dW}{dt} = \frac{\partial F}{\partial t} + \frac{\partial F_1}{\partial t}.$$

Multiply by $a^2 dv$ and integrate throughout space assuming a zero at infinity, then :

$$\iiint a^2 \frac{dW}{dt} dv = \iiint a^2 \frac{\partial F}{\partial t} dv + \iiint a^2 \frac{\partial F_1}{\partial t} dv \quad . \quad (25)$$

From (7) :

$$\iiint a^2 \frac{\partial F_1}{\partial t} dv = -\frac{h^2}{8\pi^2 m} \iiint a^2 \frac{\partial}{\partial t}\left(\frac{\nabla^2 a}{a}\right) dv \quad . \quad (26)$$

The integral (26) is zero, for by substituting in Green's formula (19) :

$$U = a, \quad V = \frac{\partial a}{\partial t}, \quad . \quad . \quad . \quad (27)$$

we obtain :

$$\iiint a \nabla^2\left(\frac{\partial a}{\partial t}\right) dv = \iiint a \frac{\partial}{\partial t}(\nabla^2 a) dv = \iiint \frac{\partial a}{\partial t} \nabla^2 a \, dv \quad (28)$$

Thus the integral (26) vanishes, since .

$$\iiint a^2 \frac{\partial}{\partial t}\left(\frac{\nabla^2 a}{a}\right) dv = \iiint \left\{ a \frac{\partial}{\partial t}(\nabla^2 a) - \nabla^2 a \frac{\partial a}{\partial t} \right\} dv \quad (29)$$

The equation (25) is thus reduced to

$$\iiint a^2 \frac{dW}{dt} dv = \iiint a^2 \frac{\partial F}{\partial t} dv, \quad . \quad (30)$$

and if the field is constant $\left(\frac{\partial F}{\partial t} = 0\right)$, we have

$$\iiint a^2 \frac{dW}{dt} dv = \frac{\overline{dW}}{dt} = 0. \quad . \quad (31)$$

The formula (31) is the statement of a theorem analogous to that of conservation of energy.

4. Calculation of the Functions ϕ and a

If the wave function is known in the form :

$$\psi = ae^{\frac{2\pi i\phi}{h}}, \quad . \quad . \quad . \quad . \quad (32)$$

where a and ϕ are real, the motion of the probability cloud and its density are determined by the formulæ of the first two paragraphs. But it often happens that ψ is known in the form :

$$\psi = \sum_k a_k e^{\frac{2\pi i}{h}\phi_k}, \quad . \quad . \quad . \quad (33)$$

which in the case of constant fields corresponds to spectral decomposition into monochromatic waves. It is thus useful to know how to calculate a and ϕ when the wave function is given in the form (33). Let us denote the complex conjugate quantity corresponding to ψ by ψ^* We have

$$\psi^* = ae^{-\frac{2\pi i}{h}\phi} = \sum_k a_k e^{-\frac{2\pi i}{h}\phi_k} \quad . \quad . \quad (34)$$

Multiplying ψ by ψ^*

$$a^2 = \psi\psi^* = \sum_{kl} a_k a_l e^{\frac{2\pi i}{h}(\phi_k - \phi_l)}$$

$$= \sum_k a_k^2 + \sum_{l<k} a_k a_l \cos \frac{2\pi}{h}(\phi_k - \phi_l) \quad . \quad (35)$$

This formula determines the resultant intensity which, according to the principle of interference, gives the probability of occurrence.

If we divide ψ by ψ^*, and take the logarithm of the quotient, we obtain :

$$\phi = \frac{h}{4\pi i}\log\frac{\psi}{\psi^*} = \frac{h}{4\pi i}\log\frac{\sum_k a_k e^{\frac{2\pi i}{h}\phi_k}}{\sum_k a_k e^{-\frac{2\pi i}{h}\phi_k}}. \quad . \quad (36)$$

Let q denote any one of the four variables x, y, z, t, then ·

$$\frac{\partial\phi}{\partial q} = \frac{h}{4\pi i}\frac{\psi^*}{\psi}\cdot\frac{\psi^*\frac{\partial\psi}{\partial q} - \psi\frac{\partial\psi^*}{\partial q}}{\psi^{*2}} = \frac{h}{4\pi i}\frac{\psi^*\frac{\partial\psi}{\partial q} - \psi\frac{\partial\psi^*}{\partial q}}{a^2}. \quad (37)$$

This formula gives us at the same time the components of grad ϕ and the derivative $\frac{\partial \phi}{\partial t}$ which represent respectively the components of momentum and the energy of the probability elements.

5. The Pilot-Wave Theory

We have seen that in the domain of application of geometrical optics we can consider the probability cloud as equivalent to a cloud of particles in a state of motion in the given field corresponding to one and the same complete integral of Jacobi's equation We can also consider one particle only and say that the probability cloud is obtained by imagining simultaneously all the possible movements corresponding to a particular form of Jacobi's function. If then we retain the classical idea of a particle localised in space and having in consequence a velocity and a path, it is possible to identify the particle with one of the probability elements In fact, these elements describe the different possible paths of the particle and consequently the particle must continually coincide with one of them.

If now we still wish to retain the classical conception of the particle in the domain proper of the new mechanics, that is to say, outside the approximation to geometrical optics, we naturally wish to maintain the identity of the particle with one of the probability elements and to represent the state of affairs by imagining on the one hand the wave, and on the other the particle to be localised in space, and we connect the motion of the particle with the propagation of the wave by the relation ·

$$\mathbf{v} = -\frac{1}{m} \operatorname{grad} \phi, \qquad . \qquad . \qquad . \quad (38)$$

where ϕ is the phase of the wave defined by (32) The velocity of the particle is thus determined at each instant if we know the initial position, and thus its path also is determined Moreover, from the formulæ of the first paragraph, if we know the form of the associated ψ-wave and if we know that initially the probability of occurrence of the particle at a point is equal to the intensity of the wave at the point, it will be so automatically at every succeeding instant ; thus the principle of interference will be satisfied. We may describe this theory as the pilot-wave theory, because we imagine the wave as guiding the motion of the particle.

This theory may at first sight appear satisfactory because it allows the retention of the classical conception of the particle while being in agreement with the principle of interference. But on closer examination it is seen to raise serious objections which we will briefly consider.

One fundamental difficulty comes from the fact that in the domain of the new dynamics the determination of the function ϕ is not independent of that of the determination of a. If, therefore, we suppose the motion of the particles to be given by (38), this motion will depend not only on the initial position but also on the probability of this initial position, since it depends upon $a(x, y, z, 0)$. This is a wider deviation at the outset from classical ideas than is apparent at first sight, for according to these ideas it is inconceivable that the order of accuracy of our knowledge of the initial state can influence the later course of the motion.

Moreover, from the moment when we accept the principle of interference in complete generality, it becomes very difficult to retain for the wave the character of a physical phenomenon in the old sense of the term For example, let us consider a particle and its associated wave incident upon an imperfectly reflecting mirror ; one part of the wave is transmitted through the mirror, another part is reflected. On account of the meaning attributed to the intensity of the wave, this division of the incident wave into transmitted and reflected waves means that the particle has a certain probability of going through the mirror and a certain probability of being turned back

Let us suppose that an experiment has just revealed the presence of the particle in the transmitted beam, then the probability of finding it in the reflected beam is zero, and this beam must from now have zero intensity ; the experiment on the transmitted beam causes the reflected one to vanish. This seems to be a necessary consequence of the interference principle applied to the case of a single particle, and it is difficult to conclude otherwise than that the wave is not a physical phenomenon in the old sense of the word It is of the nature of a symbolic representation of a probability in space and time, but the idea of a particle guided by the wave then becomes less satisfactory. So long as it was possible to regard the wave as a physical phenomenon, it was easy to adopt the view that it could guide the particle in its motion. But if the wave is merely a symbolic representation of a probability, the guidance of the particle by the wave becomes much more difficult to understand and much less in harmony with the old ideas of mechanics.

We have seen that in general there is neither conservation of energy nor of momentum for the probability elements, even in the absence of a field. This is clearly also the case for the particle if its motion is identified with that of one of the probability elements, and this results in the loss of a great part of the utility of the pilot-wave theory. Let us consider, for example, the case in which the external field is zero and in which the wave is a superposition of plane monochromatic waves. In the pilot-wave theory the energy and momentum of the particle at the point (x, y, z) at time t would be found by calculating $\frac{\partial\phi}{\partial t}$ and $-\text{grad}\,\phi$ for these values of the variables. This is easily done by means of (37), and it is found that the energy and momentum of the particle would vary in a complicated way in the course of time and would depend, moreover, on the form of the wave-train , the motion of the particle thus deduced seems hardly likely to be the correct one. Moreover, there are reasons for thinking that if we sought to measure in this case the energy of the particle we should find one or other of the values corresponding to the frequencies of the plane monochromatic waves which make up the wave-train, and not the value given by $\frac{\partial\phi}{\partial t}$. We shall return to this important point in the next chapter, where we shall be occupied with the case of light, and we shall see that herein lies one of the essential differences between the pilot-wave theory and the point of view of Bohr and Heisenberg. In short, the pilot-wave theory which localises the particle at a point of the wave, attributing to it a well-defined motion at each point, finds itself confronted with serious difficulties.

But there is no inconvenience—on the contrary there are advantages from the point of view of visual representation—in retaining the picture of the probability cloud, the elements of which possess motion defined by (5) and of which the density, equal to the intensity of the associated wave, measures at each point of space and time the probability of occurrence of the particle in agreement with the principle of interference.

CHAPTER X

THE WAVE MECHANICS OF LIGHT QUANTA

1. Photons and their Associated Waves

IN the present chapter we shall develop the conception of the probability cloud for light quanta. But as the demonstrations of the preceding chapter have been made by utilising the non-relativistic equations, we shall be obliged to go over them again, since there can be no question of applying non-relativistic equations to the motion of photons.

We have for the relativistic equation for the wave associated with a particle when there is no field of force :

$$\nabla^2\psi - \frac{1}{c^2}\frac{\partial^2\psi}{\partial t^2} = \frac{4\pi^2 m^2 c^2}{h^2}\psi. \qquad (1)$$

Introducing the notation :

$$\Box^2 = \nabla^2 - \frac{1}{c^2}\frac{\partial^2}{\partial t^2}, \qquad (2)$$

we may rewrite (1) thus :

$$\Box^2\psi = \frac{4\pi^2 m^2 c^2}{h^2}\psi \qquad (3)$$

A solution of this equation of a simple sinusoidal form corresponding to rectilinear uniform motion is

$$\psi = ae^{\frac{2\pi i}{h}\left\{Wt - (p_x x + p_y y + p_z z)\right\}} \qquad (4)$$

the energy W of the particle and its momentum **p** being expressed as a function of the mass m and of the velocity by the relativity formulæ :

$$W = \frac{mc^2}{\sqrt{1-\beta^2}}, \quad \mathbf{p} = \frac{m\mathbf{v}}{\sqrt{1-\beta^2}} \qquad (5)$$

Remembering this, let us consider a succession of particles of smaller and smaller proper masses. Simple sinusoidal solutions will always exist of the type (4) corresponding to a given value W of the energy, but in proportion as the mass m tends to zero, the velocity v tends to c, since W is kept constant. In passing to the limit we can conceive particles of mass zero the waves of which will have the frequency $\nu = \frac{W}{h}$ and of which the velocity is c It suffices to suppose that m and β tend simultaneously the one to zero and the other to unity, so that the ratio $\frac{mc^2}{\sqrt{1-\beta^2}}$ preserves the same value $h\nu$ For these particles of zero mass we have therefore ·

$$W = h\nu, \quad p = \text{Lim} \frac{mv}{\sqrt{1-\beta^2}} = \frac{h\nu}{c}. \qquad (6)$$

These are the fundamental relations of Einstein's quantum theory of light, which have made it possible to give an explanation to the photo-electric and to the Compton effect. We are thus led to consider light as made up of particles of zero mass which we shall call photons. The equation of their associated waves is obtained by making $m = 0$ in equation (3), which gives the classical equation of light waves ·

$$\Box^2\psi = 0. \qquad (7)$$

Thus we shall always associate a solution of the wave equation (7) with the photon, and we shall identify this solution with the classical luminous wave. It is, of course, to be understood in the general case that the wave will not be plane and monochromatic, but a general solution of (7)

2. The Probability Cloud Associated with a Photon

We still adopt the principle of interference that the intensity of the ψ-wave must give the probability of occurrence of the associated photon in such a way that in a case where many photons occur this intensity measures the amount of energy which can be received at any point In this way we are in agreement with the meaning attributed to the intensity of a light wave in classical theories As in the case of electrons and other material particles, it is natural to assume for the photons a probability cloud connected with the ψ-wave so that the interference principle is satisfied.

In order to avoid certain complications we shall suppose that the ψ-wave consists approximately of a super-position of plane monochromatic waves of the same frequency ν, which is the case approximately realised in practice in ordinary experiments in interference. We can then write :

$$\psi(x, y, z, t) = \sum_k a_k e^{2\pi i\nu\left(t - \frac{\alpha_k x + \beta_k y + \gamma_k z}{c}\right)} = a e^{\frac{2\pi i}{h}\phi}$$

$$= a e^{\frac{2\pi i}{h}(h\nu t - \phi_1)}, \quad . \quad . \quad . \quad . \quad . \quad . \quad (8)$$

where a and ϕ_1 are functions of (x, y, z).

If we substitute (8) in (7) and separate the real and imaginary parts we obtain :

$$\frac{h^2\nu^2}{c^2} - \sum\left(\frac{\partial\phi}{\partial x}\right)^2 = -\frac{h^2}{4\pi^2}\frac{\nabla^2 a}{a} \quad . \quad . \quad (9)$$

$$\sum\frac{\partial\phi}{\partial x}\frac{\partial a}{\partial x} + \frac{1}{2}a\nabla^2\phi = \frac{h\nu}{c^2}\frac{\partial a}{\partial t}. \quad . \quad . \quad (10)$$

Equation (10) shows at once that if we attribute to the probability elements the velocity :

$$\mathbf{v} = -\frac{c^2}{h\nu}\operatorname{grad}\phi, \quad . \quad . \quad . \quad (11)$$

the interference principle will be satisfied. We may, in fact, by using (11) and writing $a^2 = \rho$, write (10) in the form :

$$\operatorname{div}(\rho\mathbf{v}) + \frac{\partial\rho}{\partial t} = 0. \quad . \quad . \quad . \quad (12)$$

This is the equation of continuity for the motion of the probability fluid if we suppose, as the interference principle requires, that ρ is the probability density.

Equation (11) suggests the definition of the momentum and energy of the probability elements by means of :

$$\mathbf{p} = -\operatorname{grad}\phi, \quad W = \frac{\partial\phi}{\partial t} = h\nu, \quad . \quad . \quad (13)$$

for then $p = \frac{h\nu}{c^2} = \frac{Wv}{c^2}$, and we again obtain the formula which relates energy and momentum in relativistic dynamics. If we adopt the definitions of (13), equation (9) appears as the Jacobi equation of the probability elements

It is easy to write down the equations of motion of these elements, for .

$$\frac{dp_x}{dt} = \frac{\partial p_x}{\partial x}v_x + \frac{\partial p_x}{\partial y}v_y + \frac{\partial p_x}{\partial z}v_z + \frac{\partial p_x}{\partial t}$$
$$= \frac{c^2}{h\nu}\left(\frac{\partial\phi}{\partial x}\frac{\partial^2\phi}{\partial x^2} + \frac{\partial\phi}{\partial y}\frac{\partial^2\phi}{\partial x\partial y} + \frac{\partial\phi}{\partial z}\frac{\partial^2\phi}{\partial x\partial z}\right) = \frac{c^2}{2h\nu}\frac{\partial}{\partial x}\left\{\sum\left(\frac{\partial\phi}{\partial x}\right)^2\right\} \quad . \quad . \quad . \quad (14)$$

Whence by (9) .

$$\frac{dp_x}{dt} = \frac{hc^2}{8\pi^2\nu}\frac{\partial}{\partial x}\left(\frac{\nabla^2 a}{a}\right) = -\frac{\partial F_1}{\partial x}, \quad . \quad . \quad (15)$$

writing $F_1 = -\frac{hc^2}{8\pi^2\nu}\frac{\nabla^2 a}{a}$, and there are similar equations for p_y and p_z. These three equations determine the motion of the elements as a function of a and ϕ and the derivatives of F_1 may be described as the components of the quantum force derived from the quantum potential F_1. It is, of course, clear that in general the quantities (p_x, p_y, p_z) are not constant; in general the momentum is not conserved in the case of the probability elements, because the quantum force does not always vanish.

3. Interpretation of Interference Phenomena

When the wave-train is very long and no obstacle lies in its path, we can represent it by a plane monochromatic wave :

$$\psi = ae^{2\pi i\left\{\nu t - \frac{\nu}{c}(\alpha x + \beta y + \gamma z)\right\}} \quad . \quad . \quad (18)$$

and the phase is thus :

$$\phi = h\nu t - \frac{h\nu}{c}(\alpha x + \beta y + \gamma z) \quad . \quad . \quad (19)$$

The probability elements have then all the same velocity along the direction (α, β, γ) and equal to :

$$v = -\frac{c^2}{h\nu}\left|\text{grad}\,\phi\right| = c. \quad . \quad . \quad (20)$$

If we consider a large number of photons with associated waves all of the form (18), from the statistical point of view it is as if the photons described rectilinear paths with velocity c, so that we have again the linear propagation of light.

This is no longer the case when the wave encounters obstacles (mirrors, screens, etc.). The mathematical form of the wave must then be modified so as to satisfy certain conditions at the boundaries and the phenomena of interference and diffraction occur.

If we suppose that the obstacles encountered by the wave are fixed, there is no modification of the incident frequency, and it will always be possible to express the wave in the complex form :

$$\psi = ae^{\frac{2\pi i}{h}(h\nu t - \phi_1)} \quad . \quad . \quad . \quad . \quad (21)$$

The phase is a linear function in the time, and a and ϕ_1 are functions of (x, y, z) only Equation (11) can be written in this case :

$$\mathbf{v} = \frac{c^2}{h\nu} \operatorname{grad} \phi_1, \quad . \quad (22)$$

and determines the motion of the probability elements in the region where interference is taking place. The probability of occurrence of the photon in an element of volume dv is

$$\mathrm{P}dv = a^2 dv, \quad . \quad . \quad . \quad (23)$$

the constant factor of a being suitably chosen

Formula (23) makes it possible to obtain once more the explanation of the phenomena of interference and diffraction of light given by classical theories In fact, it states that if we consider an assembly of photons associated with identical waves the number of photons passing per second at the site of interference phenomena is proportional to the intensity of the wave at this point. Thus by comparing, as it is natural to do, the ψ-wave of the photons with the classical light wave, the new mechanics leads us to anticipate the same system of bright and dark fringes as the classical theory.

In order to record interference fringes, for example by photography, we can make an experiment of short duration with intense illumination or one of long duration with feeble illumination ; in the former case we take an average in space, in the latter an average in time, but the result must evidently be the same. This explains why experiments on interference and diffraction are independent of the intensity We must lay further stress upon this important point. Let us consider an experiment in which interference is obtained with very feeble illumination and a very long exposure. From time to time the source emits a photon, and these emissions are so widely separated from one another that in general there is only a single photon with its associated wave-train crossing the interference apparatus. The probability that the presence of the photon will be made known by photographic action in the apparatus is everywhere proportional to the resultant intensity of the wave-train During the very long duration of the experiment, the process of emission is repeated a very great number of times, N, and the apparatus receives in succession N identical wave-trains

Clearly the photographic effect produced is the same as if the apparatus had received a single wave-train carrying N photons distributed in the train in proportion to the square of the amplitude. Thus the experiment made with very feeble illumination and very long duration must give the same result in agreement with classical theory as a rapid experiment with intense illumination. It is almost certain that the same considerations are valid for the diffraction of material particles.

Equations (15) for the motion of the probability show that in a case where there is interference in the presence of fixed obstacles the probability elements do not move in a straight line , their path is curved by the action of the quantum force which itself results from the variation of amplitude Let us take the simple example of the diffraction of a plane wave by the straight edge of a plane semi-infinite screen The light penetrates the geometric shadow, as is known from Fresnel's principle Thus there are necessarily probability elements which bend round the edge of the screen and clearly there is not conservation of momentum in the ordinary sense. This suggests a remark of interest from the historical point of view. The supporters of Newton's corpuscular theory formerly held after the discovery of this phenomenon that the edge of a screen exerted a force on the light corpuscles . we return to some extent to this view with our quantum force. which is indeed a consequence of the presence of the screen. But the quantum force is of a very special character and without the adoption of the pilot-wave theory, of which we know already the difficulties, we cannot consider the quantum force correctly described as applied to the particle itself.

4. The Interference of Light in the Neighbourhood of a Perfectly Reflecting Plane Mirror

It is very instructive to study the probability motion in a special case of interference; that which occurs in the neighbourhood of a plane mirror struck by a beam of light. We shall take first the case of a perfectly reflecting plane mirror, the plane of the mirror being taken as that of xy, the plane of

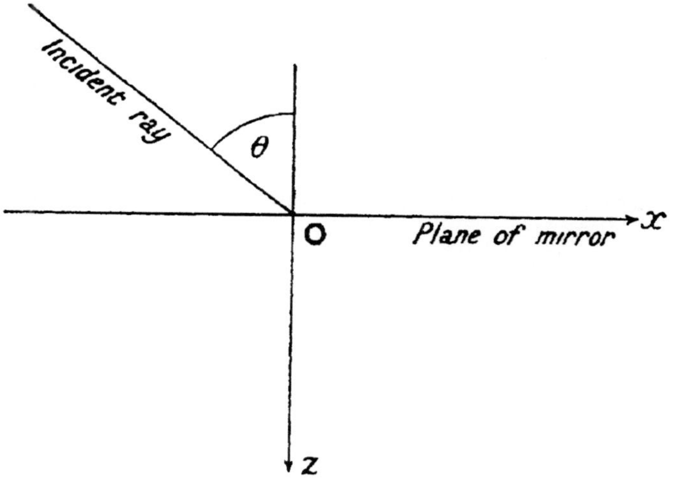

FIG. 7.

incidence or plane of the figure as zx, and the axis of z will be the normal to the mirror directed away from the incident wave.

The incident plane wave is:

$$\psi_1 = a_0 e^{2\pi i\nu\left(t - \frac{x\sin\theta + z\cos\theta}{c}\right)} \quad . \quad . \quad . \quad (24)$$

and the reflected wave:

$$\psi_2 = a_0 e^{2\pi i\nu\left(t - \frac{x\sin\theta - z\cos\theta}{c} + \alpha\right)}, \quad . \quad . \quad (25)$$

the amplitude is the same in both cases because the mirror is perfectly reflecting, and α is a constant corresponding to a possible change of phase occurring on reflection.

Near the mirror there is superposition of the waves ψ_1 and ψ_2 and we have :

$$\psi = \psi_1 + \psi_2 = ae^{\frac{2\pi i}{h}\phi}, \quad . \quad . \quad . \quad (26)$$

where

$$a = 2a_0 \cos\left(2\pi\frac{\nu}{c}z\cos\theta + \frac{\alpha}{2}\right), \quad . \quad . \quad (27)$$

$$\phi = h\nu\left(t - \frac{x\sin\theta}{c}\right) + \frac{h\alpha}{4\pi}. \quad . \quad . \quad (28)$$

According to (11) the velocity of the probability elements in the interference region has components

$$v_x = -\frac{c^2}{h\nu}\frac{\partial\phi}{\partial x} = c\sin\theta, \quad v_y = v_z = 0. \qquad (29)$$

Thus in the neighbourhood of the mirror the probability moves parallel to it and its density, a^2, has maxima and minima on planes parallel to the reflecting surface with a separation of magnitude $\frac{\lambda}{4\cos\theta}$ by (27). The probability fluid, homogeneous in the incident beam where all positions of the photon are equally probable, divides itself into parallel layers on entering the region of interference. We are, of course, in practice always concerned with limited trains of waves presenting a wave front, and the motion of the probability which we have just described exists only when, the wave front having been reflected by the mirror, the interference system is established

In the example we have just studied we may be tempted to say that the probability tracks are actually the paths of the photons themselves , this is the point of view of the pilot-wave theory. The photons uniformly distributed in the incident wave would come into the interference region and form layers which would flow parallel to the surface of the mirror. But, as we have seen, this identification of the motion of the corpuscles with that of the probability elements raises difficulties of principle. When we pass on to consider the case of an imperfectly reflecting mirror we shall see that the pilot-wave theory leads to an improbable result on the subject of the velocity of the photons.

5. The Interference of Light in the Neighbourhood of an Imperfectly Reflecting Plane Mirror

We pass on to the case of a plane mirror which is not perfectly reflecting. Some of the photons will be transmitted through the surface of the mirror into the medium situated behind, while the rest will be reflected. We shall consider the surface of the mirror as a very thin transition layer in which the partial reflection of the wave takes place

It is of little importance for what follows whether the medium behind this layer is identical with the medium (air or vacuum) situated on the side of incidence or consists, on the contrary, of a refracting body. On the side of incidence there is a region where the superposition of the incident and reflected waves gives rise to interference. We wish to understand how the probability elements are to traverse this region of interference in order that some may enter into the reflected, others into the transmitted, beam.

The incident wave ψ_1 is still given by (24), but in order to simplify the calculation somewhat we will take $a_0 = 1$. It would be quite easy to restore a_0 and a_0^2 to all the formulæ. We shall thus write :

$$\psi_1 = e^{2\pi i\nu\left(t - \frac{x \sin\theta + z\cos\theta}{c}\right)} \quad . \quad . \quad . \quad (30)$$

for the incident wave and

$$\psi_2 = \eta e^{2\pi i\nu\left(t - \frac{x \sin\theta - z\cos\theta}{c}\right) + \alpha} \quad . \quad . \quad (31)$$

for the reflected wave.

If $\eta = 1$, the mirror is perfectly reflecting and we again have the problem considered above. If $\eta = 0$ the beam is transmitted without any reflection, or the mirror does not exist In the intermediate case, $0 < \eta < 1$, the proportion of the probability elements which undergo reflection is η^2 by the interference principle. At the site of interference in the neighbourhood of the mirror on the side of incidence, the resultant wave is :

$$\psi = \psi_1 + \psi_2 = ae^{\frac{2\pi i}{h}\phi} \quad . \quad . \quad . \quad . \quad (32)$$

For the sake of brevity write :

$$\mu = \frac{4\pi\nu}{c} z\cos\theta + \alpha.$$

To determine a and ϕ we make use of (35) and (37) of the preceding chapter, and we find easily ·

$$\left.\begin{aligned} a^2 = 1 + \eta^2 + 2\eta \cos \mu \\ \frac{\partial \phi}{\partial x} = -\frac{h\nu}{c} \sin \theta, \quad \frac{\partial \phi}{\partial y} = 0, \quad \frac{\partial \phi}{\partial z} = -\frac{h\nu}{c} \cos \theta \, \frac{1-\eta^2}{a^2}, \end{aligned}\right\} \tag{33}$$

The velocity components of the probability elements are by (11):

$$v_x = c \sin \theta, \quad v_y = 0, \quad v_z = c \cos \theta \, \frac{1 - \eta^2}{a^2}. \tag{34}$$

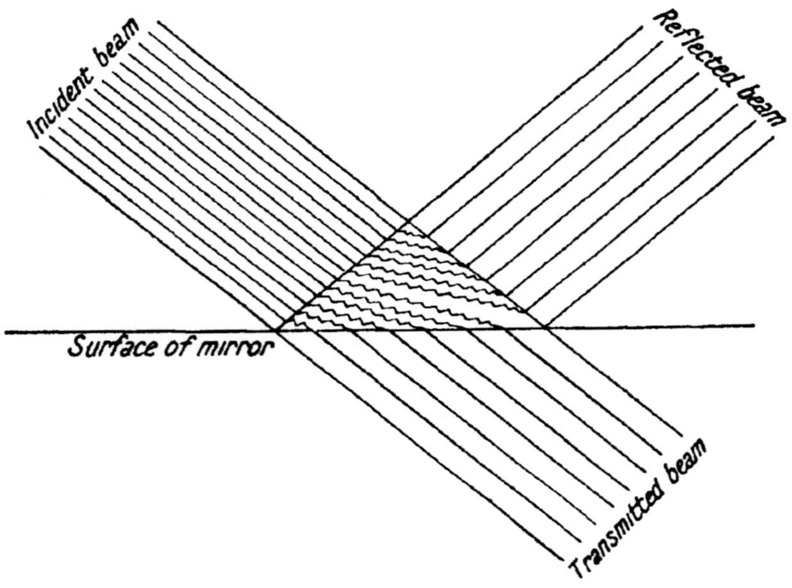

FIG. 8.

The motion of the probability elements is thus in the plane of incidence, and their velocity parallel to the mirror is the same as if the latter were perfectly reflecting But in this case v_z is no longer zero, it is a periodic function of z, and we conclude that the probability tracks in the interference region are wavy curves similar to those of Fig 8. It is easily seen that the average slope of these wavy curves lies between the value 0 corresponding to the case where $\eta = 1$, which has already been considered, and the value $\tan \theta$ corresponding to the case of total transmission, $\eta = 0$.

In Fig. 8 it is seen how the probability elements uniformly

distributed in the incident bundle come to occupy some the transmitted and others the reflected beam, the density of their redistribution in these two bundles being again uniform In the interference region the probability density is given by the value of a^2 in equation (33). Thus there are in this case bright and dark fringes parallel to the surface of the mirror, but the dark fringes are not absolutely black, since the minima of a^2 are equal to $(1 - \eta)^2$ which is always positive. Thus in the interference region there is no place where no probability element exists. These conclusions are almost evident from Fig. 8, for if the dark fringes were quite black it would be difficult to see how the probability elements would come to occupy the transmitted beam.

Here again it is tempting to imagine the photons as localised points describing probability paths. But apart from the difficulties already mentioned, another very interesting one arises here. If we examine (34) we see that the component v_z is greater than $c \cos \theta$ in the dark fringes. The result is that in these fringes the velocity v of the probability elements is greater than c for :

$$v^2 = v_x^2 + v_y^2 + v_z^2 = c^2 \sin^2 \theta + c^2 \cos^2 \theta \left(\frac{1 + \eta}{1 - \eta}\right)^2 > c^2, \quad (35)$$

so that if we wish to attribute the probability motion to the photons we are compelled to attribute to them a velocity greater than c in the dark fringes, and this would be very difficult to reconcile with the principle of relativity.

6. The Superposition of Two Plane Monochromatic Waves

Let us consider a light wave formed by superposing two plane monochromatic waves travelling in the direction of z :

$$\psi = a_1 e^{2\pi i \nu_1 \left(t - \frac{z}{c}\right)} + a_2 e^{2\pi i \nu_2 \left(t - \frac{z}{c}\right)} \quad . \quad . \quad (36)$$

If we write ψ in the form $ae^{\frac{2\pi i}{h}\phi}$ we find :

$$a^2 = a_1{}^2 + a_2{}^2 + 2a_1 a_2 \cos 2\pi(\nu_1 - \nu_2)\left(t - \frac{z}{c}\right), \quad (37)$$

and thus there are maxima and minima travelling along the z-axis at space intervals of magnitude $\frac{c}{\nu_1 - \nu_2}$. The probability of occurrence of the associated photon must be equal to a^2 by the interference principle, and thus has the same maxima and minima.

If we calculate the quantity $\frac{\partial\phi}{\partial t}$, which plays the part of energy for the elements, we find :

$$\frac{\partial\phi}{\partial t} = \frac{h}{4\pi i} \cdot \frac{1}{a^2}\left(\psi^*\frac{\partial\psi}{\partial t} - \psi\frac{\partial\psi^*}{\partial t}\right)$$

$$= \frac{a_1^2 h\nu_1 + a_2^2 h\nu_2 + a_1 a_2(h\nu_1 + h\nu_2)\cos 2\pi(\nu_1 - \nu_2)\left(t - \frac{z}{c}\right)}{a_1^2 + a_2^2 + 2a_1 a_2 \cos 2\pi(\nu_1 - \nu_2)\left(t - \frac{z}{c}\right)}$$

If $\nu_1 = \nu_2 = \nu$, we find, of course, the constant value $h\nu$ for $\frac{\partial\phi}{\partial t}$, but in the general case $\nu_1 \neq \nu_2$, $\frac{\partial\phi}{\partial t}$ is a complicated variable quantity. In the pilot-wave theory, where we attempt to identify the motion of the particle with that of the probability elements, the particle ought to have this continually varying energy $\frac{\partial\phi}{\partial t}$. Now it appears certain that if we allow the wave (36) to fall on a piece of matter, we obtain a photo-electric effect corresponding either to the quantum $h\nu_1$ or to the quantum $h\nu_2$. Everything takes place as if the associated particle had either the energy $h\nu_1$ or $h\nu_2$, but not the energy $\frac{\partial\phi}{\partial t}$ Thus to obtain the probability of occurrence of the particle we must consider the amplitude a resulting from the superposition of two monochromatic waves On the other hand, to anticipate the different amounts of energy with which the particle can appear, we must consider not the resulting phase but the frequencies of the different monochromatic waves, that is to say, the spectral distribution of the ψ-wave. There are thus several possibilities—in our example there are two—for the value of the energy of the particle We can no longer attribute a definite energy to the particle as does the pilot-wave theory, but only speak of the probability that it will appear with so much energy.

Similar considerations can be applied to the momentum.

CHAPTER XI

THE THEORY OF BOHR AND HEISENBERG

1. The Principle of Spectral Distribution

TO sum up the results obtained to this point: we have seen that it is always necessary to associate with the motion of a particle the propagation of a wave $\psi = ae^{\frac{2\pi i}{h}\phi}$ and that an essential principle, necessary for the interpretation of experimental results, is the interference principle according to which the resultant intensity of the wave, $a^2 = \psi\psi^*$, measures always and everywhere, in the case both of matter and light, the probability of occurrence of the particle. Moreover, we were led to imagine a fictitious fluid or probability fluid, the motion of which is determined by the propagation of the wave and the density a^2 of which gives the probability of occurrence according to the interference principle. The motion of the elements of the probability fluid coincides with the possible motion of the particle as described by the old dynamics when the approximations of geometrical optics are applicable to the study of the wave We were therefore led to suppose that the particles are well-defined points describing probability paths, but examination of this point of view (the pilot-wave theory) revealed difficulties. Thus the true meaning of the duality of waves and particles still remains obscure, and we can now conveniently pass on to the theory of Bohr and Heisenberg.

This theory rests on two principles. Firstly, the interference principle which we know already; and secondly, the principle of spectral distribution, to which we were introduced at the end of the last chapter, and which we will explain more fully by a consideration of the case of the zero field. The starting-point of wave mechanics is that a plane monochromatic wave corresponds to the uniform rectilinear motion of a particle. But a limited wave-train can be considered as a superposition of plane monochromatic waves of the form :

$$\psi = \sum_k a_k \psi_k = \sum_k a_k e^{2\pi i \nu_k \left\{ t - \frac{n_k}{c}(\alpha_k x + \beta_k y + \gamma_k z) \right\}}, \quad . \quad (1)$$

the constants α_k, β_k, γ_k, and n_k being related by the equations :

$$\alpha_k^2 + \beta_k^2 + \gamma_k^2 = 1, \quad n_k = \sqrt{1 - \frac{\nu_0^2}{\nu_k^2}}, \quad . \quad . \quad (2)$$

where ν_0 is the proper frequency $\frac{mc^2}{h}$ of the particle.

From the beginning of the development of wave mechanics Born has proposed to consider each quantity a_k^2 as giving the relative probability that the particle possesses the state of motion corresponding to ψ_k

Thus, contrary to the view of the pilot-wave theory, the ψ-wave would not give the motion of the particle but only the probability that it has this or that state of motion. With Born's hypothesis, the difficulties pointed out at the end of the last chapter with regard to the photo-electric effects produced by a wave, which is the superposition of two or more monochromatic waves, disappear spontaneously. We shall describe Born's postulate as the principle of spectral distribution. If we accept it the definition of the particle by its associated wave is subject to a double uncertainty , on the one hand, its position is uncertain by the interference principle, since there is a certain probability measured by a^2 that the particle may be found at any point of the region occupied by the wave-train ; on the other hand, the state of motion of the particle defined by its energy and momentum is also uncertain by the principle of spectral distribution, since there are several possible states of motion, the probability of each being given by the square of the amplitude of the corresponding monochromatic component in the spectrum of the wave-train.

How must this double uncertainty be explained ? It is this explanation which the theory of Bohr and Heisenberg attempts to offer by a subtle and profound analysis of the concepts of observation and of measurement.

2. The Theory of Bohr and Heisenberg. The Uncertainty Relations

To make an observation on a phenomenon is in some measure to disturb it. We can in fact observe only the establishment of an interaction between the phenomenon studied and the surrounding medium of which the observer himself is a part. If the measuring process disturbs the phenomenon to a relatively small extent, the value of the quantities characteristic of the phenomenon can be regarded as accurately known after the measurement, taking account, of course, of the experimental errors. But if the process changes the phenomenon to a great extent then the result of observation gives no longer any exact information of the state existing after measurement. This state is affected by an uncertainty arising from the lack of knowledge of the way in which the measurement has disturbed the phenomenon. In particular, we may very readily admit that the process of measuring a quantity A necessarily disturbs the value of a quantity B in such a way that if the process is improved in order to determine A more and more accurately, the value of B afterwards is more and more inaccurately known. The state of a particle is defined according to classical ideas by eight quantities, $x, y, z, t, p_x, p_y, p_z$, and W, which give the position and state of motion at a particular instant. These eight quantities form two groups, the co-ordinates of space and time, $x, y. z, t$, and the conjugate quantities of these co-ordinates, p_x, p_y, p_z, W. We shall show that if the principles of interference and of spectral distribution be accepted any process which measures one of the eight quantities must of necessity alter the value of the conjugate, this change being the greater the more accurately the measurement is made. The uncertainty which results must not be considered as an accidental uncertainty due to an imperfection in our methods of measurement and which could be avoided by improved methods. On the contrary, the uncertainty is an essential one, arising from the disturbance of the phenomenon studied by the act of measurement itself and a consequence of an important natural law.

To show the necessity of this uncertainty as a consequence of the acceptance of the two principles of interference and of spectral distribution, we will begin by remarking that it must always be possible to represent the result of an observation on a particle by a wave-train. The extension of the wave-train in space represents the uncertainty about the position of the particle after the observation and the extension in the spectral domain occupied by the frequencies of the simple sinusoidal waves which superimpose to form the wave-train corresponds to the uncertainty about the state of motion

According to the fundamental ideas of wave mechanics, the state of uniform rectilinear motion of the particle must be associated with the propagation of a plane monochromatic wave of frequency $\nu = \frac{W}{h}$ and of wave-length $\lambda = \frac{h}{p}$, W and p denoting the energy and momentum of the particle.

Let us introduce the vector **n**, the vector wave-number of the plane monochromatic wave, with the direction of **p** and equal in magnitude to $\frac{1}{\lambda}$. We then have:

$$\nu = \frac{W}{h}, \quad N_x = \frac{p_x}{h}, \quad N_y = \frac{p_y}{h}, \quad N_z = \frac{p_z}{h} \quad . \quad (3)$$

Now, as results from the calculations of Chapter IV, § 3 and as can be demonstrated more generally, a wave-train of dimensions δx, δy, δz in space and of which the time of passage at a point is δt, requires for its mathematical representation an assembly of plane monochromatic waves for which the components of the vector wave-number and frequency fill at least intervals δN_x, δN_y, δN_z and $\delta\nu$ related to δx, δy, δz and δt by the inequalities:

$$\delta N_x \,.\, \delta x > 1, \quad \delta N_y \,\, \delta y > 1, \quad \delta N_z \,.\, \delta z > 1, \quad \delta\nu \,.\, \delta t > 1. \quad (4)$$

As we suppose that a state of uniform rectilinear motion of the particle corresponds to each plane monochromatic wave, we must regard the quantities:

$$\delta W = h\delta\nu, \quad \delta p_x = h\delta N_x, \quad \delta p_y = h\delta N_y, \quad \delta p_z = h\delta N_z \,. \quad (5)$$

as being the uncertainties in the values of the energy and momentum. The relations then become:

$$\delta p_x \,.\, \delta x > h, \quad \delta p_y \,.\, \delta y > h, \quad \delta p_z \,.\, \delta z > h, \quad \delta W \,.\, \delta t > h, \quad (6)$$

which are the uncertainty relations of Heisenberg. The less the uncertainty in one of the eight quantities x, y, z, t, p_x, p_y, p_z, W, the greater that in the conjugate quantity by virtue of the meaning attributed to the wave.

3. The Meaning of the Wave in the Theory of Bohr and Heisenberg

We may sum up this question by a consideration of how we can regard the ψ-wave on the view of Bohr and Heisenberg. Let us suppose that at time t_0 an initial observation has been made which allows us to fix the position and state of motion of the particle within certain limits; we admit that the uncertainty about the conjugate quantities resulting from this observation satisfies Heisenberg's relations (6) in the most favourable case. To represent the results of this first observation, we must form a wave-train of which the resultant intensity at each point is equal to the probability that the particle is at the point and of which the spectral distribution indicates the relative probabilities of the different states of motion of the particle. In order to see as far as possible what may result from this imperfectly known initial state, we must follow the propagation of the wave-train and remember that during the whole of its course the probability of occurrence is always measured at each point by the intensity a^2, and that the probability of each state of motion is measured by the intensity of the corresponding spectral component. We can therefore predict that if a second observation made later at time t has just provided new information about the position or state of motion of the particle, there is a certain probability that the corpuscle lies in a particular region of space, and some other probability that it has a certain state of motion. These predictions, which give probabilities and not certainties, are the only ones that we can obtain; according to Bohr and Heisenberg, we seek in vain a representation of the particle as a point describing a well-defined path with a definite velocity.

We can, with Heisenberg, describe the wave-train as a probability packet. We have seen that we can associate a probability cloud with it, the density of the probability fluid thus imagined being equal at each point to the intensity a^2 of a wave-train, and measuring in consequence the probability of occurrence. The probability elements describe paths which depend on the initial extension of the wave-train, that is upon the initial uncertainty of the position of the particle. That the motion of the probability depends on the knowledge of the initial state raises no difficulty, for the probability of an event depends always on the more or less exact knowledge we have of earlier states.

The study of the propagation of the wave-train allows us to state the probability of the different possible positions of the particle at the time t. If at this instant we make a new observation to determine the position of the particle, the result must agree with our expectations, but, once made, this observation will in general limit the uncertainty about the position of the particle. If, for example, the wave-train occupies a region R of space, we know before the observation that the particle must lie within this region, but in general we shall know afterwards that it lies in a region R_1 included in R. To represent the state of our knowledge after the observation it will thus be necessary to make a reduction of the probability packet in such a way that the wave-train now occupies the region R_1 only. Thus by the mere fact of a new observation a part of the old wave-train suddenly vanishes. This shows, as we have mentioned in the introduction, the abstract and symbolic character of the wave according to this view.

Moreover, a breach appears as a consequence of this theory in the old idea of determinism in physical phenomena, for this idea was based on the possibility of determining exact initial data from which subsequent phenomena could be rigorously deduced by rigorous dynamical laws. The motion of a particle could be inexorably fixed when its initial position and velocity were known. But in the theory of Bohr and Heisenberg it becomes impossible to determine simultaneously with absolute certainty the initial position and velocity of a particle, and consequently it becomes impossible to state that its motion is rigorously determined, for expectations based on a theory of probability can alone be obtained on this question.

4. Agreement with the Old Dynamics

There is nevertheless one important fact that the new theory must explain. For all mechanical phenomena on a large scale the old conceptions are sufficient, and it cannot be denied that a rigorous determinism appears to exist on our ordinary scale for these phenomena How is this part to be explained ? At the outset we must note that with the new ideas two kinds of uncertainty intervene in practice. The first of these, already admitted by classical theories, is, we may say, accidental, arising from the inevitable imperfection in our methods of measurement, and one which could be indefinitely diminished by a continued improvement in experimental technique. The second is the essential and irreducible uncertainty introduced by Heisenberg's uncertainty relations (6). Now, in the cases where the old mechanical conception is well verified, the accidental is much greater than the essential uncertainty and masks it completely The result is that events take place practically as if Heisenberg's uncertainty did not exist, that is to say, as if, *except for experimental errors*, all the deterministic conceptions of the old dynamics were exact But if a continually improved experimental technique were to make it possible to confine the values of the dynamical magnitudes to narrower and narrower limits a point would at last be reached where we should come up against the Heisenberg uncertainty.

We will illustrate this by a numerical example

Consider the motion along the x-axis of a small billiard ball weighing a milligramme and of negligible dimensions. To determine the initial state we must find the position of its centre and its velocity. Suppose that we have found the abscissa of the centre to within a thousandth of a millimetre, which would be a good determination. Heisenberg's relation tells us that we shall be unable to know the velocity of the ball at this instant with an uncertainty less than :

$$\delta v = \frac{h}{m\delta x} = \frac{6{\cdot}55 \times 10^{-27}}{10^{-3} \times 10^{-4}} = 6{\cdot}55 \times 10^{-20} \text{ cm. per sec.}$$

It is evident that there is no practical method of measurement which would permit of the attainment of this degree of accuracy ; the Heisenberg uncertainty will be completely masked by the experimental error, and it will be as if this uncertainty did not exist.

The mathematical agreement between the new mechanics, as conceived by Bohr and Heisenberg, and the old mechanics is, moreover, shown very elegantly by means of Ehrenfest's theorem (Chap. IX, § 3). We have seen that the old mechanics corresponds to the case where geometrical optics is applicable when the conditions of propagation do not vary appreciably on a scale of the same order as the wave-length. As the wave-length in the usual cases is much smaller than anything we can measure directly, we can imagine a wave-train which occupies a region whose dimensions contain very many wave-lengths and which, nevertheless, can be regarded as a point on our ordinary scale. This wave-train can thus be represented by a wave-group moving approximately with Rayleigh's group velocity; it will form a small probability droplet with dimensions too small for our methods of measurement. The equations which express Ehrenfest's theorem are:

$$m\overline{\gamma_x} = \overline{f_x}, \qquad m\overline{\gamma_y} = \overline{f_y}, \qquad m\overline{\gamma_z} = \overline{f_z}, \qquad (7)$$

where, for example, γ_x is the time derivative of the velocity of the probability elements along the x-axis, and for all the elements of the droplet is equal to $\frac{dU_x}{dt}$, where U_x denotes the group velocity along the x-axis, and consequently $\overline{\gamma_x} = \frac{dU_x}{dt}$. The approximation of geometrical optics being applicable by hypothesis, the force is approximately constant in all the extent of the wave-train, whence $\overline{f_x} = f_x$, f_x denoting the x-component of the force in the small region occupied by the wave-train. The same arguments apply to the y- and z-components. We have:

$$m\frac{dU_x}{dt} = f_x, \quad m\frac{dU_y}{dt} = f_y \quad m\frac{dU_z}{dt} = f_z. \qquad (8)$$

The probability droplet thus moves as a whole, like a material point in a given field of force subject to the old dynamics. Of course, the position of the particle within the wave-train is uncertain, but the dimensions of the train being less than anything we can measure, in practice it is as if the particle had always a definite position and moved in accordance with Newton's equations.

We see with what degree of elegance Ehrenfest's theorem enables us to make the union between the old mechanics and the theory of Bohr and Heisenberg.

5. Einstein's Objection. Is the Particle non-Localisable or not Localised?

A conception so novel as that of Bohr and Heisenberg cannot fail to raise objections. We will consider one of these which was raised by Einstein at the Solvay Congress in Brussels in October, 1927. Let a particle and the associated plane monochromatic wave fall normally on a screen pierced by a circular hole, with a photographic film in the form of a hemisphere of large radius behind it (Fig. 9).

If the hole has sufficiently small dimensions, the wave will be diffracted in passing through it, and will spread in all directions to the right of the screen. According to the view of Bohr and Heisenberg, there is a certain probability that the particle will make itself evident by photographic action at some point A of the film. But if a photographic effect is produced at A at the instant t, no other such effect can be produced anywhere else on the film since there is only one particle present by our hypothesis. Now, with our ordinary ideas of space and time, even in the relativistic form, it is impossible to understand how the fact that a photographic effect has been produced at A can prevent instantaneously the production of an effect at any other point B unless we admit that the particle is actually localised in space and at each instant occupies a definite point in the associated wave. No other conception appears able to be reconciled with the idea that physical phenomena can be entirely represented in the framework of space and of time, or even in the space-time of Einstein.

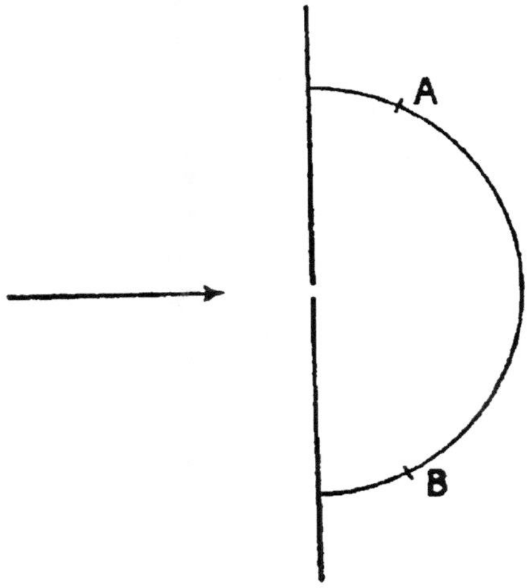

Fig. 9.

This very interesting and simple reasoning of Einstein's shows clearly that we must adopt one or other of the two following attitudes, which we denote by A and B.

(A) We retain the idea that the particle is localised at each instant in space, and that in consequence it has a path and a velocity. We must then express the ideas of Bohr and Heisenberg by saying that although the particle has always a definite position and velocity, an important natural law expressed by Heisenberg's relations (6) prevents us from being able at one and the same time to determine exactly this position and state of motion, for this reason we can only arrive at probabilities with regard to the future positions and states of motion of the particle. From this point of view there is no real indeterminacy, but merely uncertainty imposed by the very nature of things. We should not be able to assert that there is a rigorous determinism in the motion of particles since we could never determine it exactly, but neither could we deny this determinism.

(B) An opinion of a much more radical character, which appears to be held by Bohr and by many other eminent physicists, is that the particle associated with an extended wave-train is not actually localised in space and time; in a certain sense it is present throughout the extent of the wave-train. For Bohr the particles are, in fact, "unsharply defined individuals within finite space-time regions" In Einstein's example the particle would be in some sort virtually spread over the region occupied by the diffracted wave-train, at the moment when the photographic effect is produced at A, the particle would be, as it were, condensed at this point to produce an observable effect. No mechanism in harmony with our ordinary motion of space-time can, so it seems, explain this instantaneous condensation. If we adopt the opinion B, we must say that the space-time frame is insufficient for the complete interpretation of natural phenomena.

Further, the effect produced by the particle always obeys the law of conservation of energy. If, for example, the particle is a photon, the photo-electric effect produced at A will verify Einstein's photo-electric law. It is this property of the particle to condense at a point and produce an effect there in conformity with the causal laws of conservation that Bohr has expressed by saying: "The individuality of the particles transcending the space-time description meets the claim of causality."

At the moment when the particle enters into relation with

the surrounding medium to produce an observable phenomenon, according to the opinion B, it makes, as it were, a choice between several possibilities. Let us consider the reflection on an imperfectly reflecting mirror, M (Fig. 10).

The incident wave divides into a reflected and a transmitted wave. We must not say that the particle on arriving at the mirror makes a choice between the reflected and transmitted wave, for the arrival of the particle at the mirror is not an observable phenomenon. The transmitted and reflected beams both exist until the instant when the particle manifests its presence in one or the other by an observable phenomenon;

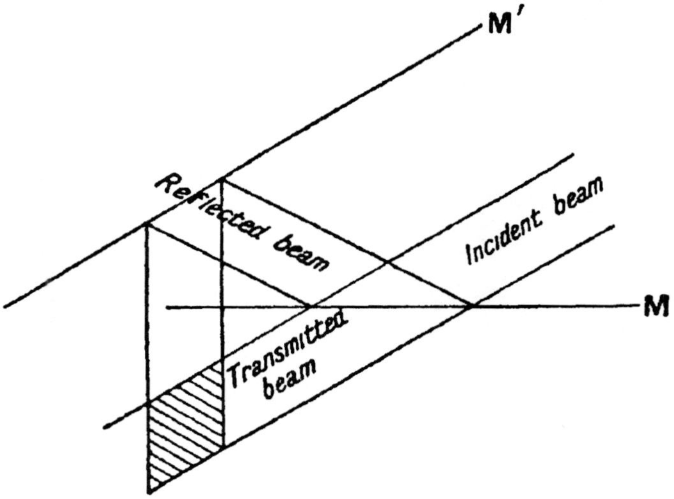

Fig. 10.

only at this moment does the choice operate, for, according to a remark of Heisenberg's, so long as no manifestation of the particle has been produced, interference can be obtained in the shaded parts of Fig 10 by sending back the reflected beam by means of a mirror M′ on to the transmitted beam, which proves the necessity of considering the two beams.

6. Conclusion

These are the broad outlines of the theory of Bohr and Heisenberg on the nature of the reciprocal relation of particles and waves. The theory certainly contains many difficulties and obscurities. In particular we cannot yet explain in a satisfactory way how it can take account of the experiments of Geiger and Bothe and of those of Compton and Simon which have verified the exactness of the conservation of energy and momentum in individual encounters between photons and electrons.

We must perhaps hope that the introduction of some new idea will help to discover an interpretation of the dualism of waves and particles which will prove more lucid than that proposed by Bohr and Heisenberg.

Nevertheless, it appears certain that there is something fundamental in the uncertainty relations.

CHAPTER XII

THE POSSIBILITY OF MEASUREMENT AND HEISENBERG'S RELATIONS

1. Methods of Measurement and Heisenberg's Relations

THROUGHOUT the preceding chapter we have admitted that no observation is capable at one and the same time of determining a co-ordinate and its conjugate momentum with an accuracy greater than that expressed by Heisenberg's uncertainty relations. We must now verify this statement by criticising the methods of measurement at our disposal. This form of criticism was first offered by Heisenberg.

Let us consider a material particle, for example an electron. To determine its position with great accuracy we have only one means, and that is to employ optical methods ; but these allow us to measure a co-ordinate only to an approximation of the order of the wave-length. To increase the accuracy of measurement of the co-ordinates of the particle, we are thus led to employ a shorter and shorter wave-length, but then the particle is subject to a more and more accentuated Compton effect, for the energy of the incident photons is greater and greater and the momentum of the particle is more and more changed by the act of locating it. If, conversely, we propose to measure the velocity and momentum, we shall be able to use the Doppler effect, but this, as we shall see later, is always accompanied by a Compton effect which changes the velocity. To reduce the Compton effect we are led to employ a large wave-length, but then the position of the particles at the instant of measurement will be inaccurately defined.

2. Heisenberg's Microscope

The first illustration of these general considerations is one given by Heisenberg. Let us imagine that an electron in motion is under examination by a microscope illuminated from below by monochromatic light of frequency ν (Fig. 11).

When the electron scatters a photon, a divergent wave enters the microscope. By the well-known theory of the resolving power in classical optics, if the object glass subtends an angle 2ϵ at the object, a length in the object plane can only be determined with a possible inaccuracy of $\frac{\lambda}{2 \sin \epsilon}$ or approximately $\frac{\lambda}{2\epsilon}$.

Let the y-axis lie along the axis of the microscope, which is, of course, the direction of the incident light, and let the x-axis lie along the direction of the velocity of the electron in the plane of the object carrier. The measurement will only be able to determine the position of the electron on the x-axis at the instant of scattering with a possible inaccuracy of $\delta x = \frac{\lambda}{2\epsilon}$.

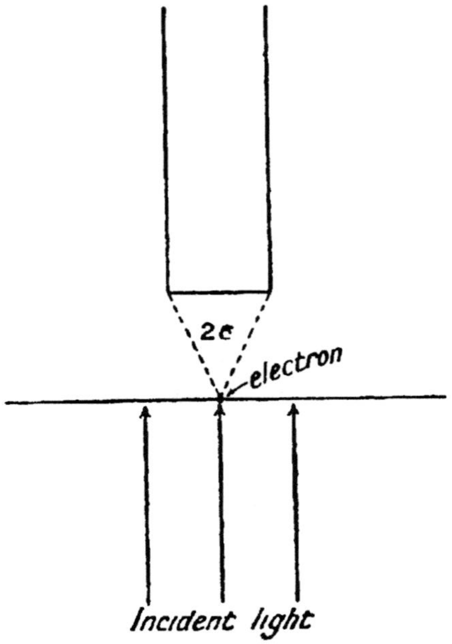

FIG. 11.

Before the scattering, the photon has energy $h\nu$ and momentum $\frac{h\nu}{c}$ directed along the y-axis; the electron has velocity $\mathbf{v}$ directed along the x-axis, and if v is small compared with c, its momentum is $m\mathbf{v}$ and its kinetic energy $\frac{1}{2}mv^2$. By the Compton effect we know that the scattering modifies the frequency of the photon and the velocity of the electron. After scattering, the photon has frequency ν', energy $h\nu'$ and momentum $\frac{h\nu'}{c}$, making with the axis of the microscope a very small angle α necessarily less than ϵ, since the scattered photon must pass through the objective. The velocity of the electron has become $\mathbf{v}'$, its momentum $m\mathbf{v}'$, and its energy $\frac{1}{2}mv'^2$. Following Compton's method, we shall apply the principles of conservation of energy and momentum to the process of scattering, and taking α^2 as a small fraction we obtain :

$$\left.\begin{aligned} h\nu + \tfrac{1}{2}mv_x^2 &= h\nu' + \tfrac{1}{2}m(v_x'^2 + v_y'^2) \\ \frac{h\nu}{c} &= \frac{h\nu'}{c} + mv_y' \\ mv_x &= \frac{h\nu'}{c}\alpha + mv_x' \end{aligned}\right\} \quad . \quad . \quad . \quad (1)$$

Substituting in the first equation the value of $\frac{1}{2}m(v_x'^2 + v_y'^2)$ obtained from the other two, we find :

$$\frac{h^2}{mc^2}(\nu - \nu')^2 - 2h(\nu - \nu') - 2\alpha h\nu'\frac{v}{c} + \alpha^2\frac{h^2\nu'^2}{mc^2} = 0. \quad (2)$$

Equation (2) shows that ν differs from ν' only by terms of order α, so that to the first order in α we may write the last equation of (1) :

$$mv_x - mv_x' = p_x - p_x' = \frac{\alpha h\nu}{c} = \frac{\alpha h}{\lambda}. \quad . \quad . \quad (3)$$

As we do not know the exact value of α which may vary from $-\epsilon$ to $+\epsilon$, there is an uncertainty in the value of p_x after scattering of amount :

$$\delta p_x = \frac{2\epsilon h}{\lambda}. \quad . \quad . \quad . \quad . \quad . \quad (4)$$

Thus, under the most favourable conditions we have :

$$\delta x \times \delta p_x = \frac{\lambda}{2\epsilon} \times \frac{2\epsilon h}{\lambda} = h, \quad . \quad . \quad . \quad (5)$$

and this is Heisenberg's uncertainty relation.

3. Measurement of the Velocity of an Electron by Means of the Doppler Effect

We pass on to examine the determination of the velocity of an electron by the Doppler effect. An electron is considered with a velocity **v** along the positive direction of the x-axis. A train of light waves of average wave-length λ travelling along the negative direction of the x-axis is projected upon it. If scattering occurs, the scattered photon may undergo a reversal of its velocity and be sent along the positive direction of the

x-axis. Let us suppose that this happens and that we measure the frequency ν' of the scattered radiation exactly. For the sake of simplicity, we suppose the velocity of the electron much smaller than that of light. The principles of conservation of energy and momentum give :

$$\left.\begin{aligned} h\nu + \tfrac{1}{2}mv^2 &= h\nu' + \tfrac{1}{2}mv'^2 \\ mv - \frac{h\nu}{c} &= mv' + \frac{h\nu'}{c} \end{aligned}\right\}, \quad . \quad . \quad (6)$$

v' being the velocity of the electron after scattering. By elimination of v' from the equations, we have :

$$h(\nu - \nu') = \frac{1}{2m}\left\{\frac{h^2}{c^2}(\nu + \nu')^2 - 2mv\frac{h}{c}(\nu + \nu')\right\}. \quad . \quad (7)$$

In the scattering process the frequency is changed very little, and we can thus write $\nu' = \nu - \epsilon$, and neglect $\epsilon\frac{v}{c}$ and ϵ^2. Hence

$$\epsilon\left(1 + \frac{2h\nu}{mc^2}\right) = \frac{2h\nu^2}{mc^2} - 2\nu\frac{v}{c}. \quad . \quad . \quad (8)$$

In ordinary cases, $\frac{h\nu}{mc^2}$ is very small, since for light $h\nu$ is of the order 10^{-13} and mc^2 is about 8×10^{-7}. We can thus neglect the fraction $\frac{2h\nu}{mc^2}$ on the left side of (8) and write :

$$\nu' = \nu - \epsilon = \nu\left(1 - \frac{2h\nu}{mc^2} + 2\frac{v}{c}\right). \quad . \quad . \quad (9)$$

The term $\frac{2v}{c}$ corresponds to the Doppler effect, and would exist if h were infinitely small. The term $-\frac{2h\nu}{mc^2}$ expresses the Compton effect for the case considered and the two effects are superposed. Since the Compton effect alters the velocity of the electron, we must try to make it negligible and take the wave-length large enough to make the ratio : $\dfrac{\frac{v}{c}}{\frac{h\nu}{mc^2}} = \frac{mv}{h}\lambda$ very large. In this case the Doppler effect alone is appreciable, and we may write :

$$\nu' = \nu\left(1 + \frac{2v}{c}\right) \text{ or } \lambda' = \lambda\left(1 - \frac{2v}{c}\right). \quad . \quad (10)$$

But the incident wave-train has necessarily a finite length l; consequently it is not strictly monochromatic, and if we introduce the wave-number $\frac{1}{\lambda}$, this quantity will vary for the different monochromatic waves of the train by the amount $\delta\left(\frac{1}{\lambda}\right)$ where :

$$\delta\left(\frac{1}{\lambda}\right) \sim \frac{1}{l} \quad . \quad . \quad . \quad . \quad (11)$$

the sign $\sim$ denoting "of the order of."

Thus, even if λ' be measured without any experimental error, there would still remain an uncertainty in the value of v, since according to (10) we have :

$$v = \frac{c}{2}\left(1 - \frac{\lambda'}{\lambda}\right), \quad . \quad . \quad . \quad (12)$$

and the uncertainty in λ implies an uncertainty in v equal to :

$$|\delta v| = \frac{c}{2}\lambda'\delta\left(\frac{1}{\lambda}\right). \quad . \quad . \quad (13)$$

Thus the uncertainty in the momentum of the electron after measurement is :

$$\delta p_x = \frac{mc\lambda}{2l}. \quad . \quad . \quad . \quad (14)$$

But the simultaneous value of the co-ordinate is itself also subject to an uncertainty.

In fact, the Compton effect, although by hypothesis small in comparison with the Doppler effect, nevertheless exists and causes a change in the velocity of the electron equal by the second of equations (6) to :

$$\begin{aligned} v' - v &= -\frac{h}{mc}(\nu + \nu') \\ &= -\frac{2h}{m\lambda} \text{ (approximately)}. \quad . \quad . \quad (15) \end{aligned}$$

Let us consider the most favourable case, which is that in which the initial position is known. There will be an uncertainty in the position after measurement, since it is not known at what instant in the interval $\frac{l}{c}$, during which the wave-train passes the electron, the scattering occurs, and according as this instant is at the beginning or end of the interval there will be a difference $(v - v')\frac{l}{c} = \frac{2hl}{m\lambda c}$ in the position of the electron. Thus, after the measurement has been made, the co-ordinate of the electron is subject to an uncertainty :

$$\delta x = \frac{2hl}{m\lambda c}, \quad . \quad . \quad . \quad . \quad (16)$$

and combining (14) and (16) we find that in the most favourable case :

$$\delta x \, \delta p_x = \frac{mc\lambda}{2l} \frac{2hl}{m\lambda c} = h, \quad . \quad . \quad . \quad (17)$$

so that we arrive once more at Heisenberg's uncertainty relation.

4. The Passage of a Particle through a Diaphragm

As another example we will take the determination of the position of a particle, for example a photon, by studying its passage through an opening in a plane screen. In order to fix the co-ordinates of the particle accurately we tend to make the opening very small, but the smaller the opening is made the more pronounced the diffraction phenomena which, according to the ideas of wave mechanics, are associated with the passage of the particle through the hole. Moreover, to find the instant when the particle passes into the plane of the screen we will make use of a movable shutter which will make it possible to uncover the hole for a very short interval. The more rapidly we work the shutter, the better will be the determination of the instant when the particle traverses the hole, but at the same time, the associated wave-train being proportionately shortened, the monochromatic property of the train will be more and more changed and consequently the energy of the particle will be less and less well-defined. We will consider in detail the simple case where the incident particle falls normally on the screen and where the opening is a rectangle of sides $2a$ and $2b$.

Let the centre of the opening be taken as origin of co-ordinates, the axis of x being parallel to the longer side $2a$ and the axis of y parallel to the shorter side $2b$, while the axis of z is perpendicular to the plane of the screen in the direction away from the incident wave (Fig. 12). Let M be a point of the opening with co-ordinates (X, Y, 0), and let (dX, dY) be the sides of a small rectangle about this point. Let us determine by Huygen's principle the elementary wave sent by the small

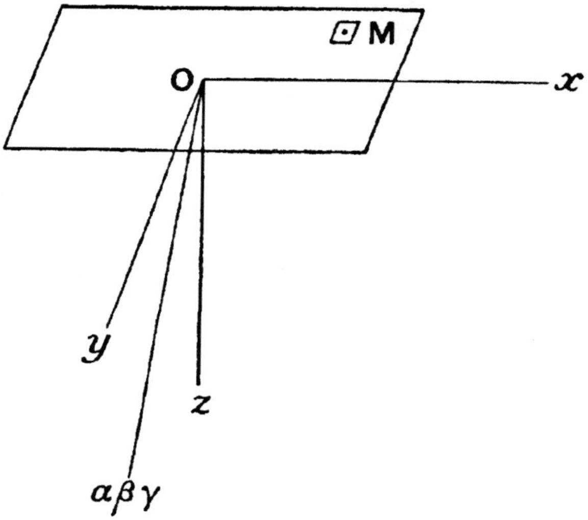

FIG. 12.

rectangle $dX\,dY$ in the direction (α, β, γ) which makes a very small angle with the z-axis. If (x, y, z) denote the co-ordinates of a very distant point in this direction the elementary wave is expressed by:

$$d\psi_{\alpha\beta} = K\,dX\,dY \cos 2\pi\left\{\nu t - \frac{\alpha(x - X) + \beta(y - Y) + z}{\lambda}\right\}, \quad (18)$$

where K is a coefficient which varies with (α, β, γ) but much more slowly than the cosine term and where γ has been written equal to unity. The resulting wave in the direction (α, β, γ) from all points of the aperture is

$$\psi_{\alpha\beta} = \iint d\psi_{\alpha\beta} = \text{A} \cos 2\pi\left(\nu t - \frac{\alpha x + \beta y + z}{\lambda}\right) + \text{B} \sin 2\pi\left(\nu t - \frac{\alpha x + \beta y + z}{\lambda}\right), \quad (19)$$

where

$$\text{A} = \text{K}\iint \cos 2\pi\frac{\alpha\text{X} + \beta\text{Y}}{\lambda} d\text{X}\, d\text{Y}\,; \qquad \text{B} = \text{K}\iint \sin 2\pi\frac{\alpha\text{X} + \beta\text{Y}}{\lambda} d\text{X}\, d\text{Y}. \quad (20)$$

B vanishes because in the integral two elements situated symmetrically with respect to O make equal and opposite contributions In A we can write :

$$\cos 2\pi\frac{\alpha\text{X} + \beta\text{Y}}{\lambda} = \cos 2\pi\frac{\alpha\text{X}}{\lambda} \cos 2\pi\frac{\beta\text{Y}}{\lambda} - \sin 2\pi\frac{\alpha\text{X}}{\lambda} \sin 2\pi\frac{\beta\text{Y}}{\lambda}, \quad (21)$$

and the integral of the product of the sines again vanishes. Thus :

$$\left.\begin{aligned} \text{A} &= 4\text{K}\int_0^a \cos 2\pi\frac{\alpha\text{X}}{\lambda} d\text{X}\int_0^b \cos 2\pi\frac{\beta\text{Y}}{\lambda} d\text{Y} \\ &= \frac{\text{K}\lambda^2}{\pi^2\alpha\beta} \sin 2\pi\frac{\alpha a}{\lambda} \sin 2\pi\frac{\beta b}{\lambda} \end{aligned}\right\}. \quad (22)$$

whence

$$\psi_{\alpha\beta} = \frac{\text{K}\lambda^2}{\pi^2\alpha\beta} \sin 2\pi\frac{\alpha a}{\lambda} \sin 2\pi\frac{\beta b}{\lambda} \cos 2\pi\left(\nu t - \frac{\alpha x + \beta y + z}{\lambda}\right). \quad (23)$$

Thus $\psi_{\alpha\beta}$ vanishes in directions for which $2\pi\frac{\alpha a}{\lambda} = m\pi$ or $2\pi\frac{\beta b}{\lambda} = n\pi$, where m and n are integers, that is for directions for which $\alpha = \frac{m\lambda}{2a}$, or $\beta = \frac{n\lambda}{2b}$. On the other hand, $\psi_{\alpha\beta}$ has maximum values in the directions for which

$$\alpha = (2m + 1)\frac{\lambda}{2a}, \text{ or } \beta = (2n + 1)\frac{\lambda}{2b}.$$

In this way we obtain what is known as a diffraction phenomenon localised at infinity.

To observe it, we shall place a lens of which the optic axis coincides with the axis of z. If there were no diffraction, only an image of the rectangular aperture would be observed situated in the focal plane of the lens on the optic axis. But on account of the existence of plane monochromatic waves inclined to the optic axis, a series of other images are also obtained corresponding to the maxima of $\psi_{\alpha\beta}$. The intensity of these images decreases rapidly when the order is raised.

In short, the plane wave which falls on the screen is of the form :

$$\psi = a \cos 2\pi\left(\nu t - \frac{z}{\lambda}\right). \quad . \quad . \quad (24)$$

In passing through the rectangular aperture it is transformed into a group of plane waves slightly inclined to the z-axis and of the form :

$$\psi = \sum a_{\alpha\beta} \cos 2\pi\left(\nu t - \frac{\alpha x + \beta y + z}{\lambda}\right), \quad . \quad (25)$$

the partial amplitudes $a_{\alpha\beta}$ representing the successive maxima and minima as functions of α and β. Since the intensity of the successive waves diminishes rapidly we see that the group extension with respect to the variable α is measured by :

$$\delta\alpha = k_1 \frac{\lambda}{2a} > \frac{\lambda}{2a}, \quad . \quad . \quad . \quad (26)$$

k_1 denoting a small integer which corresponds to the highest order of diffraction for which the intensity is appreciable. In the same way the group extension with respect to β will be

$$\delta\beta = k_2 \frac{\lambda}{2b} > \frac{\lambda}{2b}. \quad . \quad . \quad . \quad (27)$$

If **N** denotes the wave-number vector for the monochromatic wave characterised by the angles α and β we have :

$$\mathrm{N}_x = \frac{\alpha}{\lambda}, \quad \mathrm{N}_y = \frac{\beta}{\lambda}, \quad \mathrm{N}_z = \frac{1}{\lambda}. \quad . \quad . \quad (28)$$

The greatest variations of N_x and N_y in the wave group after passage through the screen are :

$$\delta\mathrm{N}_x = \frac{\delta\alpha}{\lambda} = \frac{k_1}{2a}, \quad \delta\mathrm{N}_y = \frac{\delta\beta}{\lambda} = \frac{k_2}{2b}. \quad . \quad . \quad (29)$$

We have, therefore, the following relations in orders of magnitude :

$$\delta N_x > \frac{1}{2a}, \quad \delta N_y > \frac{1}{2b}. \qquad (30)$$

Now the position of the particle at the instant of its passage through the rectangular aperture is defined with an uncertainty δx equal to $2a$ and an uncertainty δy equal to $2b$. We have therefore the relations in orders of magnitude ·

$$\delta N_x \delta x > 1, \quad \delta N_y \delta y > 1. \qquad (31)$$

According to the principle of spectral distribution, the uncertainties in the components p_x and p_y of the momentum are connected with the uncertainties δN_x and δN_y by the equations :

$$\delta p_x = h\delta N_x, \quad \delta p_y = h\delta N_y, \qquad (32)$$

and (31) thus takes the form of Heisenberg's relations :

$$\delta p_x \delta x > h, \quad \delta p_y \delta y > h \qquad (33)$$

Moreover, if we wish to determine the z-co-ordinate of the particle and the time t of the passage through the screen, we must employ a movable shutter in the manner explained above. Let τ denote the interval during which the shutter is raised. The uncertainty in t is clearly equal to τ, that in z is $v\tau$, v denoting the group velocity which we know is equal to that of the particle. Thus :

$$\delta t = \tau, \quad \delta z = v\tau. \qquad (34)$$

But in opening the shutter for the time τ only, we allow only a limited wave-train to pass through the aperture, and this train is composed of monochromatic waves occupying an interval in the spectrum at least of the order $\frac{1}{\tau}$. The corresponding interval in wave-length is such that $\delta\left(\frac{1}{\lambda}\right) = \frac{\delta\left(\frac{1}{\lambda}\right)}{\delta\nu}\delta\nu$ is of the order $\frac{1}{v\tau}$ since $v = \frac{\delta\left(\frac{1}{\lambda}\right)}{\delta\nu}$ by definition. We have then :

$$\delta\nu > \frac{1}{\tau}, \quad \delta\left(\frac{1}{\lambda}\right) > \frac{1}{v\tau}. \qquad (35)$$

Now by the principle of spectral distribution, the uncertainty in the final energy of the particle is $h\delta\nu$, and that in the final value of the component p_z of the momentum is $h\delta N_z = h\delta\left(\frac{1}{\lambda}\right)$ by (28). We have thus ·

$$\delta W\,\delta t > h, \quad \delta p_z \delta z > h. \qquad (36)$$

These are the other two Heisenberg relations.

5. A Note on the Measurement of Velocity

We have just confirmed by means of examples that the processes of measurement which we are able to use all lead to Heisenberg's uncertainty relations. We might, however, be tempted to reason in the following way. It is possible to make an experiment at a time t_1 showing that the particle is situated in the immediate neighbourhood of a point A of space, then at a later time t_2 another experiment showing that it is then in the immediate neighbourhood of another point B. If the time $t_2 - t_1$ is sufficiently long, we shall obtain a very good value of the velocity by taking ·

$$\mathbf{v} = \frac{\mathbf{AB}}{t_2 - t_1}, \qquad (37)$$

and the value of the momentum mv does not appear in this way to be affected by the Heisenberg uncertainty.

But we must note, in the first place, that if we repeat the same measurement of the velocity under exactly the same conditions we shall obtain each time a different result. In fact, as we shall show rigorously in the next chapter, the wave-train of very small dimensions, which corresponds at the time t_1 to the localisation of the particle near the point A by the first experiment, spreads during its propagation and occupies a large extent at the end of the long interval $t_2 - t_1$, when the second experiment is made. By the principle of interference there is a large region of space where the particle can possibly be found and a series of identical experiments would give a series of different points B.

Moreover, and this is an essential point, the velocity **v** given by (37) corresponds only to the motion between the instants t_1 and t_2; we cannot in any way consider it as the velocity which the particle possesses *after* the second experiment, since this second localisation near the point B completely disturbs its motion. The velocity is in no sense the initial velocity of the particle after the second observation, consequently it can give no information of what will happen after the time t_2. We have not been able to determine simultaneously the position and momentum of the particle by our two measurements of its position. The first observation permits us to localise the particle at A at time t_1, but it gives us no information about its momentum at this instant; the second permits us to localise the particle at B at t_2 and to find the velocity $\mathbf{v}$ with which the particle would be carried from A to B, but the momentum $m\mathbf{v}$ is not that which the particle possesses after the observation. We may say, if we wish, that the particle has passed from A to B with velocity $\mathbf{v}$, but that does not allow us in any way to *anticipate* exactly the motion of the particle in the interval $t_2 - t_1$ as the old deterministic dynamics claimed to do, since $\mathbf{v}$ has a value defined only at the end of the phenomenon to be anticipated.

In the next chapter we shall study by means of calculations the method of measurement of velocity which we have just discussed.

CHAPTER XIII

THE PROPAGATION OF A TRAIN OF ψ-WAVES IN THE ABSENCE OF A FIELD OF FORCE AND IN A UNIFORM FIELD

1. Rigorous Solution of the Equation of Propagation in the Absence of a Field of Force

WE pass on to study rigorously the propagation of a ψ-wave-train when there is no field of force, contenting ourselves with the non-relativistic equations. We must begin with the equation .

$$\nabla^2\psi = \frac{4\pi i}{h} m \frac{\partial\psi}{\partial t}. \quad . \quad . \quad . \quad (1)$$

This equation has the same form as the classical equation of thermal conductivity, but here the conductivity is represented by an imaginary coefficient. We can use a method of solution exactly like that applied to the thermal equation.

Equation (1) being of the first order in the time, we must know the value of $\psi(x, y, z, t)$ at an initial instant taken as the zero time in order to determine which integral is to be chosen. The problem before us is therefore to find $\psi(x, y, z, t)$ when $\psi(x, y, z, 0)$ is known We will write $\psi(x, y, z, 0) = f(x, y, z)$. The method of solution is to determine a "transformation function" $T(x, y, z, x_0, y_0, z_0, t)$ of two sets of variables x, y, z and x_0, y_0, z_0 and of the time such that ·

$$\psi(x, y, z, t) = \iiint f(x_0, y_0, z_0)\, T(x, y, z, x_0, y_0, z_0, t)\, dx_0, dy_0, dz_0, \quad . \quad . \quad . \quad (2)$$

where the limits of integration are $-\infty$ to $+\infty$ (Kennard, Heisenberg). It is necessary that two conditions should be satisfied.

1. The function $\psi(x, y, z, t)$ defined by (2) must satisfy the

equation (1); this requires that T considered as a function of x, y, z, t shall itself satisfy this equation.

2. The function ψ defined by (2) must reduce to $f(x, y, z)$ at $t = 0$.

We begin by seeking a function T which is a solution of the wave equation. We have seen in the study of the classical motion of a particle in a zero field of force that the function:

$$S(x, y, z, t, x_0, y_0, z_0) = -\frac{m}{2t}\{(x-x_0)^2 + (y-y_0)^2 + (z-z_0)^2\}, \quad . \quad . \quad . \quad (3)$$

depending upon the three initial co-ordinates, is a complete integral of Jacobi's equation, and therefore it is possible to determine the motion which transforms the initial co-ordinates x_0, y_0, z_0 at the instant zero to x, y, z at the instant t. We can therefore expect the function S to play an important part in the problem.

But, on the other hand, the function of transformation T must satisfy the wave-equation; we have:

$$\nabla^2 T = \frac{4\pi i}{h} m \frac{\partial T}{\partial t}, \quad . \quad (4)$$

and if we write:

$$T = Re^{\frac{2\pi i}{h}S}, \quad . \quad . \quad (5)$$

where R and S are real functions not yet determined, we find by substituting (5) in (4) and separating real and imaginary parts:

$$\frac{1}{2m}\left\{\left(\frac{\partial S}{\partial x}\right)^2 + \left(\frac{\partial S}{\partial y}\right)^2 + \left(\frac{\partial S}{\partial z}\right)^2\right\} = \frac{\partial S}{\partial t} + \frac{h^2}{8\pi^2 m}\frac{\nabla^2 R}{R}, \quad . \quad . \quad (6)$$

$$\frac{\partial R}{\partial x}\frac{\partial S}{\partial x} + \frac{\partial R}{\partial y}\frac{\partial S}{\partial y} + \frac{\partial R}{\partial z}\frac{\partial S}{\partial z} + \frac{1}{2}R\nabla^2 S = m\frac{\partial R}{\partial t}. \quad . \quad (7)$$

Let us take the expression (3) for the function S. Since (3) satisfies Jacobi's equation:

$$\frac{1}{2m}\sum\left(\frac{\partial S}{\partial x}\right)^2 = \frac{\partial S}{\partial t}, \quad . \quad . \quad . \quad (8)$$

it is necessary that $\nabla^2 R$ vanish in order that (6) may be satisfied. The simplest hypothesis is thus to suppose that R does not depend on the variables (x, y, z), but only upon the time t. With this assumption equation (7) reduces to :

$$\frac{dR}{dt} = \frac{1}{2m} R \nabla^2 S. \qquad (9)$$

This equation can be satisfied since the function (3) which we have chosen for S is a quadratic in (x, y, z), so that $\nabla^2 S$ is a function of t only. We have :

$$\nabla^2 S = -\frac{m}{2t}\nabla^2\{\sum(x-x_0)^2\} = -\frac{3m}{t}, \qquad (10)$$

and R is thus given by :

$$\frac{dR}{dt} = -\frac{3}{2t}R \qquad (11)$$

or

$$R = Ct^{-\frac{3}{2}}. \qquad (12)$$

We thus obtain by (5), (3) and (12) the function T .

$$T(x, y, z, x_0, y_0, z_0) = \frac{C}{t^{\frac{3}{2}}} e^{-\frac{\pi i m}{ht}\sum(x-x_0)^2}. \qquad (13)$$

The function

$$\psi(x, y, z, t) = \iiint f(x_0, y_0, z_0)\frac{C}{t^{\frac{3}{2}}} e^{-\frac{\pi i m}{ht}\sum(x-x_0)^2} dx_0\, dy_0\, dz_0 \qquad (14)$$

therefore satisfies the wave equation, but it must also reduce to $f(x, y, z)$ for $t = 0$. In order to verify this we make a change in the variables :[1]

$$r_1 = \frac{x_0 - x}{\sqrt{t}}, \quad r_2 = \frac{y_0 - y}{\sqrt{t}}, \quad r_3 = \frac{z_0 - z}{\sqrt{t}}. \qquad (15)$$

The triple integral (14) then becomes :

$$\iiint f\{(r_1\sqrt{t} + x), \ (r_2\sqrt{t} + y), \ (r_3\sqrt{t} + z)\} \frac{C}{t^{\frac{3}{2}}} e^{-\frac{\pi i m}{h}(r_1^2 + r_2^2 + r_3^2)} \frac{\partial(x_0, y_0, z_0)}{\partial(r_1, r_2, r_3)} dr_1\, dr_2\, dr_3. \qquad (16)$$

[1] The calculation which follows is due to Fourier. The passage to the limit leading to (18) is not quite rigorous but the reasoning may be made quite sound. Reference may be made to "Leçons sur quelques types simples d'équations aux dérivées partielles," by Emile Picard. Gauthier-Villars, Paris, 1927, 2° leçon.

But the Jacobian on evaluation gives :

$$\frac{\partial(x_0, y_0, z_0)}{\partial(r_1, r_2, r_3)} = \begin{vmatrix} \sqrt{t} & 0 & 0 \\ 0 & \sqrt{t} & 0 \\ 0 & 0 & \sqrt{t} \end{vmatrix} = t^{\frac{3}{2}}, \qquad (17)$$

so that .

$$\psi(x, y, z, t) = \mathrm{C}\iiint f e^{-\frac{\pi i m}{h}(r_1^2 + r_2^2 + r_3^2)} dr_1\, dr_2\, dr_3. \qquad (18)$$

If t be now made to approach zero the value of f becomes $f(x, y, z)$ and we have in the limit :

$$\psi(x, y, z, 0) = f(x, y, z)\mathrm{C}\int_{-\infty}^{\infty} e^{-\frac{\pi i m}{h}r_1^2} dr_1 \int_{-\infty}^{\infty} e^{-\frac{\pi i m}{h}r_2^2} dr_2$$
$$\int_{-\infty}^{\infty} e^{-\frac{\pi i m}{h}r_3^2} dr_3, \qquad (19)$$

since, as we mentioned above, the limits of integration are $-\infty$ and $+\infty$ These are well-known integrals, and we have in fact :

$$\int_{-\infty}^{\infty} e^{-\frac{\pi i m}{h}r^2} dr = \sqrt{\frac{h}{im}}. \quad . \qquad (20)$$

If the arbitrary constant C is given the value $\left(\frac{im}{h}\right)^{\frac{3}{2}}$, we then have :

$$\psi(x, y, z, 0) = f(x, y, z), \quad . \quad . \qquad (22)$$

so that finally the function

$$\psi(x, y, z, t) = \left(\frac{im}{ht}\right)^{\frac{3}{2}} \iiint f(x_0, y_0, z_0) e^{-\frac{\pi i m}{ht}\{\Sigma(x - x_0)^2\}} dx_0\, dy_0\, dz_0, \quad . \quad . \quad . \qquad (23)$$

the limits of integration being $-\infty$ and $+\infty$ for each of the variables, is the solution of the wave-equation (1) which reduces to $f(x_0, y_0, z_0)$ for $t = 0$.

The problem of the propagation of the wave-train associated with a particle is thus solved rigorously.

2. The Calculations Applied to a Special Case (Darwin)

In order to work out the results we shall make a special assumption in regard to the form of the initial wave-train. We shall suppose that $f(x, y, z)$ is of the form:

$$f(x, y, z) = e^{-\frac{r^2}{2\sigma^2}} e^{-\frac{2\pi i}{h}(mv_x x + mv_y y + mv_z z)}, \quad . \quad (24)$$

where r^2 is written for $(x^2 + y^2 + z^2)$.

The explanation of this particular choice of f will be clear from the following considerations We suppose that at instants in the neighbourhood of $t = 0$ the wave-train is of the form studied above (Chap IV, § 3), viz :

$$\psi(x, y, z, t) = A(x, y\ z, t) e^{2\pi i\left(\nu t - \frac{\alpha x + \beta y + \gamma z}{\lambda}\right)}, \quad . \quad (25)$$

where $\lambda = \frac{h}{mv}$. Thus at the time $t = 0$, this wave-train is reduced to:

$$\psi(x, y, z, 0) = A(x, y, z\ 0) e^{-\frac{2\pi i}{h}(mv_x x + mv_y y + mv_z z)}, \quad . \quad (26)$$

and the probability that at this instant the particle will be situated at the point (x, y, z) is $A^2(x, y, z, 0)$ Now we take the instant $t = 0$ as the starting-point for the calculation, since it is supposed that an observation has been made upon the particle at that time The result of this initial observation makes it possible for us to state that the most probable position of the particle after the observation is a certain point P which for simplicity we shall choose as the origin of co-ordinates. But there will be a certain possible error and by the Gaussian law of errors, the result of the observation must be stated thus: the probability that the particle is situated at the point (x, y, z) is $e^{-\frac{r^2}{\sigma^2}}$, σ being the smaller the more accurately the experiment is made. As soon as the distance from the point (x, y, z) to the origin is a small multiple of σ the probability that the initial co-ordinates are (x, y, z) becomes very small; we can thus say that the region in which the particle can be found at the initial instant has dimensions of the order of σ. According to the interference principle we have:

$$A^2(x, y, z, 0) = e^{-\frac{r^2}{\sigma^2}}; \quad A(x, y, z, 0) = e^{-\frac{r^2}{2\sigma^2}}, \quad . \quad (27)$$

and finally we are led to adopt the form proposed in (24) for f. The general form (23) becomes in this case :

$$\psi(x, y, z, t) = \left(\frac{im}{ht}\right)^{\frac{3}{2}} \prod_{xyz} \int_{-\infty}^{+\infty} e^{-\left\{\frac{x_0^2}{2\sigma^2} + \frac{2\pi i}{h} mv_x x_0 + \frac{\pi im}{ht}(x - x_0)^2\right\}} dx_0, \quad (28)$$

where the symbol $\prod_{xyz}$ denotes the product of the factor which follows it by those obtained by replacing x_0 and x, by y_0 and y, then by z_0 and z respectively.

Writing :

$$a = \frac{1}{2\sigma^2} + \frac{\pi im}{ht}, \quad b_x = \frac{2\pi im}{ht}(x - v_x t), \quad . \quad (29)$$

the formula (28) may be written more simply :

$$\psi(x, y, z, t) = \left(\frac{im}{ht}\right)^{\frac{3}{2}} \prod_{xyz} e^{-\frac{\pi im}{ht}x^2} \int_{-\infty}^{+\infty} e^{-(ax_0^2 - b_x x_0)} dx_0. \quad (30)$$

But

$$\int_{-\infty}^{+\infty} e^{-(a_0 x^2 - b_x x_0)} dx_0 = e^{\frac{b_x^2}{4a}} \int_{-\infty}^{+\infty} e^{-a\left(x_0 - \frac{b_x}{2a}\right)^2} dx_0$$

$$= \frac{e^{\frac{b_x^2}{4a}}}{\sqrt{a}} \int_{-\infty}^{+\infty} e^{-z^2} dz = e^{\frac{b_x^2}{4a}} \sqrt{\frac{\pi}{a}}, \quad . \quad (31)$$

and consequently

$$\psi(x, y, z, t) = \left(\frac{\pi im}{aht}\right)^{\frac{3}{2}} \prod_{xyz} e^{\left(\frac{b_x^2}{4a} - \frac{\pi im}{ht}x^2\right)}, \quad . \quad (32)$$

the factor $\sqrt{\frac{\pi}{a}}$ occurring three times.

We have

$$\left(\frac{\pi im}{aht}\right)^{\frac{3}{2}} = \frac{1}{\left(1 + \frac{ht}{2\pi im\sigma^2}\right)^{\frac{3}{2}}} = \left(\frac{\sigma}{\sqrt{\sigma^2 + \frac{ht}{2\pi im}}}\right)^3, \quad . \quad (33)$$

and

$$\frac{b_x^2}{4a} = \frac{\frac{\pi im}{ht}(x - v_x t)^2}{1 - \frac{iht}{2\pi m\sigma^2}}. \quad . \quad . \quad . \quad (34)$$

If we get rid of the imaginary in the denominator we obtain :

$$\frac{b_x^2}{4a} = \frac{\frac{\pi i m}{ht}\sigma^2 - \frac{1}{2}}{\sigma^2 + \left(\frac{ht}{2\pi m\sigma}\right)^2}(x - v_x t)^2, \quad . \quad . \quad (35)$$

thus finally ·

$$\psi(x, y, z, t) = \left(\frac{\sigma}{\sqrt{\sigma^2 + \left(\frac{ht}{2\pi i m}\right)^2}}\right)^3 e^{-\frac{1}{2}\cdot\frac{(x - v_x t)^2 + (y - v_y t)^2 + (z - v_z t)^2}{\sigma^2 + \left(\frac{ht}{2\pi m\sigma}\right)^2}}$$

$$e^{\frac{\pi i m}{ht}\frac{\sigma^2\{(x - v_x t)^2 + (y - v_y t)^2 + (z - v_z t)^2\}}{\sigma^2 + \left(\frac{ht}{2\pi m\sigma}\right)^2}} \times e^{-\frac{\pi i m}{ht}(x^2 + y^2 + z^2)}. \quad (36)$$

If we write as usual $\psi = ae^{\frac{2\pi i\phi}{h}}$, a and ϕ being real quantities, we find :

$$a(x, y, z, t) = \sqrt{\psi\psi^*}$$

$$= \left\{\frac{\sigma}{\sqrt{\sigma^2 + \left(\frac{ht}{2\pi m\sigma}\right)^2}}\right\}^3 e^{-\frac{1}{2}\cdot\frac{(x - v_x t)^2 + (y - v_y t)^2 + (z - v_z t)^2}{\sigma^2 + \left(\frac{ht}{2\pi m\sigma}\right)^2}}, \quad (37)$$

$$\phi(x, y, z, t) =$$

$$\frac{m}{2t}\left[\frac{\sigma^2}{\sigma^2 + \left(\frac{ht}{2\pi m\sigma}\right)^2}\{(x - v_x t)^2 + (y - v_y t)^2 + (z - v_z t)^2\} - (x^2 + y^2 + z^2)\right]$$

$$+ F(t), \quad (38)$$

where $F(t)$ is a certain function of the time which we need not determine.

If we suppose that the dimensions of the wave-train are very large with respect to the wave-length $\lambda = \frac{h}{mv}$, then $\sigma \gg \frac{h}{mv}$. If we consider a value of t which is not very large compared with the reduced period $\frac{h}{\frac{1}{2}mv^2}$, we have :

$$\frac{h^2}{m^2v^2} \sim \frac{ht}{m},$$

where the symbol denotes that the two sides are of the same

order Thus, since $\sigma^2 \gg \frac{h^2}{m^2v^2}$, we can neglect $\frac{ht}{2\pi m\sigma}$ in comparison with σ, and (36) is reduced to :

$$\psi(x, y, z, t) = e^{-\frac{(x - v_xt)^2 + (y - v_yt)^2 + (z - v_zt)^2}{2\sigma^2}} \cdot e^{\frac{2\pi i}{h}\{\frac{1}{2}m(v_x^2 + v_y^2 + v_z^2)t - mv_xx - mv_yy - mv_zz\}} \quad (39)$$

The wave-train will have preserved the same form as it had at the beginning, the amplitude being carried forward in the direction of propagation with the velocity (v_x, v_y, v_z). These are the conditions under which the approximate results of Chapter IV are valid. But here we see that they are valid for a limited time only. A time arrives in every case when the factor $\frac{ht}{2\pi m\sigma}$ is no longer negligible compared with σ and the amplitude round the point with co-ordinates $x = v_xt$, $y = v_yt$, $z = v_zt$, is again expressed by a Gaussian function in which σ^2 must be replaced by $\sigma^2 + \left(\frac{ht}{2\pi m\sigma}\right)^2$. There is a continuous spreading of the wave-train

The same result may be obtained by considering the motion of the probability.

The velocity of the probability elements is equal to $-\frac{1}{m}$ grad ϕ, its components are denoted by (ξ, η, ζ) to avoid confusion with (v_x, v_y, v_z), which are given constants. We have therefore by (38) .

$$\xi = -\frac{1}{m}\frac{\partial\phi}{\partial x} = v_x + \left(\frac{x}{t} - v_x\right)\frac{\left(\frac{ht}{2\pi m\sigma}\right)^2}{\sigma^2 + \left(\frac{ht}{2\pi m\sigma}\right)^2} \quad (40)$$

together with similar equations for η and ζ.

When t is sufficiently small, all the probability elements move approximately with the velocity **v** ; the probability cloud moves as a whole in the direction of propagation with this velocity. But with increase of time the probability elements acquire a velocity component perpendicular to the direction of propagation which tends to extend the wave-train. At the same time the probability elements situated in the forward part of the wave-train acquire in the direction of propagation a velocity greater than that of the elements situated behind, so that there is a progressive lengthening of the train. This is readily seen from the equations (40) by taking the z-axis as the direction of propagation and $v_x = v_y = 0$. The wave-train thus spreads slowly in all directions.

3. The Measurement of Velocity by Two Successive Observations

We retain the hypothesis (24) concerning the form of $f(x, y, z)$ and consequently the expression (36) for ψ The probability that an experiment made at time t will locate the particle in a volume element $dx\,dy\,dz$ is therefore by (37) :

$$P(x, y, z, t)dx\,dy\,dz = a^2\,dx\,dy\,dz. \quad . \quad . \quad (41)$$

We shall make use of this formula to discuss by means of a calculation the question of the determination of the velocity of the particle by two successive determinations of its position which was raised at the end of the last chapter

We suppose that an initial observation made at zero time has made it possible to locate the particle at the origin of co-ordinates with a possible error of the order of σ. A second observation at time t attributes to the particle a position (x, y, z), so that it is natural to say that the particle had the velocity u after the first observation with components given by ·

$$u_x = \frac{x}{t}, \quad u_y = \frac{y}{t}, \quad u_z = \frac{z}{t}. \quad . \quad (42)$$

and that the momentum had the three components :

$$p_x = \frac{mx}{t}, \quad p_y = \frac{my}{t}, \quad p_z = \frac{mz}{t} \quad . \quad . \quad (43)$$

It is true that these values are subject to an uncertainty of the order $\frac{\sigma}{t}$ on account of the uncertainty about the exact initial position, but if there is a long interval between the two observations, it will be possible to make this uncertainty negligible. Since the wave-train in this case has time to spread considerably between the two observations, the second observation might locate the particle in any point of an extended region of the space and the result is that in repeating the same observation under identical conditions, different values of x, y, z, and consequently of p_x, p_y, p_z, would be found. We cannot therefore say that p_x, p_y and p_z have well-defined values and there are only certain probabilities for particular values.

We can construct a "momentum space" by means of the three variables (p_x, p_y, p_z) Each determination of (x, y, z) provides by (43) a point of this space, and to each element of volume $dx\,dy\,dz$ corresponds by a well-known analytical theorem a volume dw of the momentum space given by :

$$dw = \frac{\partial(p_x, p_y, p_z)}{\partial(x, y, z)}\,dx\,dy\,dz$$

$$= \frac{m^3}{t^3}\,dx\,dy\,dz. \qquad (44)$$

The probability $P(p_x, p_y, p_z, t)$ that an observation made at the time t will give a value of the components of momentum corresponding to a point in dw is equal to the probability of finding the particle in $dx\,dy\,dz$

Thus

$$P(p_x, p_y, p_z, t)dw = a^2(x, y, z, t)\,dx\,dy\,dz, \qquad (45)$$

whence

$$P(p_x, p_y, p_z, t) = \frac{t^3}{m^3}a^2(x, y, z, t) \qquad (46)$$

Since t is supposed very large, we may be content to write .

$$a^2(x, y, z, t) = \left(\frac{2\pi m\sigma^2}{ht}\right)^3 e^{-\frac{4\pi^2 m^2\sigma^2}{h^2t^2}\{(x - v_xt)^2 + (y - v_yt)^2 + (z - v_zt)^2\}}, \qquad (47)$$

so that by (43)

$$\frac{t^3}{m^3}a^2 = P = \left(\frac{2\pi\sigma^2}{h}\right)^3 e^{-\frac{4\pi^2\sigma^2}{h^2}\{(p_x - mv_x)^2 + (p_y - mv_y)^2 + (p_z - mv_z)^2\}}. \qquad (48)$$

The most probable values of p_x, p_y, p_z are thus mv_x, mv_y, mv_z, and if we denote the differences between the true and most probable values by δp_x, δp_y, δp_z and the uncertainties in the initial co-ordinates by δx_0, δy_0, δz_0 which are equal to σ, we have :

$$P(\delta p_x, \delta p_y, \delta p_z) = \left(\frac{2\pi\sigma^2}{h}\right)^3 e^{-4\pi^2\left\{\left(\frac{\delta x_0\,\delta p_x}{h}\right)^2 + \left(\frac{\delta y_0\,\delta p_y}{h}\right)^2 + \left(\frac{\delta z_0\,\delta p_z}{h}\right)^2\right\}}. \qquad (49)$$

It follows at once from (49) that the product of the uncertainty in the co-ordinates by that in the corresponding momenta after the first observation must be regarded as being of the order of magnitude of h. We arrive again at Heisenberg's conception.

4. Rigorous Solution of the Propagation of a ψ-Wave-train in a Uniform Constant Field of Force

The propagation of a wave-train in a uniform constant field of force is defined by the potential function :

$$F(x, y, z) = -(k_x x + k_y y + k_z z). \qquad (50)$$

We shall in this case again try to find a transformation function The wave-equation is .

$$\nabla^2 \psi + \frac{8\pi^2 m}{h^2}(k_x x + k_y y + k_z z)\psi = \frac{4\pi i m}{h}\frac{\partial \psi}{\partial t}, \qquad (51)$$

and $\psi(x, y, z, t)$ is completely determined if the initial value $\psi(x, y, z, 0) = f(x, y, z)$ is given The transformation function $T(x, y, z, t, x_0, y_0, z_0)$ must be such that .

$$\psi(x, y, z, t) = \iiint f(x_0, y_0, z_0) T\, dx_0\, dy_0\, dz_0. \qquad (52)$$

the limits of integration being $-\infty$ to $+\infty$.

Thus T considered as a function of (x, y, z) must satisfy the equation :

$$\nabla^2 T + \frac{8\pi^2 m}{h^2}(k_x x + k_y y + k_z z)T = \frac{4\pi i m}{h}\frac{\partial T}{\partial t}. \qquad (53)$$

As before, let us write

$$T = Re^{\frac{2\pi i}{h}S}, \qquad (54)$$

where R is a function of t and S of $x, y, z, t, x_0, y_0, z_0$.

We find on substituting (54) in (53).

$$\frac{1}{2m}\sum\left(\frac{\partial S}{\partial x}\right)^2 + \sum k_x x = \frac{\partial S}{\partial t}, \qquad (55)$$

$$m\frac{dR}{dt} = \frac{1}{2}R\nabla^2 S. \qquad (56)$$

We can thus take for S Jacobi's function in the old mechanics which, as we have seen (Chap. II, § 6) is:

$$S = -\frac{m}{2t}\sum(x - x_0)^2 - \frac{1}{2}t\sum k_x(x + x_0) + \frac{t^3}{24m}\sum k_x^2, \qquad (57)$$

and is a solution of equation (55) As in § 1 we find.

$$\nabla^2 S = -\frac{3m}{t}. \qquad (58)$$

and by (56):

$$R = Ct^{-\frac{3}{2}}. \qquad (59)$$

It remains to verify that the function:

$$\psi = C\iiint\frac{f}{t^{\frac{3}{2}}}e^{\frac{2\pi i}{h}S}dx_0\,dy_0\,dz_0 \qquad (60)$$

reduces to $f(x, y, z)$ at $t = 0$.

We again make the change of variables (15) and make use of (17) so that (60) becomes

$$\psi = C\iiint f e^{\frac{2\pi i}{h}S}dr_1\,dr_2\,dr_3, \qquad (61)$$

where in f and S it is supposed that x_0, y_0 and z_0 have been replaced.

In the limit when t approaches zero it is found that:

$$\psi(x, y, z, 0) = Cf(x, y, z)\int_{-\infty}^{+\infty}e^{-\frac{\pi i m}{h}r_1^2}dr_1\int_{-\infty}^{\infty}e^{-\frac{\pi i m}{h}r_2^2}dr_2 \int_{-\infty}^{\infty}e^{-\frac{\pi i m}{h}r_3^2}dr_3. \qquad (62)$$

and again it is only necessary to write $C = \left(\frac{im}{h}\right)^{\frac{3}{2}}$ to obtain

$$\psi(x, y, z, 0) = f(x, y, z)$$

Finally, the expression :

$$\psi(x, y, z, t) = \left(\frac{im}{ht}\right)^{\frac{3}{2}} \iiint f\, e^{\frac{2\pi i}{h}S}\, dx_0\, dy_0\, dz_0 \qquad . \quad (63)$$

is the solution of the wave-equation which assumes the value $f(x, y, z)$ at $t = 0$, and is therefore the solution required.

5. Development of the Calculations in a Special Case

Let us adopt the form for f given by .

$$f = e^{-\frac{r^2}{2\sigma^2}} e^{-\frac{2\pi i m}{h}\sum v_{0x} x}, \quad . \quad . \quad . \quad (64)$$

where $r^2 = x^2 + y^2 + z^2$ and v_{0x}, etc , are the initial velocity components.

If we write S_x for that part of S which depends upon x and x_0 we find :

$$\psi = \left(\frac{im}{ht}\right)^{\frac{3}{2}} \prod_{xyz} \int_{-\infty}^{\infty} e^{-\frac{x_0^2}{2\sigma^2} - \frac{2\pi i m}{h} v_{0x} x_0} e^{\frac{2\pi i}{h}S_x}\, dx_0 \qquad . \quad (65)$$

After making the substitutions

$$a = \frac{1}{2\sigma^2} + \frac{\pi i m}{ht}, \quad b_x = \frac{2\pi i m}{ht}\left(x - v_{0x}t - \frac{k_x}{2m}t^2\right), \quad . \quad (66)$$

(65) becomes :

$$\psi = \left(\frac{im}{ht}\right)^{\frac{3}{2}} \prod_{xyz} e^{-\frac{\pi i m}{ht}x^2 - \frac{\pi i k_x t}{h}x + \frac{\pi i t^3 k_x^2}{12mh}} \int_{-\infty}^{\infty} e^{-a x_0^2 + b_x x_0}\, dx_0, \quad (67)$$

and the calculations made above give us in this case :

$$\psi = \left(\frac{\pi i m}{hta}\right)^{\frac{3}{2}} \prod_{xyz} e^{\frac{b_x^2}{4a} - \frac{\pi i m}{ht}x^2 - \frac{\pi i k_x t}{h}x + \frac{\pi i t^3}{12mh}k_x^2}. \qquad . \quad (68)$$

The value of $\left(\frac{\pi i m}{hta}\right)^{\frac{3}{2}}$ is that given in (33), and (35) is replaced by :

$$\frac{b_x^2}{4a} = \frac{\frac{\pi i m}{ht}\sigma^2 - \frac{1}{2}}{\sigma^2 + \left(\frac{ht}{2\pi m\sigma}\right)^2}\left(x - v_{0x}t - \frac{1}{2}\frac{k_x}{m}t\right)^2. \qquad . \quad (69)$$

Thus the value of ψ is given by :

$$\psi = \left(\frac{\sigma}{\sqrt{\sigma^2 + \frac{ht}{2\pi mi}}}\right)^3 e^{-\frac{1}{2}\sum \frac{\left(x - v_{0x}t - \frac{k_x}{2m}t^2\right)^2}{\sigma^2 + \left(\frac{ht}{2\pi m\sigma}\right)^2}}$$

$$\times\, e^{\frac{\pi i m}{ht}\left\{\frac{\sigma^2 \sum\left(x - v_{0x}t - \frac{k_x}{2m}t^2\right)^2}{\sigma^2 + \left(\frac{ht}{2\pi m\sigma}\right)^2} - \sum\left(x^2 + \frac{k_x x t^2}{m} - \frac{k_x^2 t^4}{12m^2}\right)\right\}} . \quad (70)$$

According to the interference principle, the probability that the particle is situated at (x, y, z) at time t is :

$$a^2 = \psi\psi^* = \left(\frac{\sigma}{\sqrt{\sigma^2 + \left(\frac{ht}{2\pi m\sigma}\right)^2}}\right)^3 e^{-\frac{\sum\left(x - v_{0x}t - \frac{k_x t^2}{m}\right)^2}{\sigma^2 + \left(\frac{ht}{2\pi m\sigma}\right)^2}} , \quad (71)$$

and when it is permissible to neglect $\left(\frac{ht}{2\pi m\sigma}\right)^2$ in comparison with σ^2, which would always be possible if h were infinitesimal, we have :

$$a^2 = e^{-\sum\left(x - v_{0x}t - \frac{k_x}{2m}t^2\right)^2} . \quad (72)$$

In this case the wave-train has the same form about the point with co-ordinates :

$$x = v_{0x}t - \frac{k_x}{2m}t^2, \quad y = v_{0y}t - \frac{k_y}{2m}t^2, \quad z = v_{0z}t - \frac{k_z}{2m}t^2,$$

at time t as it had about the origin at zero time. The wave-train moves as a whole and has throughout the same motion as in the classical theory, but when the term $\left(\frac{ht}{2\pi m\sigma}\right)^2$ can be no longer neglected the dimensions of the wave-train increase, since σ is replaced by $\sigma^1 = \sqrt{\sigma^2 + \left(\frac{ht}{2\pi m\sigma}\right)^2}$ and there is continuous spreading.

We arrive at the same conclusion by calculating the velocity of the probability elements. Let (ξ, η, ζ) again denote the components of this velocity. The expression (70) shows that the phase is given by:

$$\phi = \frac{m}{2t}\left\{\frac{\sigma^2}{\sigma^2 + \left(\frac{ht}{2\pi m\sigma}\right)^2}\sum\left(x - v_{0x}\,t - \frac{k_x}{2m}\,t^2\right)^2 \right.$$
$$\left. - \sum\left(x^2 + \frac{k_x}{m}\,xt^2 - \frac{k_x^2}{12m^2}\,t^4\right)\right\} \quad (73)$$

omitting the additional term of the form $F(t)$ which contributes nothing to (ξ, η, ζ).

From (73) we deduce

$$\xi = -\frac{1}{m}\frac{\partial\phi}{\partial x} = v_{0x} + \frac{k_x}{m}t + \frac{\left(\frac{ht}{2\pi m\sigma}\right)^2}{\sigma^2 + \left(\frac{ht}{2\pi m\sigma}\right)^2}\left(\frac{x}{t} - v_{0x} - \frac{k_x}{2m}\,t\right) \quad . \quad . \quad . \quad (74)$$

together with similar expressions for η and ζ.

These expressions show that if $\left(\frac{ht}{2\pi m\sigma}\right)^2$ is negligible as before, the probability elements move as a whole with the velocity anticipated for the particles by the classical theory. But the situation changes when the term is appreciable and in addition to these classical velocities there appear centrifugal velocity components with respect to the point:

$$x = v_{0x}\,t + \frac{k_x}{2m}t^2, \quad y = v_{0y}\,t + \frac{k_y}{2m}t^2, \quad z = v_{0z}\,t + \frac{k_z}{2m}t^2,$$

and the wave-train tends to spread in all directions.

Let it be supposed that the velocity of the particle is determined by two observations made at zero time and at time t and let the second observation locate the particle at the point (x, y, z). We can consider the initial velocity components as equal to .

$$U_{0x} = \frac{x}{t} - \frac{k_x}{2m}t, \quad U_{0y} = \frac{y}{t} - \frac{k_y}{2m}t, \quad U_{0z} = \frac{z}{t} - \frac{k_z}{2m}t. \quad (75)$$

The possible error due to the uncertainty σ in the original position can be diminished as much as we please by taking for t a sufficiently large value. By the argument of the preceding paragraph we again find that the probability that a second observation will give values (p_{0x}, p_{0y}, p_{0z}) for the original components of momentum is given by

$$P(p_{0x}, p_{0y}, p_{0z}) = \left(\frac{2\pi\sigma^2}{h}\right)^3 e^{-\frac{4\pi^2\sigma^2}{h^2}\sum(p_{0x} - mv_{0x})^2} \quad . \quad (76)$$

The most probable values for p_{0x}, p_{0y} and p_{0z} are therefore mv_{0x}, mv_{0y} and mv_{0z}. Let us denote by δp_{0x}, δp_{0y} and δp_{0z} the deviations between the true and most probable values, and let δx_0, δy_0 and δz_0 be the uncertainties, which are equal to σ, in the initial co-ordinates, so that

$$P(\delta p_{0x}, \delta p_{0y}, \delta p_{0z}) = \left(\frac{2\pi\sigma^2}{h}\right)^3 e^{-4\pi^2\sum\left(\frac{\delta p_{0x}\,\delta x_0}{h}\right)^2} \quad . \quad (77)$$

We have once more the Heisenberg relations between the uncertainties in the co-ordinates and in the conjugate momenta in the initial state after the first observation.

CHAPTER XIV

WAVE MECHANICS OF SYSTEMS OF PARTICLES

1. Summary of the Principles of the Old Dynamics of Systems

HITHERTO we have been occupied only with the case of a single particle moving in a given field of force. But we have often to consider the case of an assembly of particles acting upon one another. We cannot then consider the field as given, since, if attention is paid to one of the particles of the system, that particular particle is subject to forces generated by the others, and these possess a motion dependent upon the particle itself. Thus it is necessary to determine at one and the same time the motion of all the particles, and this determination is the solution of the rather complicated problem which constitutes the subject of what is known as the dynamics of systems. We shall recall the principles of this, limiting ourselves to Newtonian mechanics

In classical mechanics we pass very simply from the dynamics of a single material point to the dynamics of systems by admitting the principle of the equality of action and re-action, according to which the force exerted by a particle A on a particle B is equal and opposite to that exerted by B on A.

Let us consider a system of N particles numbered from 1 to N to which co-ordinates (x_i, y_i, z_i) are assigned, where i may have any value from 1 to N

The Lagrangian function for the ith particle is:

$$L_i(x_i, y_i, z_i, \dot{x}_i, \dot{y}_i, \dot{z}_i, t) = T_i - F_i(x_1 \ldots z_N, t), \quad . \quad (1)$$

T_i being the kinetic energy $\frac{1}{2}m_i(\dot{x}_i^2 + \dot{y}_i^2 + \dot{z}_i^2)$ of the particle.

F_i is the potential energy of the ith particle depending upon the position of all the particles of the system and on the external field of force to which the assembly may be subject. We will write it in the form:

$$F_i = \sum_j F_{ij} + f_i, \quad (j = 1 \text{ to } N), \qquad (2)$$

where F_{ij} denotes that part of the potential energy of the ith particle which arises from the action of the jth particle upon it, F_{ii} being zero, since the particle is not considered to act upon itself f_i denotes the action of the external field on the ith particle.

The principle of equality of action and reaction is expressed by the formula

$$F_{ij} = F_{ji}.[1] \qquad (3)$$

In other words, the quantities F_{ij} form a symmetrical table with diagonal terms zero

We can write down the Lagrangian equations for each particle as follows

$$\frac{d}{dt}\left(\frac{\partial L_i}{\partial \dot{x}_i}\right) = \frac{\partial L_i}{\partial x_i} \qquad (4)$$

with similar equations in y_i and z_i, and there are 3N equations of this type in the assembly.

The classical dynamics of systems condenses these 3N equations by introducing a Lagrangian function L defined by.

$$L(x_1, y_1, \ldots z_N\ \dot{x}_1, \dot{y}_1, \ldots z_N, t) = \sum T_i - \tfrac{1}{2}\sum F_{ij} - \sum f_i$$
$$= T - F. \qquad (5)$$

where $\sum F_{ij}$ denotes a double summation over i and j and $T = \sum T_i$, $F = \frac{1}{2}\sum F_{ij} + f_i$.

L is the Lagrangian function for the whole system, and is not the sum of the individual Lagrangian functions, since it contains each term of mutual action once only. In the same way F is called the potential energy of the whole system; it is

[1] F_{ij} and F_{ji} are, in fact, functions of r_{ij} alone, where $r_{ij} = \sqrt{(x_i - x_j)^2 + (y_i - y_j)^2 + (z_i - z_j)^2}$ is the distance between the ith and jth particles and the assumption of (3) implies that $\frac{\partial F_{ij}}{\partial x_i} = -\frac{\partial F_{ji}}{\partial x_j}$ or the principle of action and reaction is satisfied.

not the sum of the potential energies of the various particles By means of L the 3N Lagrangian equations become .

$$\frac{d}{dt}\left(\frac{\partial L}{\partial \dot{x}_i}\right) = \frac{\partial L}{\partial x_i}, \quad (i = 1 \text{ to } N) \quad . \quad (6)$$

with the corresponding equations in y and z.

As we have now Lagrangian equations with a single function L depending upon all the co-ordinates of the particles of the system, we shall be able to find a principle of stationary action for the whole system. Consider therefore a space of 3N + 1 dimensions built up by the 3N co-ordinates and the time. The motion of the whole system is represented by a line in this space, each point of the line corresponding to an arrangement of the system at a particular time The line representing the motion between two points P and Q from time t_0 to time t_1 is defined by the Hamiltonian principle that the integral

$$\int_{t_0}^{t_1} L\, dt \quad . \quad (7)$$

taken along it is stationary for all infinitely small displacements from it with the extremities fixed. This principle is valid, since it takes us by the classical procedure of the calculus of variations to the 3N Lagrangian equations (6). Moreover, this Hamiltonian principle has an intrinsic significance independent of the choice of variables assigned to the system. Thus, if the 3N co-ordinates (x_i, y_i, z_i) are expressible in terms of n variables, q_k, in the form

$$x_i = f_i(q_1 \ldots q_n), \quad y_i = \phi_i(q_1 \ldots q_n), \quad z_i = \psi_i(q_1 \ldots q_n), \quad (8)$$

the function L will be expressible in terms of the $(2n + 1)$ variables q_k, $\dot{q}_k$ and t. We shall have therefore :

$$\delta\int_{t_0}^{t_1} L(q_k, \dot{q}_k, t)dt = 0 \quad . \quad (9)$$

the limits t_0 and t_1 not being subject to variation In general n is equal to 3N, but if there are any constraints, that is to say, if certain relations [1] exist between the co-ordinates of the N particles, n may be less than 3N The number of independent

[1] We suppose, for the sake of simplicity, that the constraints are independent of the time.

variables which are necessary to define the system is called the number of degrees of freedom.

As in the case of the single material point we define certain momenta p_i conjugate to the co-ordinates q_i by the relations:

$$p_i = \frac{\partial L}{\partial q_i} \quad (i = 1 \text{ to } n), \qquad (10)$$

which makes it possible to write the Lagrangian equations in the form:

$$\frac{dp_i}{dt} = \frac{\partial L}{\partial q_i}, \quad (i = 1 \text{ to } n) \qquad (11)$$

In the same way we shall describe as the energy the quantity

$$W = \sum p_i \dot{q}_i - L \qquad (12)$$

and since by (10) and (11) we have

$$\frac{dW}{dt} = \sum \frac{dp_i}{dt} q_i + \sum p_i \frac{dq_i}{dt} - \sum \frac{\partial L}{\partial q_i} q_i - \sum \frac{\partial L}{\partial q_i} \frac{dq_i}{dt} - \frac{\partial L}{\partial t}$$
$$= -\frac{\partial L}{\partial t}, \qquad (13)$$

we conclude that if the external field is independent of the time, or $\frac{\partial f_i}{\partial t} = 0$, the quantity W remains constant.

By the definition (12) of W we can express the Hamiltonian integral as a line integral in the space of $(n + 1)$ dimensions formed by the n co-ordinates q_i and the time, for we have:

$$\int_{t_0}^{t_1} L\, dt = \int_P^Q (\sum p_i dq_i - W\, dt), \qquad (14)$$

P and Q being the extremities of the line representing the path of the motion in the q-t space.

In the case in which the external field of force does not depend on the time, and where in consequence the energy remains constant, the Hamiltonian principle leads to the principle of least action of Maupertuis. Let us consider a generalised space formed by the q co-ordinates alone; this space will play an important part in what follows. The assembly of positions of the particles of the system at a given instant is denoted by a representative point in this space, and the motion of the particles of the system is represented by a curve or trajectory of the representative point in the generalised space. The principle of least action of Maupertuis may be described by the statement that the trajectory of the representative point between two points A and B of the generalised space is such that the line integral $\int_A^B \sum p_i dq_i$ taken along the trajectory is stationary for any infinitely small variation which leaves unaltered the limits A and B and the energy W The proof by Hamilton's principle is exactly the same as that of Chapter I, § 4, except for the circumstance that there are now n variables instead of 3

Similarly, by resuming the proofs of Chapter I, §§ 5-6, by merely changing $\sum_1^3$ to $\sum_1^n$ we shall find first the Hamiltonian equations

$$\frac{dp_i}{dt} = -\frac{\partial H}{\partial q_i}, \quad \frac{dq_i}{dt} = \frac{\partial H}{\partial p_i}, \quad (i = 1 \ . \ . \ n) \quad . \quad (15)$$

then the theorem of contact transformations which is now expressed in the statement that the transformations $\alpha_i = f_i(q_k, p_k, t)$ and $\beta_i = \phi_i(q_k, p_k, t)$, subject to the condition,

$$\sum_1^n p_i dq_i - \sum_1^n \beta_i d\alpha_i = -[dS]_t, \quad . \quad (16)$$

maintain the canonical form of the Hamilton equations if H is replaced by $K = H - \frac{\partial S}{\partial t}$, expressed in the new variables. Here, as in the earlier chapter, the notation means that the differential of S is made without varying t

By means of this theorem we can develop as before the theory of Jacobi's equation (Chap. II) and arrive at Jacobi's theorem that if it is possible to obtain a complete integral, i.e one depending upon n arbitrary constants α_i, of the first order partial differential equation

$$H\left(q_i - \frac{\partial S}{\partial q_i}, t\right) = \frac{\partial S}{\partial t} \quad . \quad (17)$$

we shall have

$$p_i = -\frac{\partial S}{\partial q_i}, \quad \beta_i - \frac{\partial S}{\partial \alpha_i}, \quad (i = 1 \ . \ \ n) \quad . \quad (18)$$

where S depends upon q_i, α_i and t and the β's are n new constants. The equations (18), which define the $2n$ quantities q_i and p_i as functions of the time and the $2n$ constants α_i and β_i, give completely the motion of the system of n degrees of freedom.

2. Transition from the Old to the New Dynamics of Systems

To pass from the wave mechanics of a single particle to the wave mechanics of systems of particles, we cannot proceed as in the old mechanics. If we wished to follow this route it would be necessary to consider the motion of each particle and its associated wave under the action of the fields created by the other particles and of the external field, if it exists. Then by introducing the principle of action and reaction it would be necessary to solve simultaneously the problem of the propagation of the N waves associated with the N particles of the system. It appears hardly possible to proceed in this way, the chief reason being the difficulty of locating each particle at a point in its wave, we cannot express the field of force acting upon a particle in terms of the positions of the others, since these positions are not well defined. In order to construct the wave mechanics of systems Schrodinger has followed a quite different path which, while raising certain difficulties of principle, has given very good results and with which we have at present to be content. But he has in his attempt succeeded in obtaining only the non-relativistic equations; the relativistic wave mechanics of systems is still lacking.

Schrodinger assumes the existence of the generalised space of n dimensions formed by the variables $q_1 \ldots q_n$, which define the system of n degrees of freedom to be considered.

He associates with the motion of the system not as many waves travelling in ordinary space as there are particles, but a single wave travelling in the generalised space He has sought an equation for this wave which, to the approximation of geometrical optics, is in harmony with the old mechanics Following Schrodinger's idea we must therefore seek a wave equation depending upon the variables $q_1 \ldots q_n, t$, such that, if the solution be written in the form .

$$\psi = ae^{\frac{2\pi i}{h}\phi}, \qquad \ldots \qquad (19)$$

where ψ, a and ϕ depend upon the variables and the time, the conditions are realised (1) that when the approximations of geometrical optics are realised, in particular, when h is considered infinitely small, the function ϕ will coincide with Jacobi's function of the old mechanics, (2) that if the system consists of a single particle we must obtain the wave equation for a single particle, and (3) if the system consists of N particles which do not interact, the wave equation must split up into N separate equations of the type valid for a single particle.

But before studying a propagation in generalised space we must complete the definition of it by attributing to it a metric in the Riemannian sense, that is to say we must assume that the square of the element of length corresponding to a variation of the co-ordinates q_i of amount dq_i is given at each point by the quadratic expression $ds^2 = \sum_{ik} g_{ik} dq_i dq_k$, where as usual summation over the possible values of i and k is implied. We shall see how the g_{ik} must be chosen but must first recall certain mathematical formulæ which we require

3. Mathematical Results

Let us consider a space of n dimensions and suppose, in the first place, that the points have n co-ordinates $(x_1, \ldots x_n)$ such that the surfaces, $x_i =$ constant, cut one another at right angles, which simply means that we have chosen a system of orthogonal co-ordinates. In the neighbourhood of each point it is as if we had chosen a rectangular Cartesian system of co-ordinates and the square of the element of length takes the form :

$$ds^2 = \sum dx_i^2. \qquad (20)$$

The element of volume will be

$$d\tau = dx_1 dx_2 \ldots dx_n \qquad (21)$$

By means of a transformation of the variables.

$$q_i = f_i(x_1 \ldots x_n),$$

we then define any n curvilinear co-ordinates Conversely, the x_i may be considered as functions of the q_i and the expression for dx_i^2 may be written .

$$dx_i^2 = \sum_{jk} \frac{\partial x_i}{\partial q_j} \frac{\partial x_i}{\partial q_k} dq_j dq_k \qquad (22)$$

and in consequence we have .

$$ds^2 = \sum_{ijk} \frac{\partial x_i}{\partial q_j} \frac{\partial x_i}{\partial q_k} dq_j dq_k = \sum g_{jk} dq_j dq_k, \quad . \quad (23)$$

where

$$g_{jk} = \sum_i \frac{\partial x_i}{\partial q_j} \frac{\partial x_i}{\partial q_k}, \quad . \quad . \quad (24)$$

and evidently

$$g_{jk} = g_{kj} \quad . \quad . \quad . \quad . \quad . \quad (25)$$

Let $\left|\frac{\partial x_k}{\partial q_i}\right|$ denote the determinant with the general term $\frac{\partial x_k}{\partial q_i}$, it is the Jacobian $\frac{\partial(x_1, \ldots x_n)}{\partial(q_1, \ldots q_n)}$ of the x's with respect to the q's. By the multiplication rule of determinants .

$$\left|\frac{\partial x_k}{\partial q_i}\right|^2 = \left|\sum_j \frac{\partial x_j}{\partial q_i} \frac{\partial x_j}{\partial q_k}\right| = |g_{ik}|, \quad . \quad . \quad (26)$$

so that if g denotes the determinant of the terms g_{ik}, we have ·

$$g = \left\{\frac{\partial(x_1, \ldots x_n)}{\partial(q_1, \ldots q_n)}\right\}^2 . \quad . \quad . \quad (27)$$

The well-known analytical theorem for change of variables then gives .

$$d\tau = dx_1 \ldots dx_n = \sqrt{g}\, dq_1 \ldots dq_n, \quad (28)$$

and in this way we obtain the element of volume in terms of the q_i's and g_{ik}'s.

γ_{ik} being the minor of g_{ik} in the determinant g, we write .

$$g^{ik} = \frac{\gamma_{ik}}{g} \quad . \quad . \quad (29)$$

whence $g^{ik} = g^{ki}$ and by the properties of determinants ·

$$\sum_k g^{ik} g_{kl} = 1 \text{ or } 0 \quad . \quad . \quad (30)$$

according as $i = l$ or $i \neq l$.

This formula represents n^2 linear equations which completely determine the n^2 quantities g^{ik} as functions of the g_{ik}, and we can readily verify that .

$$g^{kl} = \sum_j \frac{\partial q_k}{\partial x_j} \frac{\partial q_l}{\partial x_j}. \quad . \quad . \quad . \quad (31)$$

We have by (24) ·

$$\sum_k g^{ik} g_{kl} = \sum_k \left(\sum_j \frac{\partial q_i}{\partial x_j} \frac{\partial q_k}{\partial x_j} \sum_m \frac{\partial x_m}{\partial q_k} \frac{\partial x_m}{\partial q_l} \right)$$

$$= \sum_{jm} \frac{\partial q_i}{\partial x_j} \frac{\partial x_m}{\partial q_l} \sum_k \frac{\partial q_k}{\partial x_j} \frac{\partial x_m}{\partial q_k}, \qquad . \quad (32)$$

and the product under $\sum_k$ vanishes unless $j = m$, when it is equal to unity. We have, therefore :

$$\sum_k g^{ik} g_{kl} = \sum_j \frac{\partial q_i}{\partial x_j} \frac{\partial x_j}{\partial q_l} = \frac{\partial q_i}{\partial q_l}, \qquad . \quad . \quad (33)$$

which vanishes unless $i = l$ and is then equal to unity. The equations (30) are thus satisfied by (31).

We pass on finally to determine the general expression for the Laplacian operator in terms of general co-ordinates, q_i, the operation on a function f being by definition $\sum_i \frac{\partial^2 f}{\partial x_i^2}$ We will begin with the statement that if f is a function of the n co-ordinates, which is finite, uniform and continuous throughout the n-dimensional space considered and which is zero at infinity, the equation .

$$\sum \frac{\partial^2 f}{\partial x_i^2} = 0 \qquad . \quad . \quad (34)$$

is the expression of the fact that the integral $\int \sum_i \left(\frac{\partial f}{\partial x_i} \right)^2 d\tau$ extended throughout all space is stationary for any infinitely small variation in the form of f which does not violate the continuity and uniformity of this function. The integral and the space are, of course, n-dimensional and $d\tau$ is an element of volume $dx_1\, dx_2 \,.\,.\, dx_n$. If f varies by δf at each point of this space the above integral undergoes the change :

$$\delta \int \sum_i \left(\frac{\partial f}{\partial x_i} \right)^2 d\tau = \int 2 \sum_i \frac{\partial f}{\partial x_i} \delta \left(\frac{\partial f}{\partial x_i} \right) d\tau = - \int 2 \sum_i \frac{\partial^2 f}{\partial x_i^2} \delta f \, d\tau, \quad (35)$$

and in order that this change may be zero whatever the value of δf, it is both necessary and sufficient that equation (34) be true.

We can also express the integral to be varied in terms of the q co-ordinates by a change of variables from x to q We have:

$$\frac{\partial f}{\partial x_i} = \sum_k \frac{\partial f}{\partial q_k}\frac{\partial q_k}{\partial x_i}, \quad \left(\frac{\partial f}{\partial x_i}\right)^2 = \sum_{k,l} \frac{\partial f}{\partial q_k}\frac{\partial f}{\partial q_l}\frac{\partial q_k}{\partial x_i}\frac{\partial q_l}{\partial x_i}, \tag{36}$$

and

$$\sum_i \left(\frac{\partial f}{\partial x_i}\right)^2 = \sum_{kl} \frac{\partial f}{\partial q_k}\frac{\partial f}{\partial q_l}\sum_i \frac{\partial q_k}{\partial x_i}\frac{\partial q_l}{\partial x_i} = \sum_{kl} g^{kl}\frac{\partial f}{\partial q_k}\frac{\partial f}{\partial q_l} \tag{37}$$

by (31) From this we deduce:

$$\delta\int\sum_i \left(\frac{\partial f}{\partial x_i}\right)^2 d\tau = \delta\int\sum_{k,l} g^{kl}\frac{\partial f}{\partial q_k}\frac{\partial f}{\partial q_l}\sqrt{g}\,dq_1 \ldots dq_n$$

$$= \int 2\sum_{k,l} g^{kl}\frac{\partial f}{\partial q_k}\delta\left(\frac{\partial f}{\partial q_l}\right)\sqrt{g}\,dq_1 \ldots dq_n$$

$$= -\int 2\sum_{k,l}\frac{\partial}{\partial q_l}\left(\sqrt{g}\,g^{kl}\frac{\partial f}{\partial q_k}\right)\delta f\,dq_1 \ldots dq_n \tag{38}$$

If we compare this with (35) the latter being another expression of the same quantity, remembering that:

$$d\tau = \sqrt{g}\,dq_1 \ldots dq_n. \tag{39}$$

we see that:

$$\sum_i \frac{\partial^2 f}{\partial x_i^2} = \frac{1}{\sqrt{g}}\sum_{kl}\frac{\partial}{\partial q_l}\left(\sqrt{g}\,g^{kl}\frac{\partial f}{\partial q_k}\right) \tag{40}$$

This is the generalised expression of the Laplace operation in n dimensions in any co-ordinates, q Of course, if $n = 3$, we have the ordinary operation in curvilinear co-ordinates

4. The Wave Equation in Generalised Space

A metric must be associated with the space before we can consider propagation in it, and for this purpose we begin with the kinetic energy of the system, and since Schrodinger's wave mechanics is non-relativistic we shall begin with the expression:

$$T = \sum_i \tfrac{1}{2}m_i(\dot{x}_i^2 + \dot{y}_i^2 + \dot{z}_i^2) \tag{41}$$

for the kinetic energy, where (x_i, y_i, z_i) denote the rectangular co-ordinates of the ith particle, m_i its mass and the number of particles is N. If the system has n degrees of freedom, the 3N co-ordinates may be expressed by n co-ordinates $q_1 \ldots q_n$. The velocities are expressible linearly in the $\dot{q}$'s and T becomes a homogeneous quadratic in these quantities, since it is assumed that t does not occur explicitly in the relations between the x's and the q's :

$$T = \tfrac{1}{2}\sum_{i,k}\mu_{ik}\dot{q}_i\dot{q}_k, \qquad . \quad . \quad . \quad (42)$$

where the quantities μ_{ik} are in general functions of the q's and $\mu_{ik} = \mu_{ki}$.

The Lagrangian function, $L = T - F$, depends upon the $\dot{q}$'s through T only, so that .

$$p_i = \frac{\partial L}{\partial \dot{q}_i} = \frac{\partial T}{\partial \dot{q}_i} = \sum_k \mu_{ik}\dot{q}_k, \quad (i = 1, 2 \ldots n). \qquad (43)$$

This equation represents a system of n linear equations expressing the p's in terms of the $\dot{q}$'s and they can in general be solved to give the $\dot{q}$'s in terms of the p's Let ν_{ik} denote the minor of μ_{ik} in the determinant $|\mu_{ik}| = \mu$ and write .

$$\mu^{ik} = \frac{\nu^{ik}}{\mu}, \qquad . \quad . \quad (44)$$

so that we find .

$$\dot{q}_i = \sum_k \mu^{ik}p_k. \quad (i = 1, 2, \ldots n). \quad . \qquad (45)$$

We may easily find the classical form of Jacobi's equation. The energy expressed as a function of the q's, p's and the time is :

$$H(q_i, p_i, t) = \sum \tfrac{1}{2}\mu_{ik}\mu^{ij}p_j\mu^{kl}p_l + F(q_i, t), \quad . \quad (46)$$

where the summation applies to all the suffixes and F is the potential energy of the system

By the theory of determinants .

$$\sum_k \mu_{ik}\mu^{kl} = 1 \text{ or } 0 \qquad . \qquad (47)$$

according as $i = l$ or $i \neq l$, and therefore

$$H(q_i, p_i, t) = \tfrac{1}{2}\sum_{ij}\mu^{ij}p_ip_j + F(q_i, t) \quad . \quad . \quad (48)$$

and (17) may be written

$$\frac{1}{2}\sum_{ij}\mu^{ij}\frac{\partial S}{\partial q_i}\frac{\partial S}{\partial q_j} + F(q_i, t) = \frac{\partial S}{\partial t}. \qquad (49)$$

The metric of this space will be defined by making μ_{ik}, μ^{ik} and μ play the part of g_{ik}, g^{ik} and g in the last paragraph, or we define the expression ds^2 by the formula :

$$ds^2 = \sum_{ik}\mu_{ik}dq_i dq_k. \qquad (50)$$

The element of volume is then

$$d\tau = \sqrt{\mu}\, dq_1 \ldots dq_n \qquad (51)$$

and the generalised Laplacian operatoi

$$\frac{1}{\sqrt{\mu}}\sum_{ik}\frac{\partial}{\partial q_i}\left(\sqrt{\mu}\,\mu^{ik}\frac{\partial}{\partial q_k}\right). \qquad (52)$$

We have assumed that the non-relativistic equation for a single particle of mass m which the wave function satisfies is .

$$\frac{1}{m}\nabla^2\psi - \frac{8\pi^2}{h^2}F\psi = \frac{4\pi i}{h}\frac{\partial\psi}{\partial t}. \qquad (53)$$

Schrödinger has transposed this expression and adopted as the wave equation in the generalised space

$$\frac{1}{\sqrt{\mu}}\sum_{ik}\frac{\partial}{\partial q_i}\left(\sqrt{\mu}\,\mu^{ik}\frac{\partial\psi}{\partial q_k}\right) - \frac{8\pi^2}{h^2}F(q_i, t)\psi = \frac{4\pi i}{h}\frac{\partial\psi}{\partial t} \qquad (54)$$

We must make sure that this expression satisfies the three conditions stated in § 2 of this chapter.

1. When the conditions of geometrical optics are satisfied and in particular when h can be considered infinitely small, the function ϕ satisfies Jacobi's equation

Let us write as usual $\psi = ae^{\frac{2\pi i}{h}\phi}$ where the variables are the q's and t and a and ϕ are real. Substituting in (54) and equating to zero the real terms, then neglecting in the equation thus obtained the terms which do not contain h^2 in the denominator, we find :

$$\frac{1}{2}\sum_{ij}\mu^{ij}\frac{\partial\phi}{\partial q_i}\frac{\partial\phi}{\partial q_j} + F(q_i, t) = \frac{\partial\phi}{\partial t} \qquad (55)$$

The function ϕ thus satisfies Jacobi's equation (49) and to this degree of approximation it may be regarded as the Jacobian function of the old mechanics.

2. If the system consists of a single particle we obtain once more equation (53).

Let us denote the mass of the particle by m and take rectangular axes of co-ordinates. We have $T = \frac{1}{2}m(\dot{x}^2 + \dot{y}^2 + \dot{z}^2)$, and therefore in this case :

$$\mu_{ik} = \begin{cases} m \text{ for } i = k \\ 0 \text{ for } i \neq k \end{cases}, \quad \mu = m^3, \quad \mu^{ik} = \begin{cases} \frac{1}{m} \text{ for } i = k \\ 0 \text{ for } i \neq k \end{cases}, \quad \begin{cases} i \\ k \end{cases} = 1\ 2.\ 3 \qquad . \quad . \quad . \quad (56)$$

The equation (54) when applied to this special case becomes (53)

3. If the system is formed by N particles which do not react upon one another the wave equation splits up into N separate equations of the type valid for a single particle

Let m_i denote the mass of the ith particle, and let the co-ordinates be chosen rectangular

We have .

$$T = \sum_i \tfrac{1}{2}m(\dot{x}_i^2 + \dot{y}_i^2 + \dot{z}_i^2),$$

and in this case :

$$\left.\begin{aligned} &\mu_{ik} = 0 \text{ for } i \neq k \quad \mu_{11} = \mu_{22} = \mu_{33} = m_1 \quad \text{and in general} \\ &\mu_{3i-2,\,3i-2} = \mu_{3i-1,\,3i-1} = \mu_{3i,\,3i} = m_i \quad \mu = m_1{}^3 m_2{}^3 \ \ldots\ m_N^3 \\ &\mu^{ik} = 0 \text{ for } i \neq k, \quad \mu^{11} = \mu^{22} = \mu^{33} = \frac{1}{m_1} \quad \text{and in general} \\ &\mu^{3i-2,\,3i-2} = \mu^{3i-1,\,3i-1} = \mu^{3i,\,3i} = \frac{1}{m_i} \end{aligned}\right\} \quad (57)$$

F in this case becomes $\sum_i F_i(x_i, y_i, z_i, t)$, and equation (54) is reduced to the form

$$\sum_i \left\{ \frac{1}{m_i}\left(\frac{\partial^2\psi}{\partial x_i^2} + \frac{\partial^2\psi}{\partial y_i^2} + \frac{\partial^2\psi}{\partial z_i^2} \right) - \frac{8\pi^2}{h^2} F_i \psi \right\} = \frac{4\pi i}{h} \frac{\partial\psi}{\partial t} \quad (58)$$

If we write ψ in the form :

$$\psi = \psi_1 \psi_2 \ldots \psi_N, \qquad (59)$$

where ψ is a function of all the variables while ψ_i is a function of x_i, y_i, z_i and t only, we obtain N equations of the form :

$$\frac{1}{m_i}\left(\frac{\partial^2 \psi_i}{\partial x_i^2} + \frac{\partial^2 \psi_i}{\partial y_i^2} + \frac{\partial^2 \psi_i}{\partial z_i^2}\right) - \frac{8\pi^2}{h^2} F_i \psi_i = \frac{4\pi i}{h}\frac{\partial \psi_i}{\partial t}. \quad (i = 1, 2, \ldots N) \qquad (60)$$

and these are the equations of the particles valid when they are considered separately.

Thus (54) satisfies the conditions laid down.

If the system is composed of N particles acting upon one another but not subject to constraints we can build up the generalised space by the 3N rectangular co-ordinates and the μ_{ik} and μ^{ik} have the values (57) The wave equation takes the form :

$$\sum_i \frac{1}{m_i}\left(\frac{\partial^2 \psi}{\partial x_i^2} + \frac{\partial^2 \psi}{\partial y_i^2} + \frac{\partial^2 \psi}{\partial z_i^2}\right) - \frac{8\pi^2}{h^2} F \psi = \frac{4\pi i}{h}\frac{\partial \psi}{\partial t}. \qquad (61)$$

where F now depends upon the 3N variables x_1, x_2, . . . z_N and the time t

All these formulæ are non-relativistic, and it has not yet been possible to find a wave equation fulfilling the requirements of the theory of relativity. Moreover, we have, in agreement with Schrödinger's work, considered wave propagation in the fictitious generalised space It has not yet been possible to connect this propagation of a single wave in a fictitious space with that of one or several waves in ordinary space.

This impossibility seems to strengthen the view that no physical reality is to be attached to the associated wave, but that it is simply a symbolic representation of probability.

CHAPTER XV

THE INTERPRETATION OF THE WAVE ASSOCIATED WITH THE MOTION OF A SYSTEM

1. The Approximation of Geometrical Optics

IN order to explain the meaning of the many-dimensional wave associated with a system we begin with the wave equation :

$$\frac{1}{\sqrt{\mu}}\sum_{ik}\frac{\partial}{\partial q_i}\left(\sqrt{\mu}\,\mu^{ik}\frac{\partial\psi}{\partial q_k}\right) - \frac{8\pi^2}{h^2}F\psi = \frac{4\pi i}{h}\frac{\partial\psi}{\partial t} \qquad (1)$$

We shall write ψ in the form $ae^{\frac{2\pi i}{h}\phi}$, when by substitution in (1) and equating the real and imaginary parts to zero, we find

$$\frac{1}{2}\sum_{ik}\mu^{ik}\frac{\partial\phi}{\partial q_i}\frac{\partial\phi}{\partial q_k} + F = \frac{\partial\phi}{\partial t} + \frac{h^2}{8\pi^2 a}\frac{1}{\sqrt{\mu}}\sum_{ik}\frac{\partial}{\partial q_i}\left(\sqrt{\mu}\,\mu^{ik}\frac{\partial a}{\partial q_k}\right), \qquad (2)$$

$$\sum_{ik}\mu^{ik}\frac{\partial a}{\partial q_i}\frac{\partial\phi}{\partial q_k} + \frac{1}{2}\frac{a}{\sqrt{\mu}}\sum_{ik}\frac{\partial}{\partial q_i}\left(\sqrt{\mu}\,\mu^{ik}\frac{\partial\phi}{\partial q_k}\right) = \frac{\partial a}{\partial t}. \quad . \qquad (3)$$

In the present section of this chapter we shall neglect the last term of (2), since we are limiting ourselves to the approximation of geometrical optics. The function ϕ then satisfies Jacobi's equation, as we have seen, and we may regard the classical mechanics as valid in this case and define the Lagrangian momenta by :

$$p_i = \sum_k \mu_{ik}\dot{q}_k = -\frac{\partial S}{\partial q_i} = -\frac{\partial\phi}{\partial q_i}. \quad . \quad . \qquad (4)$$

By solving these equations for the $\dot{q}$'s we find

$$\dot{q}_i = \sum_k \mu^{ik}p_k = -\sum_k \mu^{ik}\frac{\partial\phi}{\partial q_k} \quad . \quad . \qquad (5)$$

By substitution in (3) .

$$\frac{\partial a}{\partial t} + \sum_i \frac{\partial a}{\partial q_i}\dot{q}_i + \frac{a}{2\sqrt{\mu}}\sum_i \frac{\partial}{\partial q_i}(\sqrt{\mu}\,\dot{q}_i) = 0 \qquad (6)$$

and after multiplication by $2a$.

$$\frac{\partial a^2}{\partial t} + \frac{1}{\sqrt{\mu}}\sum_i \frac{\partial}{\partial q_i}(\sqrt{\mu}\,a^2\dot{q}_i) = 0. \qquad . \quad (7)$$

We shall interpret this equation in the same way as we interpreted that for a single particle.

We know that ϕ satisfies Jacobi's equation to our degree of approximation Let $\phi = \phi(q_1, \ldots q_n, t, \alpha_1 \ldots \alpha_n)$, according to Jacobi's theory the classical equations of motion are .

$$\frac{\partial \phi}{\partial \alpha_i} = \beta_i \quad (i = 1, 2 \ldots n). \qquad . \quad . \quad (8)$$

To a particular function ϕ with the same set of constants α_i there corresponds an infinity of possible motions dependent upon the choice of the constants β_i. We shall again describe these motions as being of the same class The motion of the whole system is defined by the motion of its representative point in generalised space, and this motion is determined by the equations (8). Instead of considering a system, we can consider an assembly of identical systems performing motions of the same class and to this assembly there will correspond a cloud of points in the generalised space associated with the same ψ-wave The velocities of these representative points are given by the equations (5)

The motion of this cloud of points must satisfy the hydrodynamical equation of continuity of which it is easy to find an explanation in the generalised space Let us consider a small volume bounded by the surfaces

$$q_i = c_i, \qquad q_i = c_i + dq_i, \qquad (i = 1, 2 \ldots n) \qquad (9)$$

The sides of this small parallelepiped are in the directions of the co-ordinate axes q_i, and are of lengths dq_i Consider a particular co-ordinate q_k. The number of representative points which cross the face $q_k = c_k$ in time dt is equal to the number contained in an element with this face as base and with side

$\dot{q}_k dt$. If ρ denote the density of the cloud at the face considered the flux is:

$$\sigma = \rho\sqrt{\mu}\, dq_1 \ldots dq_{k-1} dq_{k+1} \ldots dq_n \dot{q}_k dt \quad . \quad (10)$$

The flux across the parallel face $q_k = c_k + dq_k$ is in the same way:

$$\sigma + \frac{\partial \sigma}{\partial q_k} dq_k$$

and the difference is:

$$-\frac{\partial}{\partial q_k}(\rho\sqrt{\mu}\, \dot{q}_k) dq_1 \ldots dq_n dt. \quad . \quad . \quad (11)$$

In the same way, by considering each face of the parallelepiped, we obtain for the excess of the cloud entering over that which leaves the element the quantity

$$-\sum_k \frac{\partial}{\partial q_k}(\rho\sqrt{\mu}\, \dot{q}_k) dq_1 \ldots dq_n dt. \quad . \quad (12)$$

Expressed as a change of density this may also be written $\frac{\partial \rho}{\partial t} dt \sqrt{\mu}\, dq_1 \ldots dq_n$ and by equating the two expressions we obtain the equation of continuity

$$\frac{\partial \rho}{\partial t} + \frac{1}{\sqrt{\mu}} \sum_k \frac{\partial}{\partial q_k}(\sqrt{\mu}\, \rho\, \dot{q}_k) = 0 \quad . \quad . \quad (13)$$

A comparison of (13) with (7) leads us to write:

$$\rho = \mathrm{K}\, a^2 \quad . \quad . \quad . \quad . \quad (14)$$

This result may be expressed in terms of probability by considering a system of n degrees of freedom, the motion of which is known to belong to a certain class, but of which the initial configuration is not exactly known. The intensity of the associated wave in the generalised space measures at each point of the space the probability of occurrence of the representative point of the system.

The cloud of representative points may be replaced by a probability fluid of which the elements describe the various trajectories which are possible, according to the old dynamics, for the representative point, the density of the fluid being proportional to a^2 and being a measure of the probability of occurrence at each point of the space It is thus possible to the approximation of geometrical optics to satisfy the principle of interference and at the same time to retain the view that the particles of the system have a definite position in space, and in consequence that the representative point itself has a definite position at each instant in the generalised space. For systems as for single particles the difficulties begin when we leave the realm of geometrical optics

2. The General Case. Motion of Probability

When the approximations of the last paragraph cease to be valid, we can no longer neglect the last term in equation (2) The principle of interference will still be adopted according to which the square of the amplitude of the wave is a measure of the probability of occurrence of the representative point at each point of the space and at each instant It will thus be necessary to associate a probability cloud with the ψ-wave, and the motion of the cloud in the space will be such that the principle of interference is satisfied. This result is attained by defining the velocity of the probability elements by the relations:

$$\dot{q}_i = - \sum_k \mu^{ik} \frac{\partial \phi}{\partial q_k}. \qquad (15)$$

The equation of continuity is still satisfied on account of (3) by writing $\rho = a^2$.

The motion of the probability elements defined by (15) can be studied as in Chapter IX Equation (2), which takes the place of Jacobi's equation, may be written .

$$\frac{1}{2} \sum_{ik} \mu^{ik} \frac{\partial \phi}{\partial q_i} \frac{\partial \phi}{\partial q_k} + F + F_1 = \frac{\partial \phi}{\partial t}, \qquad (16)$$

where

$$F_1 = - \frac{h^2}{8\pi^2 a} \frac{1}{\sqrt{\mu}} \sum_{ik} \frac{\partial}{\partial q_i} \left(\sqrt{\mu}\, \mu^{ik} \frac{\partial a}{\partial q_k} \right). \qquad (17)$$

We can say that the probability elements move in the same way as if there were a supplementary potential energy of magnitude F_1, which may be described as quantum potential, and which depends upon the amplitude a of the wave, and hence upon the density of the probability cloud. We may define a function of the q's, $\dot{q}$'s and t by the formula .

$$L = \tfrac{1}{2}\sum_{ik}\mu_{ik}\dot{q}_i\dot{q}_k - F - F_1, \qquad (18)$$

described as the Lagrangian function of the probability elements. The derivatives

$$p_i = \frac{\partial L}{\partial \dot{q}_i} = \sum_{ik}\mu_{ik}\dot{q}_k \qquad (19)$$

are the conjugate momenta of the elements corresponding to the variables q_i

By (15) we have

$$p_i = -\sum_{kj}\mu_{ik}\mu^{kj}\frac{\partial\phi}{\partial q_j} = -\frac{\partial\phi}{\partial q_i} \qquad (20)$$

and the quantity

$$W = \sum_i p_i\dot{q}_i - L = \tfrac{1}{2}\sum_{ik}\mu_{ik}\dot{q}_i\dot{q}_k - F - F_1 \qquad (21)$$

plays the part of the energy.

We shall determine the equations of motion as in Chapter IX for the probability elements by calculating $\frac{dp_i}{dt}$

$$\begin{aligned}\frac{dp_i}{dt} &= \sum_k \frac{\partial p_i}{\partial q_k}\dot{q}_k + \frac{\partial p_i}{\partial t} = \sum_{kj}\mu^{kj}\frac{\partial\phi}{\partial q_j}\frac{\partial^2\phi}{\partial q_i\partial q_k} - \frac{\partial^2\phi}{\partial q_i\partial t}\\ &= \frac{\partial}{\partial q_i}\left(\sum_{kj}\frac{1}{2}\mu^{kj}\frac{\partial\phi}{\partial q_k}\frac{\partial\phi}{\partial q_j} - \frac{\partial\phi}{\partial t}\right) - \frac{1}{2}\sum_{kj}\frac{\partial\mu^{kj}}{\partial q_i}\frac{\partial\phi}{\partial q_k}\frac{\partial\phi}{\partial q_j},\end{aligned} \qquad (22)$$

whence by (2), (19) and (20)

$$\frac{dp_i}{dt} = -\frac{\partial}{\partial q_i}(F + F_1) - \frac{1}{2}\sum_{kj}\frac{\partial\mu^{kj}}{\partial q_i}\sum_l \mu_{jl}\dot{q}_l\sum_m \mu_{km}\dot{q}_m, \qquad (23)$$

but

$$\sum_j \mu^{kj}\mu_{jl} = \begin{cases}0 \text{ if } k \neq l\\ 1 \text{ if } k = l\end{cases} \quad \sum_j \frac{\partial\mu^{kj}}{\partial q_i}\mu_{jl} = -\sum_j \mu^{kj}\frac{\partial\mu_{jl}}{\partial q_i} \qquad (24)$$

and formula (23) is then written :

$$\frac{dp_i}{dt} - \frac{1}{2}\sum \mu^{kj}\frac{\partial \mu_{jl}}{\partial q_i}\mu_{km}\dot{q}_l q_m - \frac{\partial}{\partial q_i}(F + F_1)$$

(where the summation applies to j, k, l and m)

$$= \frac{1}{2}\sum_{jl} \frac{\partial \mu_{jl}}{\partial q_i}\dot{q}_j\dot{q}_l - \frac{\partial}{\partial q_i}(F + F_1). \qquad (25)$$

Finally, by the definition (18) :

$$\frac{dp_i}{dt} = \frac{\partial L}{\partial q_i}, \quad (i = 1, 2, \quad . . n), \qquad (26)$$

which is the Lagrangian set of equations.

The term $-\frac{\partial F}{\partial q_i}$ in (25) is the q_i-component of force in the ordinary sense.

The term $\frac{1}{2}\sum_{jl}\frac{\partial \mu_{jl}}{\partial q_i}\dot{q}_j q_l$ is introduced by the choice of co-ordinates, and corresponds to centrifugal forces and forces of constraint. Both these terms occur in the equations of motion of ordinary mechanics and, if one may neglect $-\frac{\partial F_1}{\partial t}$, the motions of the probability elements in the generalised space are identical with the motions of the same class of representative points in classical dynamics If, however, $-\frac{\partial F_1}{\partial t}$ may not be neglected the elements move as if subject to an additional force derived from the quantum potential F_1 Thus, even in the absence of a force in the old classical sense, the principles of conservation of energy and of momentum do not hold for the probability elements.

3. Ehrenfest's Theorems

In the case of a system formed of N particles, subject to no constraints, we can eliminate the terms in F by means of an integration extended throughout the space and obtain once more theorems similar to those of Ehrenfest for a single particle (see Chapter IX, § 3).

We shall suppose the ψ-wave to be limited in the space in such a way that the amplitude a and its derivatives are zero at infinity and we begin with a mathematical result which generalises formula (21) of Chapter IX.

Let U and V be two functions of the co-ordinates q. Then if they be finite and continuous and vanish at infinity in the space, we shall have :

$$\int \frac{U}{\sqrt{\mu}} \sum_{ik} \frac{\partial}{\partial q_i}\left(\sqrt{\mu}\, \mu^{ik} \frac{\partial V}{\partial q_k}\right) d\tau = \int \frac{V}{\sqrt{\mu}} \sum_{ik} \frac{\partial}{\partial q_i}\left(\sqrt{\mu}\, \mu^{ik} \frac{\partial U}{\partial q_k}\right) d\tau, \quad (28)$$

where the integral is n-dimensional, $d\tau$ being the element of volume in the n-dimensional space, and the integration is extended throughout the whole space.

For an account of the vanishing of U and V at infinity, the integral on the left can be transformed by partial integration as follows :

$$\int U \sum_{ik} \frac{\partial}{\partial q_i}\left(\sqrt{\mu}\, \mu^{ik} \frac{\partial V}{\partial q_k}\right) dq_1 \ldots dq_n = -\int \sqrt{\mu} \sum_{ik} \mu^{ik} \frac{\partial V}{\partial q_k} \frac{\partial U}{\partial q_i} dq_1 \ldots dq_n$$

$$= \int V \sum_{ik} \frac{\partial}{\partial q_k}\left(\sqrt{\mu}\, \mu^{ik} \frac{\partial U}{\partial q_i}\right) dq_1 \ldots dq_n$$

$$= \int \frac{V}{\sqrt{\mu}} \sum_{ik} \frac{\partial}{\partial q_i}\left(\sqrt{\mu}\, \mu^{ik} \frac{\partial U}{\partial q_k}\right) d\tau \quad (29)$$

and (28) is thus established.

We shall describe the quantity :

$$\bar{f} = \int f a^2 d\tau \quad . \quad . \quad (30)$$

as the mean value of the function f in the probability cloud at time t. If we suppose that the system is without constraints we can choose for the q co-ordinates the 3N rectangular coordinates of the system, and we have then :

$$\mu_{ik} = \mu^{ik} = 0 \text{ if } i \neq k, \quad \mu_{jj} = \frac{1}{\mu^{jj}} = m_i \text{ for } j = 3i - 2, 3i - 1, 3i,$$

$$\mu = (m_1 m_2 \ldots m_N)^3, \quad . \quad . \quad . \quad . \quad . \quad . \quad . \quad (31)$$

the quantity m_i being the mass of the ith particle. Since the μ_{ik} are constants, the equations of motion of the probability (25) reduce to :

$$\frac{dp_\iota}{dt} = -\frac{\partial F}{\partial q_\iota} - \frac{\partial F_1}{\partial q_\iota} = f_\iota + \frac{h^2}{8\pi^2}\frac{\partial}{\partial q_\iota}\left\{\frac{1}{a\sqrt{\mu}}\sum_{kl}\frac{\partial}{\partial q_k}\left(\sqrt{\mu}\,\mu^{kl}\frac{\partial a}{\partial q_l}\right)\right\}. \quad (32)$$

In this equation we have taken account of the definition (17) of F_1 and have denoted the q_ι-component of the force in the classical sense by f_ι.

If we multiply (32) by $a^2 d\tau$ and integrate throughout the space we obtain:

$$\overline{\frac{dp_\iota}{dt}} = \overline{f_\iota} + \frac{h^2}{8\pi^2}\int a^2\frac{\partial}{\partial q_\iota}\left\{\frac{1}{a\sqrt{\mu}}\sum_{kl}\frac{\partial}{\partial q_k}\left(\sqrt{\mu}\,\mu^{kl}\frac{\partial a}{\partial q_l}\right)\right\}d\tau. \quad (33)$$

The integral in this expression vanishes, for on account of (31) it can be written:

$$\int a^2\frac{\partial}{\partial q_\iota}\left(\frac{1}{a}\sum_k \mu^{kk}\frac{\partial^2 a}{\partial q_k^2}\right)d\tau = \int\left\{a\frac{\partial}{\partial q_\iota}\left(\sum_k \mu^{kk}\frac{\partial^2 a}{\partial q_k^2}\right) - \frac{\partial a}{\partial q_\iota}\sum_k \mu^{kk}\frac{\partial^2 a}{\partial q_k^2}\right\}d\tau$$

$$= \int\left(a\sum_k \mu^{kk}\frac{\partial^3 a}{\partial q_\iota \partial q_k^2} - \frac{\partial a}{\partial q_\iota}\sum_k \mu^{kk}\frac{\partial^2 a}{\partial q_k^2}\right)d\tau \quad (34)$$

and (28) gives by virtue of (31):

$$\int U\sum_k \mu^{kk}\frac{\partial^2 V}{\partial q_k^2}d\tau = \int V\sum_k \mu^{kk}\frac{\partial^2 U}{\partial q_k^2}d\tau. \quad (35)$$

In this formula write $U = a$, $V = \frac{\partial a}{\partial q_\iota}$, since a and its derivatives satisfy the conditions imposed upon U and V in the development of (28), and it follows immediately that the right-hand side of (34) vanishes. (33) now gives .

$$\overline{\frac{dp_\iota}{dt}} = \overline{f_\iota}, \quad (\iota = 1, 2, \ldots N). \quad (36)$$

If there is no external field of force or if the external field is independent of the time, a theorem analogous to that of the conservation of energy may be established It may be shown, as in the preceding chapter, by means of the definition (21) of the energy of the probability elements, that:

$$\frac{dW}{dt} = -\frac{\partial L}{\partial t} = \frac{\partial F}{\partial t} + \frac{\partial F_1}{\partial t}. \quad (37)$$

After multiplying by a^2 and integrating throughout the space, it is found that:

$$\frac{\overline{dW}}{dt} = \frac{\overline{\partial F}}{\partial t} - \frac{h^2}{8\pi^2}\int a^2 \frac{\partial}{\partial t}\left\{\frac{1}{a\sqrt{\mu}}\sum_{ik}\frac{\partial}{\partial q_i}\left(\sqrt{\mu}\,\mu^{ik}\frac{\partial a}{\partial q_k}\right)\right\}d\tau \qquad (38)$$

and the integral may be written:

$$\int a^2\frac{\partial}{\partial t}\left(\frac{1}{a}\sum_k \mu^{kk}\frac{\partial^2 a}{\partial q_k^2}\right)d\tau = \int\left(a\sum_k \mu^{kk}\frac{\partial^3 a}{\partial q_k^2 \partial t} - \frac{\partial a}{\partial t}\sum_k \mu^{kk}\frac{\partial^2 a}{\partial q_k^2}\right)d\tau. \qquad (39)$$

If the same substitutions be made for U and V as above, we obtain from (38):

$$\frac{\overline{dW}}{dt} = \frac{\overline{\partial F}}{\partial t}, \qquad . \qquad (40)$$

and in the case when the external field is independent of the time, $\frac{\partial F}{\partial t}$ is zero and therefore:

$$\frac{\overline{dW}}{dt} = 0. \qquad . \quad . \quad . \qquad (41)$$

This is the theorem in the case of elements of probability which replaces that of conservation of energy.

4. The Explanation of Bohr and Heisenberg

Here, as in the case of the single particle, we might be tempted to develop a pilot-wave theory, at the same time maintaining that the particles of the system have a definite position in space and that, consequently, the representative point has also a definite position at each instant in the generalised space. We should then admit that the representative point associated with a ψ-wave has the motion defined by (15), coinciding always with one of the probability elements. If we do not know with which of the probability elements the point coincides, the probability that it occupies a volume $d\tau$ at time t will be equal to the number of elements then contained within the volume and by (14) the interference principle will be automatically satisfied. Unfortunately all the difficulties arise once more which we discovered in the pilot-wave theory of a particle, and it is even more difficult to consider the theory as offering an actual physical picture of the phenomena because of the abstract and fictitious character of the propagation of a wave in generalised space.

We therefore leave the pilot-wave theory and turn to that of Bohr and Heisenberg to see how it will apply to systems. We shall accept as fundamental hypotheses the interference principle, according to which the intensity $\psi\psi^*$ of the associated wave measures at each instant and at each point the probability of occurrence of the representative point, and the principle of spectral decomposition, according to which the relative intensities of the different monochromatic components of which the ψ-wave train is composed give the relative probabilities of the different states of motion. All the considerations developed in the case of a single particle may be extended to the case of N particles and the uncertainty relations again obtained :

$$\delta q_i \delta p_i \geqslant h \quad . \quad . \quad . \quad (42)$$

The cause of this uncertainty is always to be sought in the perturbation introduced of necessity in the process of measurement

The transition from the old to the new mechanics conceived after the manner of Bohr and Heisenberg can also be made by means of Ehrenfest's theorem, as in Chapter XI. When geometrical optics is valid for the propagation of the wave in generalised space trains of waves may exist occupying a region of dimensions large compared with the wave-length and which can, therefore, be represented by a group of nearly monochromatic waves. Although comprising many wave-lengths, these trains may on our scale still be considered of negligible dimensions, and they may be compared with a small probability element in the space Within such an element the quantities p_i and $-\frac{\partial F}{\partial q_i}$ are appreciably constant, and Ehrenfest's theorem then gives

$$\frac{dp_i}{dt} = -\frac{\partial F}{\partial q_i}. \quad . \quad . \quad . \quad . \quad (43)$$

Thus the probability element moves as a whole in the space like the representative point in the classical theory The position of this point must, of course, be regarded as indeterminate within the element, but this indeterminateness is so small on our scale that it can be neglected in practice. Actually it appears as if the configuration and state of motion were exactly defined at any instant and as if the system followed rigorously the laws of the old mechanics.

5. Concluding Remark

We make a last remark on this subject in the case where the system consists of particles exercising no action upon one another. From the last chapter it appears that we must take for ψ the product of the functions for the different particles considered separately, $\psi = \psi_1\psi_2 \ldots$ This is in agreement with the interference principle and with the statistical meaning of intensity. For the probability that the representative point of the system shall occupy the position $(x_1, y_1, \ldots z_N)$ at time t is :

$$\psi(x_1, y_1, \ldots z_N, t)\psi^*(x_1, y_1, \ldots z_N, t) \quad . \quad (44)$$

and the probability that the ith particle is at (x_i, y_i, z_i) at this instant is :

$$\psi_i(x_i, y_i, z_i, t)\psi^*(x_i, y_i, z_i, t), \quad . \quad . \quad (45)$$

but since the motions of the particles are independent, there being no mutual action. the probability that the particles will occur simultaneously at the corresponding points is $\Pi\psi_i\psi_i^*$

This is equal to $\psi\psi^*$, since

$$\psi = \Pi\psi_i. \quad . \quad . \quad . \quad (46)$$

CHAPTER XVI

THE OLD QUANTUM THEORY AND THE STABILITY OF PERIODIC MOTION

1. Early Examples of Quantisation in Periodic Motion

IN atomic phenomena periodic motion plays a great part, and we must study the special characteristics of this type of motion in wave mechanics We shall begin by recalling how the conception of a quantum of action was introduced into the study of periodic phenomena in the atom and point out some of the chief results of the old quantum theory.

It is well known that the idea of the quantum was introduced into dynamics by Planck in his researches into the state of thermodynamical equilibrium between matter and radiation As this state cannot depend upon the mechanism of the energy exchange he assumed, for the sake of simplicity, that it was brought about by means of electrons vibrating about a position of equilibrium to which they were attracted by a force proportional to the displacement. A particle of this kind oscillating in a straight line under this law of force is called a linear oscillator. In order to obtain the experimental laws of complete radiation Planck was led to make the assumption that the oscillators could not be in possession of arbitrary amounts of energy, but that only those amounts were permissible which were related to the frequency of oscillation by the formula

$$E = nh\omega, \qquad \dots \qquad (1)$$

n being an integer, h the constant of action introduced by Planck into physics, and ω the frequency of the oscillator, which, as we shall show, is independent of the energy.

We can obtain another expression of this quantum postulate

from a consideration of the linear oscillator The potential function, F, is :

$$F = \frac{k}{2}x^2, \qquad . \qquad . \qquad . \quad (2)$$

x being the displacement, and the classical equation of motion is

$$m\frac{d^2x}{dt^2} = -kx. \qquad . \qquad . \quad (3)$$

The solution is :

$$x = A \sin\left(\sqrt{\frac{k}{m}}t + \alpha\right), \qquad . \qquad . \quad (4)$$

where A and α are two arbitrary constants.

The frequency

$$\omega = \frac{1}{2\pi}\sqrt{\frac{k}{m}} \qquad . \qquad . \qquad . \quad (5)$$

is independent of A, the energy of the motion

The momentum is $p_x = m\frac{dx}{dt} = mv$, and the integral of action of Maupertuis is .

$$S_1 = \int_{x_0}^{x_1} p_x dx = m\int_{x_0}^{x_1} v\, dx \qquad . \qquad . \qquad . \quad (6)$$

and if this be calculated for a complete period we find .

$$J = \oint dS_1 = \oint mv\, dx = m\int_0^{\frac{1}{\omega}} v^2\, dt$$

$$= 2\pi^2\omega m A^2 \qquad . \qquad . \qquad . \quad (7)$$

by (4)

The energy, E, is equal to the kinetic energy of the particle at the instant it passes through the position of equilibrium, since at this point the potential energy is zero.

Thus

$$E = \tfrac{1}{2}m\dot{x}_0^2 = \tfrac{1}{2}kA^2 = 2\pi m\omega^2 A^2, \qquad . \qquad . \quad (8)$$

whence

$$\frac{E}{\omega} = 2\pi m\omega A^2 = J. \qquad . \qquad . \qquad . \quad (9)$$

The condition (1) may be written in the form .

$$J = nh, \qquad . \qquad . \qquad . \qquad . \quad (10)$$

but this is much more general, since it is not necessary to make the special assumption that the frequency of the oscillator is independent of its energy. Moreover, the quantum restriction of energy values for all motion with one degree of freedom can be expressed in this form. The condition (10) is the condition of quantisation.

The most important application of (10) is that made by Bohr to the case of an electron of charge $-e$ rotating about a positive nucleus of charge $+e$, as in the atom of hydrogen. In his first work on this subject in 1913 Bohr limited himself to the study of circular trajectories. The azimuth θ is in this case the only variable necessary for locating the particle and (10) can be applied. The kinetic energy is:

$$T = \tfrac{1}{2}mr^2\dot{\theta}^2 \quad . \quad . \quad . \quad (11)$$

and the momentum conjugate to θ is:

$$p_\theta = \frac{\partial T}{\partial \dot{\theta}} = mr^2\dot{\theta}, \quad . \quad . \quad . \quad (12)$$

hence the integral of action is:

$$\int p_\theta\, d\theta = \int mr^2\theta\, d\theta. \quad . \quad . \quad . \quad (13)$$

Since the angular velocity θ is constant on a circular path in a central field of force the value of the integral for a complete period is:

$$J = \int_0^{2\pi} mr^2\theta\, d\theta = 2\pi mr^2\dot{\theta} \quad . \quad . \quad (14)$$

Condition (10) becomes in this case:

$$2\pi mr^2\dot{\theta} = nh. \quad . \quad . \quad . \quad (15)$$

$mr^2\dot{\theta}$ is the moment of momentum of the electron with respect to the nucleus, and if this be denoted by M, (15) may be written:

$$M = \frac{nh}{2\pi}, \quad . \quad . \quad . \quad . \quad (16)$$

which is the formula which led Bohr to his brilliant explanation of the hydrogen spectrum. To obtain the formula for this spectrum we may write the equation of motion in the form:

$$mr\theta^2 = \frac{e^2}{r^2}, \quad . \quad . \quad . \quad . \quad (17)$$

and eliminating $\dot{\theta}$ between (16) and (17) we obtain :

$$\frac{1}{r} = \frac{4\pi^2 me^2}{n^2h^2}. \qquad (18)$$

The energy of the electron in its path is :

$$E = \frac{1}{2}mr^2\dot{\theta}^2 - \frac{e^2}{r} = -\frac{e^2}{2r}, \qquad (19)$$

whence

$$E_n = -\frac{2\pi^2 me^4}{n^2h^2}. \qquad (20)$$

This is the well-known formula for the energies in the various quantum states for the hydrogen atom.

At this point Bohr introduced another postulate known as the law of frequencies, according to which the atom emits radiation of frequency ν_{nm} when it passes from one stable quantum state with energy E_n to another with less energy E_m, the frequency being given by

$$\nu_{nm} = \frac{E_n - E_m}{h} = \frac{2\pi^2 me^4}{h^3}\left(\frac{1}{m^2} - \frac{1}{n^2}\right) \qquad (21)$$

If m is made equal to 2, that is if all those changes of state are considered which terminate in a final state characterised by this number, the experimental formula for the Balmer series is obtained :

$$\nu = R\left(\frac{1}{4} - \frac{1}{n^2}\right). \quad (n = 3, 4, \ldots) \qquad (22)$$

If the two formulæ are identical it must follow that .

$$R = \frac{2\pi^2 me^4}{h^3} \qquad (23)$$

and the great success of Bohr's theory is that the experimental value of R agrees with formula (23)

Equation (21) gives the frequencies of the members of another series in the hydrogen spectrum known as the Lyman and Paschen series, and from a consideration of the circular orbits of an electron about a doubly charged nucleus, Bohr has also succeeded in explaining the spectrum of ionised helium.

2. The Wilson-Sommerfeld Conditions

The satisfactory enunciation of the quantum conditions in the periodic motion of a particle in a constant field of force required an extension beyond the case where the motion is defined by a single variable. W. Wilson and Sommerfeld found a form of enunciation applicable to all periodic motion where there is separation of the variables, that is to say, where it is possible to choose the co-ordinates in such a way that each conjugate component of momentum depends only upon the corresponding co-ordinate :

$$p_i = f(q_i) \quad . \quad . \quad . \quad . \quad (24)$$

The action of Maupertuis, $\int \sum_i p_i dq_i$, is thus a sum of functions each of which depends upon a single variable. It may be shown that, in the course of the motion, some of the variables oscillate between two limits, while the others are angles with a period 2π For example, in Keplerian motion the radius vector is a variable of the first kind, the azimuth one of the second We shall say that a variable of the first kind has completed its cycle when it has increased from the lower to the upper limit and has returned to the lower ; in the same way we shall say that a variable of the second kind has described its cycle when it has increased by 2π. With these definitions in mind we can pass on to state the quantum conditions of Wilson and Sommerfeld The variables, q_i, having been chosen so that the variables can be separated, each of the integrals $\int p_i dq_i$ taken over a complete cycle of q_i is equal to an integral multiple of the constant h The conditions may be written :

$$\oint p_i dq_i = n_i h. \quad (n_i = \text{an integer.}) \quad . \quad . \quad (25)$$

A particle in motion in a constant field of force has, in general, three degrees of freedom and will require, in general, three integers for the definition of its quantised motion

We may note an important point. When q_i is a variable of the first kind like the radius vector in the Kepler problem, it oscillates during the motion between values q_{i0} and q_{i1} and the integral in this case is :

$$\int_{q_{i0}}^{q_{i1}} p_i dq_i + \int_{q_{i1}}^{q_{i0}} p_i dq_i. \qquad (26)$$

This integral would clearly be zero if p_i were a uniform function of the variable q_i ; but this is not the case, for it can be shown that in the motion with which we are concerned the conjugate momentum of a variable of the first kind is of the form :

$$p_i = \pm \sqrt{\phi_i(q_i)}, \qquad (27)$$

the function ϕ_i being positive in the interval q_{i0} to q_{i1}, and vanishing at the limits and then changing sign. p_i is thus a

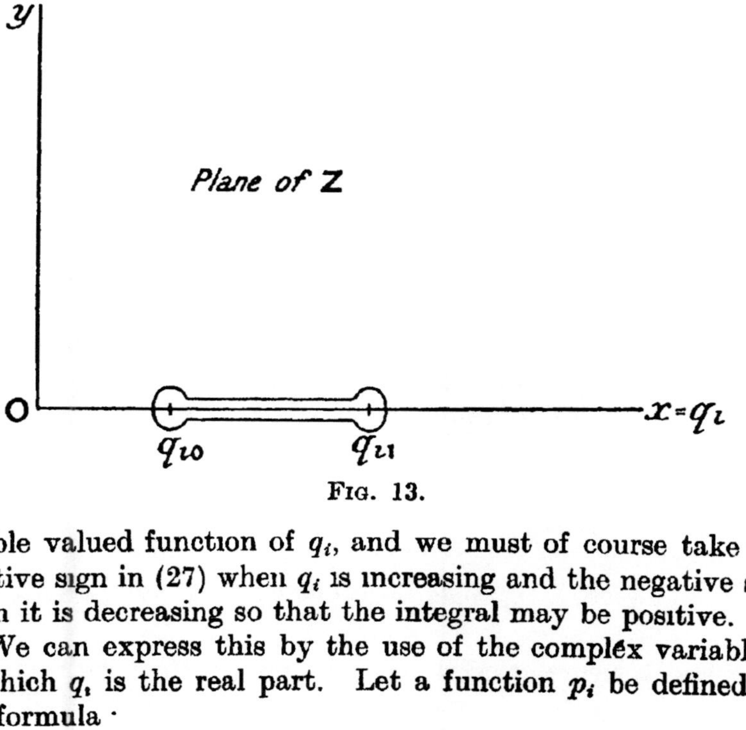

FIG. 13.

double valued function of q_i, and we must of course take the positive sign in (27) when q_i is increasing and the negative sign when it is decreasing so that the integral may be positive.

We can express this by the use of the complex variable z, of which q_i is the real part. Let a function p_i be defined by the formula ·

$$p_i = \pm \sqrt{\phi_i(z)}. \qquad (28)$$

Along the real axis this expression is identical with (28) and p_i is the momentum conjugate to q_i. The function has two branch points on the real axis and the integral must be taken along a closed contour extending from the position $q_{i0} + \epsilon$ to $q_{i1} - \epsilon$ on the real axis and completed by two infinitely small circles of radii ϵ about the branch points (Fig. 13).

There is no corresponding process for the variables of the second kind which vary from 0 to 2π; for these the momentum has a constant sign.

3. Einstein's Statement of the Quantum Conditions

The Wilson-Sommerfeld conditions can be stated independently of the choice of variables in a form given by Einstein in 1917.

In the case of a particle the action is given by:

$$dS_1 = \sum_1^3 p_i dq_i$$

This expression is invariant for any change of space co-ordinates, for it represents what may be described as the work of the momentum vector. Throughout the region R, where the motion takes place, each component $p_k = \frac{\partial S_1}{\partial q_k}$ is in general a function of the three variables, for we are no longer limiting ourselves to co-ordinates which are separable The quantum conditions are equivalent to the statement that the integral of action, taken over any closed curve C situated wholly within R, is equal to an integral multiple of Planck's constant.

To calculate this integral it is necessary to choose a system of co-ordinates, for example one in which the variables are separable. We can then write:

$$\int_C dS_1 = k_1\int p_1 dq_1 + k_2\int p_2 dq_2 + k_3\int p_3 dq_3 \tag{29}$$

k_1, k_2 and k_3 being integers and by virtue of the conditions (25) Einstein's statement is satisfied. The Wilson-Sommerfeld conditions thus lead to Einstein's form, but the latter is independent of the choice of co-ordinates.

As an illustration of this principle of Einstein's let us consider a motion taking place in a plane under the action of a central force. The radius vector, being a variable of the first kind, oscillates between two values r_1 and r_2, and in general the plane orbit fills the annular region included between the circles of radii r_1 and r_2.

The continuous line denotes the plane of the orbit (Fig. 14). The motion may be described by means of the azimuth θ measured about O and the radius vector r , to these correspond the conjugate momenta p_θ and p_r ($= \pm\sqrt{\phi(r)}$). Let us imagine the annular area to be replaced by a surface formed of two plane sheets which have been bent to fit along the circles $r = r_1$ and $r = r_2$, making in this way a Riemannian surface. The upper sheet will be associated with the positive, the lower with the negative sign. In Fig. 14 these sheets are represented

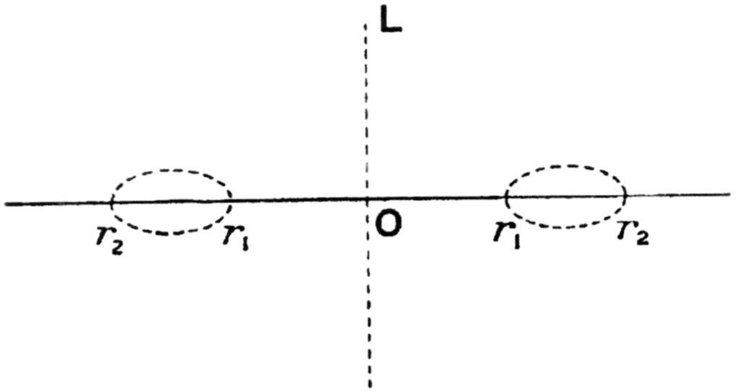

FIG. 14.

by dotted lines and for convenience they are shown displaced from one another. The annular area is thus replaced by a sort of flattened anchor ring on which p_r is a uniform function.

It is possible to distinguish three types of curves on this surface :—

1. Those which can be reduced to a point by a continuous change of shape. For these $\int_C dS_1 = 0$.
2. Those which can be made by a continuous deformation to coincide with a circle about the axis through O perpendicular to the plane of the ring and for which

$$\int_C dS_1 = \int_0^{2\pi} p_\theta \, d\theta = n_1 h.$$

3. Finally, those which can be made by a continuous deformation to coincide with a section of the surface by a plane containing the axis and for which

$$\int_C dS_1 = \oint p_r\,dr = n_2 h.$$

Moreover, any curve traced on the Riemann surface can be referred to a series of curves of these three types and Einstein's enunciation results.

4. Quantisation of Keplerian Motion

As an example of the application of the quantum conditions we will consider the case of Keplerian motion.

In polar co-ordinates the classical kinetic energy is :

$$T = \tfrac{1}{2}m(\dot{r}^2 + r^2\dot{\theta}^2) \quad . \quad . \qquad (30)$$

and the conjugate momenta are :

$$p_r = \frac{\partial T}{\partial \dot{r}} = m\dot{r}, \quad p_\theta = \frac{\partial T}{\partial \dot{\theta}} = mr^2\dot{\theta}. \quad . \qquad (31)$$

But by the law of areas p_θ is equal to a constant C, and Newton's or Coulomb's law of force makes it possible to write :

$$E = \frac{1}{2}m(\dot{r}^2 + r^2\dot{\theta}^2) - \frac{K}{r}, \quad . \qquad (32)$$

from which we may deduce by replacement of p_θ by C ·

$$p_r = m\dot{r} = \pm\sqrt{2mE - \frac{C^2}{r^2} + \frac{2mK}{r}} = \pm\sqrt{\phi(r)} \qquad (33)$$

If E is negative ϕ has two positive roots r_1 and r_2 and the radius-vector must always be included between these roots if p_r is not to become imaginary. Thus if E is negative the motion is periodic and p_r is of the form (27).

The quantum condition for the azimuth is :

$$\int_0^{2\pi} p_\theta\,d\theta = 2\pi C = n_1 h, \quad (n_1 = \text{an integer}) \quad . \qquad (34)$$

or

$$C = n_1\frac{h}{2\pi}. \quad . \quad . \quad . \quad . \qquad (35)$$

where n_1 is called the azimuthal quantum number.

This is the condition of stability (16) used by Bohr in the case of circular motion, for C is the constant moment of momentum of the " planet " about the " sun."

But in the present case we have in addition a second quantum condition which Bohr did not require, since he restricted himself to circular orbits. This second condition is :

$$\oint p_r dr = n_2 h, \quad . \quad . \quad . \quad (36)$$

where n_2 is the radial quantum number.

If r_1 and r_2 are the roots of $\phi(r)$ the integral (36) may be written :

$$\int_{r_1}^{r_2} \sqrt{\phi}\, dr + \int_{r_2}^{r_1} - \sqrt{\phi}\, dr = 2\int_{r_1}^{r_2} \sqrt{\phi}\, dr \quad . \quad (37)$$

and by equating this to $n_2 h$ a second condition is obtained to which we shall return later on.

We can easily obtain, by a general process, expressions for the p_i in terms of the q_i which are required for the calculation of the integrals from Jacobi's equation. In the special case of Keplerian motion this may be shown by writing the energy (32) in the form :

$$\mathrm{H}(q_i, p_i) = \frac{1}{2m}\left(p_r^2 + \frac{p_\theta^2}{r^2}\right) - \frac{\mathrm{K}}{r} \quad . \quad (38)$$

and Jacobi's equation for the function S_1 is .

$$\frac{1}{2m}\left\{\left(\frac{\partial S_1}{\partial r}\right)^2 + \frac{1}{r^2}\left(\frac{\partial S_1}{\partial \theta}\right)^2\right\} - \frac{\mathrm{K}}{r} = \mathrm{E}. \quad . \quad (39)$$

Substituting $\frac{\partial S_1}{\partial \theta} = C$, we find :

$$p_r = \frac{\partial S_1}{\partial r} = \sqrt{2m\mathrm{E} + \frac{2m\mathrm{K}}{r} - \frac{C^2}{r^2}}. \quad (40)$$

The function $S_1 = C\theta + \int p_r dr$ is a complete integral of (39), for it contains two arbitrary constants C and E, the values of these constants being determined by the quantum conditions (35) and (37).

5. Degeneration

We have to consider next a subject which has played a very important part in the old quantum theory ; this is the subject of degeneration. It was stated that the Wilson-Sommerfeld conditions characterised the quantised motion of a particle by means of three whole numbers But from the results given above it follows that these three numbers intervene effectively only when three variables are necessary for the description of the motion Bohr, in considering only circular motion described by a single variable, the azimuth, had to introduce only a single integer ; in the last paragraph, in the study of Keplerian motion which is plane and is described by means of a radius vector and an azimuth, we required only two integers, n_1 and n_2.

But it is important to note that the occurrence of two numbers in Keplerian motion is only accidental. This becomes clear at once by noting that the orbit in the classical theory is a closed conic, and thus if elliptic co-ordinates are chosen the motion can be described by a single variable.

These results can be generalised in the statement that every time the trajectory, instead of filling the whole of a three-dimensional region, fills only a two-dimensional or a one-dimensional region, the process of quantisation introduces only two numbers or a single number. In this case we have degeneration.

The study of Keplerian motion confirms this conclusion, as we shall appreciate by completing the calculations begun in the last paragraph. By means of Cauchy's theory of residues Sommerfeld has obtained the value of the integral

$$\oint p_r\, dr = \oint \sqrt{2mE + \frac{2mK}{r} - \frac{c^2}{r^2}}dr. \qquad (41)$$

He has found the energy of the orbit characterised by the numbers n_1 and n_2 by equating the result to n_2h and substituting the value $\frac{n_1h}{2\pi}$ for C. The result is .

$$E_{n_1n_2} = -\frac{2\pi^2me^4}{h^2(n_1+n_2)^2}. \qquad (42)$$

By making $n_2 = 0$ we obtain again Bohr's result for circular orbits, but Sommerfeld's result shows that the energy of the quantised elliptic orbits is also characterised by a single integer,

$n_1 + n_2$. The consideration of elliptic orbits does not introduce a single new term into the list of stable energy levels. The separate introduction of the two quantum numbers n_1 and n_2 appears therefore to be fictitious. This is shown better still by the fact that in the case of classical Keplerian motion it is possible to realise separation of the variables in other ways than by means of the radius vector and the azimuth. Each choice of variables which brings about separation of the variables leads to different forms for the stable elliptic orbits, but gives the same values for their energies. It must be concluded that all circular or elliptic orbits with energies equal to $-\frac{2\pi^2 me^4}{n^2h^2}$ are stable. Quantisation of Keplerian orbits brings in finally only a single integer because the orbits are closed, occupying only one dimension in space, and classical Keplerian motion is degenerate.

Degenerate motions present a special kind of instability in the sense that the least perturbation causes the degeneration to disappear, at least partially. Thus it is well known in astronomy that a perturbation, even a very feeble one, can impose periodic or secular variations on the elements of a Keplerian elliptic orbit (major axis, eccentricity, inclination, longitude of the perihelion, longitude of the ascending node), the consequence of these variations being that the orbit is no longer strictly closed and that it fills completely a space domain. The introduction of the relativity correction into the theory of Keplerian orbits is equivalent to introducing perturbation terms which are in general small, and Sommerfeld has shown that the orbit remains plane and appreciably elliptic, but that there is a slow continuous rotation of the perihelion. The trajectory is thus no longer exactly closed, and it occupies the whole of the annular area between two circles of radii equal to the distances from the attracting focus to the ends of the major axis of the rotating ellipse. The degeneration thus disappears, but only partially, since the trajectory remains plane, but it is now necessary to introduce two numbers for each stable orbit. By calculations which we will not reproduce here, Sommerfeld obtains for the energy of the quantised path characterised by the numbers n_1 and n_2:

$$E_{n_1 n_2} = -\frac{2\pi^2 me^4}{n^2h^2}\left\{1 + \frac{4\pi^2 e^4}{n^2h^2c^2}\left(\frac{n}{n_1} - \frac{3}{4}\right)\right\}, \quad . \quad (43)$$

where $n = n_1 + n_2$ is the total quantum number. From this it is clear that the energy of the stable orbit depends separately upon the two numbers n_1 and n_2 and not only upon the sum $(n_1 + n_2)$.

An electric or magnetic field acting upon the hydrogen atom also causes the degeneration to disappear from the corresponding Kepler motion.

6. The Insufficiency of the Old Quantum Theory

It is impossible to examine all the calculations to which the various applications of the quantum conditions give rise We must be content with remarking that although the calculations have often led to exact results it has not always been the case, and the old theory has more than once proved to be insufficient.

Let us return to the case of the linear oscillator treated in § 1. From the formula (1) the energy E of the stable states must be equal to one of the values of the series: $0, h\omega, 2h\omega, \ldots nh\omega$, where ω is the mechanical frequency, $\frac{1}{2\pi}\sqrt{\frac{k}{m}}$ of the oscillator.

But in order to explain certain experiments, especially in the domain of band spectra, we have been obliged to admit that the sequence of quantised energies is not that we have just stated, but the following

$$\tfrac{1}{2}h\omega,\ \tfrac{3}{2}h\omega,\ \ldots\ (n + \tfrac{1}{2})h\omega. \quad (n = 0, 1, 2, \ldots)$$

This is what is sometimes called the half quantum law and is not in agreement with the quantisation required by the old quantum theory. The application of the method of quantisation of the old theory to more complex atoms than those of hydrogen and helium has also led to poor results; for example, the ionisation potential of helium as calculated by Kramers according to the old methods is not in agreement with experiment.

For some time before the appearance of the new mechanics the impression had been formed that the Wilson-Sommerfeld conditions, while affording valuable indications, could not be considered as rigorous. We pass on now to see in what sense the new mechanics modifies these methods and how it has revealed to some extent the physical meaning of the quantum conditions.

CHAPTER XVII

THE STABILITY OF QUANTISED MOTION FROM THE POINT OF VIEW OF WAVE MECHANICS

1. Meaning of Quantisation in Wave Mechanics

WE have been led by the conceptions of wave mechanics to associate with the motion of a particle in a constant field of force defined by the potential $F(x, y, z)$ the propagation of a wave given by the equation :

$$\nabla^2\psi + \frac{8\pi^2 m}{h^2}(E - F)\psi = 0. \qquad (1)$$

If the approximations of geometrical optics are valid for the study of this wave propagation we can take as the reduced wave function :

$$\psi = ae^{\frac{2\pi i}{h}(Et - S_1)}, \qquad (2)$$

where a depends upon x, y and z only and where $S_1(x, y, z)$ is a complete integral of Jacobi's equation. In order that the phase of the function (2) may have a definite value at every point it is necessary and sufficient that along any closed curve C contained in the region of propagation we have :

$$\int_{C_1} dS_1 = \int_C \sum_1^3 p_i dq_i = nh. \quad (n = \text{an integer.}) \qquad (3)$$

We thus obtain once more Einstein's result from which the Wilson-Sommerfeld conditions follow. In the special case of a closed trajectory we can take it as our closed curve C and write down the single condition :

$$\int p\, dl = nh. \qquad (4)$$

The problem is then degenerate and each stable orbit is characterised by a single integer.

Thus if geometrical optics be valid for the propagation of the associated waves in the atoms the new mechanics gives a meaning to the mysterious quantum conditions. Since according to the new view geometrical optics and the old mechanics correspond, we can say that the quantum conditions in the old quantum theory are those which must be introduced in order to preserve the equations of the old mechanics. But this makes the whole of the old quantum theory appear nothing more than a first approximation valid within the same limits as geometrical optics Now, as Schrodinger has pointed out, this approximation is insufficient in the case of intra-atomic motion. In fact, the essential condition of application of geometrical optics is that the conditions of propagation vary very little for displacements of the order of a wave-length, and since the wave-length of the wave associated with an electron in an atom is $\frac{h}{mv}$, or approximately $\frac{7 \cdot 3}{v}$, with intra-atomic velocities of the order 10^9 cm. per sec., the order of magnitude (10^{-8} cm.) is that of the dimensions of the atom. Within the intra-atomic domain the conditions of propagation vary enormously, since they are governed by the potential F which increases indefinitely when the nucleus is approached. The application of the results of geometrical optics is thus not justified.

In short, the explanation of the old quantum conditions which we have just given puts us upon the track of the solution, but it shows also that these conditions cannot be considered as rigorous, and that the whole question of quantisation must be taken up again from the wave point of view. How shall we define a stable quantum state ?

It is natural with the new ideas to suppose that a stable state corresponds to a ψ-wave having the form of a stationary wave .

$$\psi = a(x, y, z)e^{\frac{2\pi i}{h}(Et + \alpha)} \qquad . \quad . \quad . \quad (5)$$

Since ψ is a solution of (1) the amplitude must satisfy the equation :

$$\nabla^2 a + \frac{8\pi^2 m}{h^2}(E - F)a = 0. \qquad . \quad . \quad (6)$$

We shall suppose that the amplitude is a finite, uniform and continuous function. Moreover, the interference principle leads us to suppose it to vanish at infinity ; for if the amplitude did not tend to zero at infinity, the integral, $\int a^2 dv$, would be divergent, since all the elements of it are positive and the probability that the particle was situated at a finite distance from the atomic system considered would be zero. This would be contradictory to the idea that the particle forms part of the system and is in a stable state within it.

From the point of view of wave mechanics the search for the stable states of a particle becomes the problem of finding values of E for which the equation :

$$\nabla^2 a + \frac{8\pi^2 m}{h^2}(\mathrm{E} - \mathrm{F})a = 0 \quad . \qquad . \quad (7)$$

has a solution which is uniform, finite and continuous everywhere and vanishes at infinity. The values of E defined in this way are the energies in the quantum states of the particle. The mathematical problem is closely analogous to that of determining the characteristic vibrations of a string or membrane when certain boundary conditions are imposed In this case the boundary condition is that a must vanish at infinity.

To study the mathematical problem we have just stated we shall make use of the following notation :

$$\mu = \frac{8\pi^2 m\mathrm{E}}{h^2}, \qquad \mathrm{R} = \frac{8\pi^2 m}{h^2}\mathrm{F}. \quad . \quad . \quad (8)$$

Equation (7) is then written in the form :

$$\nabla^2 a + (\mu - \mathrm{R})a = 0. \quad . \quad . \quad (9)$$

We shall show that this equation admits of solutions which are uniform, finite and continuous in a region D of space and which vanish at the boundaries of this region for certain values only of μ. These special values are called the fundamental or characteristic constants of equation (9) and sometimes the proper values. In this way the existence of quantised values of the energy will be established.

In general a single solution of (9) corresponds to each proper value, fulfilling the conditions laid down ; this is the fundamental, characteristic or proper function corresponding to the particular value of μ. We shall show that if a_i and μ_i denote two fundamental functions corresponding to two fundamental constants μ_i and μ_j then :

$$\int_D a_i a_j dv = 0. \quad . \quad . \quad . \quad (10)$$

In other words, the fundamental functions form an orthogonal system.

In order to grasp the physical character of this theory it is convenient to begin with the study of some simple classical cases of equations of the form (9) in which $R = 0$.

2. Simple Examples of Characteristic Vibrations. Vibrating Strings and Membranes

(a) The Case of a String with Fixed Ends

In the propagation of an elastic wave along a string fixed at both ends, the transverse displacement u of a point of the string satisfies the wave equation :

$$\frac{\partial^2 u}{\partial x^2} = \frac{1}{V^2}\frac{\partial^2 u}{\partial t^2}. \quad . \quad . \quad . \quad . \quad (11)$$

where V denotes a constant dependent on the mechanical properties of the string. If we consider a monochromatic stationary wave of the type :

$$u = ae^{2\pi i(\nu t + \alpha)}, \quad . \quad . \quad . \quad (12)$$

the function a must satisfy the equation :

$$\frac{d^2 a}{dx^2} + \frac{4\pi^2\nu^2}{V^2}a = 0, \quad . \quad . \quad . \quad (13)$$

which is of the form (9) with $\mu = \frac{4\pi^2\nu^2}{V^2}$ and $R = 0$.

The domain D is here of one dimension formed by the string in its position of equilibrium ; if one end be taken as origin and if l is the length of the string, D extends from $x = 0$ to $x = l$, and thus $a(0) = a(l) = 0$.

Equation (13) admits of the well-known integral :

$$a = a_0 \sin\left(\frac{2\pi\nu x}{V} + \alpha\right) \quad . \quad . \quad (14)$$

with two arbitrary constants a_0 and α. In order to satisfy the boundary conditions we must take $\alpha = 0$ and $\frac{2\pi\nu l}{V} = n\pi$, where n is an integer, the particular solution becoming :

$$a_n = a_0 \sin \frac{n\pi x}{l}. \quad . \quad . \quad (15)$$

In this case the proper values are :

$$\mu_n = \frac{n^2\pi^2}{l^2} \quad . \quad . \quad . \quad (16)$$

and the functions (15) are the corresponding proper functions.

It follows from Fourier's theorem that any state of vibration of the string can be represented by the function :

$$u(x, t) = \sum_n \left(c_n \sin \frac{n\pi}{l} x \cos 2\pi\nu_n t + d_n \sin \frac{n\pi x}{l} \sin 2\pi\nu_n t\right), \quad (17)$$

where $\nu_n = \frac{nV}{2l}$, for this function satisfies the wave equation and vanishes at the boundaries Moreover, by Fourier's theorem it follows that the constants c_n and d_n can be chosen so that u and $\frac{\partial u}{\partial t}$, for the value $t = 0$, coincide with any two continuous functions vanishing at the boundaries. Since u satisfies an equation of the second order with respect to the time, this function is determined if u and $\frac{\partial u}{\partial t}$ are known for the value $t = 0$

Any state of vibration of the string can thus be represented by (17). Finally, it is a well-known fact that :

$$\int_0^l \sin \frac{n\pi}{l} x \sin \frac{n'\pi}{l} x \, dx = 0, \quad n \neq n', \quad . \quad (18)$$

so that the proper functions are orthogonal.

But the proper functions are indefinite to the extent that a_0 is arbitrary in (15). They are said to be normalised when this constant is chosen, so that .

$$\int_D a_n^2 \, dv = 1. \quad . \quad . \quad . \quad (19)$$

In the case under consideration the normalised functions are:

$$a_n = \sqrt{\frac{2}{l}} \sin \frac{n\pi}{l} x \qquad . \qquad . \qquad (20)$$

since

$$\int_0^l \sin^2 \frac{n\pi}{l} x \, dx = \frac{l}{2}$$

(*b*) *The Case of a Plane Rectangular Membrane with Fixed Edges.*

The problem to be solved in this case is that of finding a uniform, finite and continuous solution of the equation:

$$\frac{\partial^2 u}{\partial x^2} + \frac{\partial^2 u}{\partial y^2} = \frac{1}{V^2} \frac{\partial^2 u}{\partial t^2} \qquad . \qquad . \qquad . \qquad (21)$$

which vanishes at the boundaries of the region D formed by the membrane, i.e. which vanishes for $x = 0$, $x = A$, $y = 0$, $y = B$, A and B denoting the sides of the rectangle bounding the membrane.

Let us consider the stationary monochromatic waves of the form

$$u(x, y, t) = a(x, y) e^{2\pi i(\nu t - \alpha)} \qquad . \qquad (22)$$

We find:

$$\frac{\partial^2 a}{\partial x^2} + \frac{\partial^2 a}{\partial y^2} + \frac{4\pi^2 \nu^2}{V^2} a = 0, \qquad . \qquad . \qquad (23)$$

which is an equation of the type (9) with $\mu = \frac{4\pi^2\nu^2}{V^2}$ and $R = 0$. A solution fulfilling the required conditions is obtained by writing:

$$\mu = \pi^2\left(\frac{n^2}{A^2} + \frac{n'^2}{B^2}\right), \quad a_{nn'} = \sin \frac{n\pi}{A} x \sin \frac{n'\pi}{B} y. \qquad . \qquad (24)$$

These are the proper values and proper functions of equation (23). The proper functions are orthogonal, since:

$$\int_0^A \int_0^B a_{nn'} a_{mm'} \, dx \, dy = 0 \qquad . \qquad . \qquad (25)$$

except when $m = n$, $m' = n'$.

Since $\int_0^A \int_0^B a_{nn'}^2 \, dx \, dy = \frac{AB}{4}$, the normalised functions are:

$$a_{nn'} = \frac{2}{\sqrt{AB}} \sin \frac{n\pi}{A} x \sin \frac{n'\pi}{B} y. \qquad . \qquad . \qquad (26)$$

It can be shown that the proper values and functions are unique, and that any state of vibration of the membrane can be represented by a function of the form :

$$u = \sum_{nn'} \Big(c_{nn'} \sin \frac{n\pi}{A} x \sin \frac{n'\pi}{B} y \cos 2\pi\nu_{nn'} t$$

$$+ d_{nn'} \sin \frac{n\pi}{A} x \sin \frac{n'\pi}{B} y \sin 2\pi\nu_{nn'} t \Big), \quad (27)$$

where $\nu_{nn'} = \frac{V}{2}\sqrt{\frac{n^2}{A^2} + \frac{n'^2}{B^2}}$, but we shall not give a detailed proof of this.

(c) *The Case of a Plane Circular Membrane with a Fixed Border*

The centre of the membrane will be taken as origin of a system of polar co-ordinates, and the units chosen so that the radius of the membrane is unity. In this case the wave equation is .

$$\nabla^2 u = \frac{\partial^2 u}{\partial r^2} + \frac{1}{r}\frac{\partial u}{\partial r} + \frac{1}{r^2}\frac{\partial^2 u}{\partial \theta^2} = \frac{1}{V^2}\frac{\partial^2 u}{\partial t^2}, \quad . \quad (27)$$

V being a constant characteristic of the membrane.

Let us write :

$$u(r, \theta, t) = a(r, \theta) e^{2\pi i(\nu t + \alpha)} \quad . \quad . \quad . \quad (28)$$

and thus obtain for a :

$$\frac{\partial^2 a}{\partial r^2} + \frac{1}{r}\frac{\partial a}{\partial r} + \frac{1}{r^2}\frac{\partial^2 a}{\partial \theta^2} + \frac{4\pi^2\nu^2}{V^2} a = 0, \quad . \quad . \quad (29)$$

which is again an equation of the type (9) with $\mu = \frac{4\pi^2\nu^2}{V^2}$ and $R = 0$. We make the tentative substitution :

$$a = f(r)\,\phi(\theta) \quad . \quad . \quad . \quad . \quad . \quad (30)$$

which gives on substitution in (29) .

$$\frac{r^2}{f}\frac{d^2 f}{dr^2} + \frac{r}{f}\frac{df}{dr} + \mu r^2 = -\frac{1}{\phi}\frac{d^2\phi}{d\theta^2}. \quad . \quad (31)$$

The left-hand side of this equation is a function of r only and the right-hand side of θ only, and they can be equal only if they have a constant value C. Thus :

$$\frac{d^2\phi}{d\theta^2} = -C\phi, \quad . \quad . \quad . \quad . \quad (32)$$

If C be negative, ϕ is an exponential function of θ and a cannot be uniform in the circular region D. It follows that C is positive and the general solution of (32) is :

$$\phi = \text{A} \sin (\sqrt{\text{C}}\theta + \text{B}), \quad . \quad . \quad . \quad (33)$$

A and B being arbitrary constants In order that ϕ may be uniform, C must be equal to the square of some integer k. We then obtain from (31) :

$$\frac{d^2 f}{dr^2} + \frac{1}{r}\frac{df}{dr} + \left(\mu - \frac{k^2}{r^2}\right) f = 0. \quad . \quad . \quad (34)$$

By changing the variable and substituting $\rho = \sqrt{\mu}\, r$ this equation can be written :

$$\frac{d^2 f}{d\rho^2} + \frac{1}{\rho}\frac{df}{d\rho} + \left(1 - \frac{k^2}{\rho^2}\right) f = 0. \quad . \quad (35)$$

This is Bessel's equation of order k and, as is shown in works on analysis, it admits of a single solution which remains finite for $\rho = 0$; this is Bessel's function of order k which is given by the series ·

$$\text{J}_k(\rho) = \frac{\rho^k}{2^k \underline{|k}}\left\{1 - \frac{\rho^2}{2(2k+2)} + \frac{\rho^4}{2\,4(2k+2)(2k+4)} - \ldots\right\} \quad (36)$$

We can thus take :

$$f(r) = \text{J}_k(\sqrt{\mu}\, r) \quad . \quad . \quad (37)$$

but with the condition that $f(1) = \text{J}_k(\sqrt{\mu}) = 0$. Thus the proper values of μ are the squares of the roots of the Bessel function of the kth order. If α_{kn} denote the nth root of J_k, the proper functions may be written in the form :

$$a_{kn} = \text{J}_k\left(\alpha_{kn} r\right) \begin{matrix}\sin\\ \cos\end{matrix} k\theta \quad . \quad . \quad (38)$$

where k and n are integers, the proper values being $\mu_{kn} = \alpha^2_{kn}$ The functions (38) are orthogonal, i.e.

$$\int_0^{2\pi}\int_0^1 \text{J}_k(\alpha_{kn} r)\text{J}_{k'}(\alpha_{k'n'} r) \begin{matrix}\sin\\ \cos\end{matrix} k\theta \begin{matrix}\sin\\ \cos\end{matrix} k'\theta\, r dr\, d\theta = 0 \quad . \quad (39)$$

except for $k = k'$, $n = n'$.

For $\int_0^{2\pi} \begin{matrix}\sin\\ \cos\end{matrix} k\theta \begin{matrix}\sin\\ \cos\end{matrix} k'\theta\, d\theta$ is zero if $k \neq k'$, and it is still zero when $k = k'$, provided that the sine be chosen in one factor and the cosine in the other; moreover, it is known from the theory of Bessel functions that:

$$\int_0^1 J_k(\alpha_{kn}r)J_k(\alpha_{kn'}r)r\,dr = 0. \quad . \quad . \quad (40)$$

Thus the integral of the product of two different proper functions is zero.

It can again be shown in this case that the proper values and functions are unique, and that any vibration of the membrane can be represented in the form:

$$u = \sum_{nk}\{c_{kn}\sin(k\theta + \gamma_{kn})J_k(\alpha_{kn}r)\sin 2\pi\nu_{kn}t$$
$$+ d_{kn}\sin(k\theta + \delta_{kn})J_k(\alpha_{kn}r)\cos 2\pi\nu_{kn}t\}. \quad (41)$$

where $\nu_{kn} = \dfrac{V}{2\pi}\alpha_{kn}$.

3. A Study of the General Case of Equation (9)

We shall now return to equation (9) in its general form ($R \neq 0$) and seek uniform, finite and continuous solutions vanishing at the boundaries of a certain domain D. Let M be the point with co-ordinates (x, y, z); when it is necessary to call to mind that the value of a function f is being considered at the point M we shall write $f(M)$.

Thus we can write equation (9) in the form:

$$\nabla^2 a(M) + \{\mu - R(M)\}a(M) = 0 \quad . \quad . \quad (42)$$

The determination of the proper values of this equation can be referred to the solution of a homogeneous linear integral equation. This may be shown by beginning with Green's formula:

$$\iiint_D (U\nabla^2 V - V\nabla^2 U)d\tau = \iint_S \left(U\frac{\partial V}{\partial n} - V\frac{\partial U}{\partial n}\right)d\sigma, \quad (43)$$

where U and V are uniform, finite and continuous functions within the region D bounded by S. The operator $\dfrac{\partial}{\partial n}$ is taken along the normal to S, the positive direction being from within the region D outwards.

Let U denote one of the proper functions a of the equation in question ; it is by definition uniform, finite and continuous, and is zero on S. For V we shall take :

$$V(M) = G(M, P) = \frac{1}{MP} + v(M, P), \quad . \quad . \quad (44)$$

P being an arbitrarily fixed point within D and $v(M, P)$ being a uniform, finite function such that G(M, P) is zero on S and satisfies within D, except at P, the equation :

$$\nabla^2 G(M, P) = R(M)G(M, P). \quad . \quad . \quad (45)$$

In short, we take for V Green's function of the equation $\nabla^2 f = Rf$ with respect to D at the point P, admitting the existence of this function. In applying (43) we must exclude from the domain D the point P, at which V becomes infinite, by surrounding it by a very small sphere σ and thus $a(M)$ and G(M, P) are uniform, finite and continuous in the domain D outside σ ; moreover, they are both zero on S. (43) then gives

$$\iiint_D (a\nabla^2 G - G\nabla^2 a)d\tau = \iint_\sigma \left(a\frac{\partial G}{\partial n} - G\frac{\partial a}{\partial n}\right)d\sigma \quad . \quad (46)$$

Let the radius of σ approach the value zero, the second part of the surface integral tends to zero, since the value of G on σ increases as the inverse of the radius, while the surface decreases as the square of the radius. The first part of the surface integral tends to

$$-a(P)\iint_\sigma \frac{\partial}{\partial r}\left(\frac{1}{r}\right)d\sigma = 4\pi a(P) \quad . \quad (47)$$

Thus, in the limit ·

$$a(P) = \frac{1}{4\pi}\iiint_D (a\nabla^2 G - G\nabla^2 a)d\tau, \quad . \quad . \quad (48)$$

but since according to the definitions the functions a and G satisfy the relations .

$$\left.\begin{aligned} \nabla^2 a &= (R - \mu)a \\ \nabla^2 G &= RG \end{aligned}\right\} \quad . \quad . \quad . \quad . \quad (49)$$

it follows that :

$$a\nabla^2 G - G\nabla^2 a = \mu a G \quad . \quad . \quad . \quad (50)$$

Thus from (48) :

$$a(\mathrm{P}) = \frac{\mu}{4\pi}\iiint_{\mathrm{D}} a(\mathrm{M})\mathrm{G}(\mathrm{M}, \mathrm{P})d\tau, \qquad . \qquad . \quad (51)$$

this is an integral equation satisfied by the proper function $a(\mathrm{M})$. The theory of linear integral equations shows that a homogeneous integral of the type (51) admits of solutions, which are not zero, for certain values of μi only ; these values, which are infinite in number, are the fundamental constants of the integral equation and the proper values in our vibration problem.

Only a single function, a_i, determined except for a constant factor, corresponds in general to each of these values, μ_i, the functions $a_i(\mathrm{M})$ are the fundamental functions of the integral equation and the proper functions in our problem.

When the domain D is finite, the fundamental constants form a discontinuous series ; on the other hand, when D extends to infinity, as is the case in quantum problems, there may be a continuous series of fundamental constants. It is sometimes stated that the assembly of fundamental constants forms the spectrum of the integral equation (51) or of the corresponding differential equation (9) because in physics the determination of the fundamental constants corresponds in general with the determination of characteristic vibrations. If the domain D is of finite extent the spectrum is always a discontinuous spectrum, or a line spectrum ; if it is infinite there may be side by side a line and a continuous spectrum. It remains to show that the proper functions $a_i(\mathrm{M})$ form in general a system of orthogonal functions Let μ_i and μ_j denote two proper values and a_i and a_j the corresponding proper functions. Then :

$$\nabla^2 a_i + (\mu_i - \mathrm{R})a_i = 0, \quad \nabla^2 a_j + (\mu_j - \mathrm{R})a_j = 0, \quad (52)$$

whence

$$a_j\nabla^2 a_i - a_i\nabla^2 a_j = (\mu_j - \mu_i)\, a_i\, a_j \qquad . \qquad . \quad (53)$$

and integrating throughout D

$$\int_{\mathrm{D}}(a_j\nabla^2 a_i - a_i\nabla^2 a_j)\, d\tau = (\mu_j - \mu_i)\int_{\mathrm{D}} a_i\, a_j\, d\tau. \quad . \quad (54)$$

By Green's theorem (43) the volume integral is equal to a surface integral over the boundary of D, and this integral is zero, since the a_i are by definition zero on this surface.

(54) then gives :

$$(\mu_j - \mu_i)\int_D a_i\, a_j\, d\tau = 0. \quad . \quad . \qquad (55)$$

Thus the integral throughout D of the product of two different proper functions is zero , the conclusion is, however, not valid if several proper functions correspond to the same proper value, for if a_i and a_j are two such functions, $\mu_i = \mu_j$ and it is not possible to deduce from (55) that $\int_D a_i\, a_j\, d\tau = 0$ This case corresponds exactly to the case of degeneration in the old mechanics where several different motions correspond to the same quantised energy value.

If N different proper functions $(a_{i1}, a_{i2}, \ldots a_{iN})$ correspond to the same proper value, they can always be replaced by N others, by means of the linear substitution :

$$a'_{ik} = \sum_j c_j^k\, a_{ij}, \; (k = 1, 2, \ldots N). \quad . \quad . \qquad (56)$$

If the a'_{ik} are to be orthogonal, we require :

$$\int_D a'_{ik}\, a'_{il}\, d\tau = \sum_{jm} c_j^k\, c_m^l \int_D a_{ij}\, a_{im}\, d\tau = 0, \; ({}^k_l = 1, 2, \; . \; . \; N). \quad (57)$$

This gives $\frac{N(N-1)}{2}$ relations for the determination of the N^2 efficients c_j^k. It is thus possible to choose N mutually orthogonal functions for the N proper functions corresponding to the proper value μ_i. In this way the assembly of all the proper functions form an orthogonal system.

The integrals $\int_D a_i^2\, d\tau$ have, of course, always a positive value, and the system of orthogonal functions is said to be normalised when the arbitrary constant factor in each is so chosen that these integrals are equal to unity

Finally, it can be shown that the normalised proper functions of a partial differential equation with respect to a domain D possess the property that any function $f(q_i)$, uniform, finite and continuous in D and vanishing at the boundary of this region, can be represented by a series of the form :

$$f(q_i) = \sum_k c_k\, a_k\, (q_i). \quad . \quad . \qquad (58)$$

If this be admitted the coefficient c_k can be calculated by multiplying this series by a_k and integrating throughout D. On account of the orthogonal property of the a_i we obtain .

$$c_k = \int_D f(q_i)\, a_k(q_i)\, d\tau \quad . \quad . \quad . \quad (59)$$

Let us consider the case of quantised systems for which D is an infinite domain, and let A denote an operator. If the function Aa_i is uniform, finite and continuous and vanishes at infinity, it can be developed as a series of fundamental functions of the form :

$$Aa_i = \sum_k A_{ki} a_k, \quad . \quad . \quad . \quad (60)$$

where

$$A_{ki} = \int_D a_k\, Aa_i\, d\tau. \quad . \quad . \quad . \quad (61)$$

The constants A_{ik} can be regarded as the terms of a table formed of an infinite number of lines and columns , they form, in fact, an infinite matrix We say that A_{ik} is the element ik of the matrix corresponding to the operator A

In the foregoing discussion it has been supposed that the three-space variables entered into the partial differential equation and that D was a domain of three dimensions. The same formulæ are valid if the equation depends upon two variables or only upon one ; the domain D will then be of two dimensions or of one, as in the examples of the preceding paragraph, and the triple integrals may be replaced by double or simple integrals. In the case of the vibrating string, the theorem expressed by formula (58) is Fourier's theorem and (59) reduces to the well-known formula for the coefficients in Fourier's series.

4. The Quantisation of Systems of Particles

Hitherto we have supposed that the system to be quantised is a single particle placed in a given constant field of force ; this is the case with the oscillator and with the hydrogen atom when the reaction of the electron upon the nucleus is neglected. But it may be necessary to apply the process to a system of several particles with mutual interactions ; this, for example, is the case with atoms more complex than that of hydrogen where a number of electrons are present. The wave equation is then .

$$\frac{1}{\sqrt{\mu}}\sum_{ik}\frac{\partial}{\partial q_i}\left(\sqrt{\mu}\,\mu^{ik}\frac{\partial\psi}{\partial q_k}\right)-\frac{8\pi^2}{h^2}\mathrm{F}\psi=\frac{4\pi i}{h}\frac{\partial\psi}{\partial t} \quad . \quad (62)$$

If we suppose ψ to have the form of the stationary wave :

$$\psi = ae^{\frac{2\pi i}{h}(\mathrm{E}t+\alpha)}, \quad . \quad . \quad (63)$$

where a is a function of the co-ordinates q_i, the equation in a is :

$$\frac{1}{\sqrt{\mu}}\sum_{ik}\frac{\partial}{\partial q_i}\left(\sqrt{\mu}\,\mu^{ik}\frac{\partial a}{\partial q_k}\right)+\frac{8\pi^2}{h^2}(\mathrm{E}-\mathrm{F})a=0. \quad . \quad (64)$$

The function a must be uniform, finite and continuous, and must vanish at infinity in the generalised space where

$$ds^2=\sum_{ik}\mu_{ik}\,dq_i\,dq_k$$

We shall assume that an infinity of proper values exists for E, the total energy of the system ; these proper values being the energies in the stable states. To these values proper functions a_i correspond, and in general there is only one such function to each proper value. When several functions exist for one and the same value, degeneration is said to occur

It is easy to show that the proper functions are in general orthogonal For two fundamental values E_l and E_m we have :

$$\left.\begin{aligned}\frac{1}{\sqrt{\mu}}\sum_{ik}\frac{\partial}{\partial q_i}\left(\sqrt{\mu}\,\mu^{ik}\frac{\partial a_l}{\partial q_k}\right)+\frac{8\pi^2}{h^2}(\mathrm{E}_l-\mathrm{F})a_l=0,\\ \frac{1}{\sqrt{\mu}}\sum_{ik}\frac{\partial}{\partial q_i}\left(\sqrt{\mu}\,\mu^{ik}\frac{\partial a_m}{\partial q_k}\right)+\frac{8\pi^2}{h^2}(\mathrm{E}_m-\mathrm{F})a_m=0,\end{aligned}\right\} \quad . \quad (65)$$

whence

$$\int_{-\infty}^{\infty}\left\{\frac{a_m}{\sqrt{\mu}}\sum_{ik}\frac{\partial}{\partial q_i}\left(\sqrt{\mu}\,\mu^{ik}\frac{\partial a_l}{\partial q_k}\right)-\frac{a_l}{\sqrt{\mu}}\sum_{ik}\frac{\partial}{\partial q_i}\left(\sqrt{\mu}\,\mu^{ik}\frac{\partial a_m}{\partial q_k}\right)\right\}\sqrt{\mu}\,dq$$

$$=\int_{-\infty}^{\infty}\frac{8\pi^2}{h^2}(\mathrm{E}_m-\mathrm{E}_l)a_la_m\sqrt{\mu}\,dq. \quad (66)$$

where $dq = dq_1, dq_2 \ldots dq_n$ and the integral is n-dimensional, taken over the whole of the q-space.

Integrating by parts, the left-hand side becomes :

$$\int \sqrt{\mu} \sum_{ik} \mu^{ik} \left(\frac{\partial a_m}{\partial q_k} \frac{\partial a_l}{\partial q_i} - \frac{\partial a_l}{\partial q_k} \frac{\partial a_m}{\partial q_i} \right) dq,$$

which vanishes, since $\mu^{ik} = \mu^{ki}$.

Thus :

$$(E_m - E_l) \int_{-\infty}^{\infty} a_l a_m \, d\tau = 0. \quad . \quad . \quad (67)$$

When there is a single proper function for each proper value, all the proper functions are orthogonal. If there are several proper functions for each proper value, it will be possible to replace them by the same number of linear combinations and to arrange that the new functions are orthogonal. Moreover, the functions can be normalised by writing $\int a_k^2 \, d\tau = 1$. The system of proper functions can thus always be considered orthogonal and normalised.

Any function $f(q_1, q_2, \ldots q_n)$ which is uniform, finite and continuous and vanishes at infinity in generalised space can be developed as a series of fundamental functions in the form :

$$f = \sum_k c_k a_k, \quad . \quad (68)$$

where

$$c_k = \int_{-\infty}^{\infty} f a_k \, d\tau. \quad . \quad . \quad (69)$$

Finally, if A denote a certain operator, and if Aa_i is uniform, finite and continuous and vanishes at infinity in the space we can write :

$$Aa_i = \sum_k A_{ki} a_k, \quad . \quad . \quad (70)$$

where

$$A_{ki} = \int_{-\infty}^{\infty} a_k A a_i \, d\tau$$

The A_{ik} are elements of the matrix corresponding to the operator A.

CHAPTER XVIII

SOME EXAMPLES OF QUANTISATION

1. The Plane Rotator

THE simplest case of quantisation is the plane rotator. This is the description of the system formed by a particle of mass m occupying a circle of radius R, its position being located by means of a single variable, the azimuth θ, the centre of the circle being the origin. Thus, with the ordinary mechanical conceptions :

$$T = \frac{1}{2}mR^2\dot{\theta}^2, \quad p_\theta = \frac{\partial T}{\partial \dot{\theta}} = mR^2\dot{\theta} \quad . \qquad (1)$$

and the old method of quantisation gives :

$$\int_0^{2\pi} mR^2\,\dot{\theta}\,d\theta = \int_0^{2\pi} mvR\,d\theta = nh \quad . \qquad (2)$$

or

$$mvR = \frac{nh}{2\pi}, \quad (n = \text{an integer}) \quad . \quad . \qquad (3)$$

whence

$$E_n = T = \frac{1}{2}mv^2 = \frac{n^2h^2}{8\pi^2mR^2} = \frac{n^2h^2}{8\pi^2I}, \quad . \quad . \qquad (4)$$

I denoting the moment of inertia of the rotator about the centre. In the new mechanics we must begin with the wave equation :

$$\nabla^2 a + \frac{8\pi^2 m}{h^2}(E - F)a = 0, \quad . \quad . \qquad (5)$$

which in the present case takes the simple form ·

$$\frac{1}{R^2}\frac{d^2a}{d\theta^2} + \frac{8\pi^2 m}{h^2}Ea = 0 \quad . \quad . \qquad (6)$$

Thus .

$$a = A \sin \frac{2\pi}{h} \sqrt{2mE}\, R(\theta - \theta_0), \qquad . \qquad (7)$$

A and θ_0 being the two constants of integration.

In order that this may be a uniform function of θ, it is necessary that ·

$$2\pi \frac{\sqrt{2mE}}{h} R = n, \text{ or } E_n = \frac{n^2h^2}{8\pi^2 mR^2} = \frac{n^2h^2}{8\pi^2 I}. \qquad . \qquad (8)$$

We thus obtain formula (4) again

The proper functions corresponding to these values are by (7) .

$$a_n = A \sin n(\theta - \theta_0) \qquad . \quad . \quad . \qquad (9)$$

and the reduced stable waves are ·

$$\psi_n = A \sin n(\theta - \theta_0) e^{\frac{2\pi i}{h}(E_n t + \alpha)}. \qquad . \qquad (10)$$

The functions (9) form an orthogonal system, since .

$$\int_0^{2\pi} a_n a_{n'} R\, d\theta = 0 \quad \text{if } n \neq n'.$$

If the functions are to be normalised it is necessary to take $A = \frac{1}{\sqrt{\pi R}}$, since

$$R \int_0^{2\pi} \sin^2 n(\theta - \theta_0)\, d\theta = \pi R.$$

The probability cloud in this case corresponding to the stationary wave ψ_n is at rest, since the velocity, $\mathbf{v} = -\frac{1}{m} \text{grad } \phi$, of its elements is zero and the density of the cloud giving the probability of occurrence of the particle is $A^2 \sin^2 n(\theta - \theta_0)$

Instead of considering the stationary wave ψ_n, we can consider the stable waves

$$\psi'_n = A' e^{\frac{2\pi i}{h}\left\{E_n t \quad \frac{nh}{2\pi}(\theta - \theta_0) + \alpha\right\}}, \qquad . \quad . \qquad (11)$$

obtained by superposing two waves ψ_n. The probability elements associated with ψ'_n have the velocity :

$$v = -\frac{1}{mR}\frac{\partial \phi}{\partial \theta} = \pm \frac{1}{mR}\frac{nh}{2\pi}$$

i.e. by (3) the same velocity as the particle in classical mechanics. The probability of occurrence is in this case the same at all points of the circle.

2. The Rotator with a Free Axis

A rather more complicated case is that of the rotator about a movable axis. This consists of a particle of mass m which rotates on a sphere of radius R and according to ordinary mechanics it must describe a geodesic or great circle on the sphere. The quantum condition and the formula giving the energy in the stable states in the old quantum theory is thus the same as for the plane rotator.

In wave mechanics we begin with the wave equation:

$$\nabla^2 a + \frac{8\pi^2 m}{h^2} \mathrm{E} a = 0. \qquad (12)$$

a must be expressed by two variables, the colatitude θ and the longitude α.

On the sphere

$$ds^2 = \mathrm{R}^2 d\theta^2 + \mathrm{R}^2 \sin^2\theta \, d\alpha^2, \qquad (13)$$

the values of the g's in this case being .

$$\left.\begin{array}{c} g_{11} = \mathrm{R}^2, \quad g_{12} = 0, \quad g_{22} = \mathrm{R}^2 \sin^2\theta \\ g^{11} = \dfrac{1}{\mathrm{R}^2}, \quad g^{12} = 0, \quad g^{22} = \dfrac{1}{\mathrm{R}^2 \sin^2\theta} \\ g = \mathrm{R}^4 \sin^2\theta. \end{array}\right\} \qquad (14)$$

Hence :

$$\nabla^2 a = \frac{1}{\sqrt{g}} \sum_{ik} \frac{\partial}{\partial q_i}\left(\sqrt{g}\, g^{ik} \frac{\partial a}{\partial q_k}\right) = \frac{1}{\mathrm{R}^2 \sin\theta}\left\{\frac{\partial}{\partial\theta}\left(\sin\theta \frac{\partial a}{\partial\theta}\right) + \frac{\partial}{\partial\alpha}\left(\frac{1}{\sin\theta}\frac{\partial a}{\partial\alpha}\right)\right\}, \qquad (15)$$

and the final form of the wave equation is .

$$\frac{1}{\sin\theta}\frac{\partial}{\partial\theta}\left(\sin\theta\frac{\partial a}{\partial\theta}\right) + \frac{1}{\sin^2\theta}\frac{\partial^2 a}{\partial\alpha^2} + \frac{8\pi^2 m \mathrm{R}^2 \mathrm{E}}{h^2} a = 0 \qquad (16)$$

This equation has been studied and it is known that it has a uniform, finite and continuous solution over the sphere only when the coefficient of a is equal to the product of two consecutive positive numbers, including zero.

The proper values of E are therefore :

$$E_n = n(n+1)\frac{h^2}{8\pi^2 m R^2}. \quad (n = 0, 1, \ldots .) \quad . \quad (17)$$

The corresponding proper functions are the spherical functions of Laplace $Y_n(\theta, \alpha)$ They can be expressed by means of trigonometrical functions and the Legendre polynomials. The latter are defined by the formula

$$P_n(x) = \frac{1}{2^n \underline{|n}} \frac{d^n}{dx^n}(1 - x^2)^n. \quad (18)$$

By means of these we define derived polynomials .

$$P_n^k(x) = (1 - x^2)^{\frac{k}{2}} \frac{d^k}{dx^k} P_n(x). \quad (19)$$

The functions of Laplace are given by :

$$Y_n(\theta, \alpha) = \sum_{k=0}^{k=n} (A_k \cos k\alpha + B_k \sin k\alpha)\, P_n^k(\cos\theta), \quad (20)$$

A_k and B_k being constants The stable stationary waves for the rotator can now be written in the form

$$\psi_{nk}(\theta, \alpha, t) = \sum_{k=0}^{k=n} (A_k \cos k\alpha + B_k \sin k\alpha)\, P_n^k(\cos\theta)\, e^{\frac{2\pi i}{h}(E_n t + \gamma)} \quad . \quad . \quad . \quad (21)$$

It will be noticed in this case that there is degeneration, since for a single value of E_n it is possible to obtain $(2n + 1)$ different functions by choosing the $(2n + 1)$ constants, A_0, A_1, B_1, . . . B_n arbitrarily. The functions Y_n are orthogonal, since they are the proper functions of a partial differential equation, and therefore the general theorem of the last chapter applies to them.

The probability elements associated with the stationary wave ψ_{nk} are at rest and their density at a point of the sphere is Y_n^2. Since several proper functions exist for a single proper value, it is possible to form many linear combinations of stationary waves giving a resultant monochromatic wave The simplest are of the form .

$$\psi'_{nk} = A' P_n^k(\cos\theta) e^{\frac{2\pi i}{h}\left(E_n t \pm \frac{kh\alpha}{2\pi} + \gamma\right)} \quad . \quad . \quad . \quad (22)$$

The probability elements associated with ψ'_{nk} describe parallel lines on the sphere with velocity:

$$v = -\frac{1}{m}|\text{grad}\,\phi| = \frac{kh}{2\pi m R \sin\alpha}.$$

The probability density is a function of the colatitude only, and is equal to $\{A'P_n^k(\cos\theta)\}^2$

More complicated motion could be obtained for the probability elements by combining stationary solutions corresponding to different orientations of the polar axis.

3. The Harmonic Oscillator

This case is that of a particle of mass m constrained to move along a straight line Ox under a force towards the point O proportional to the displacement from O ($= -kx$). In the old mechanics, as we have seen at the beginning of Chapter XVI, the frequency of vibration is independent of the amplitude, and has the value .

$$\omega = \frac{1}{2\pi}\sqrt{\frac{k}{m}} = \frac{1}{T}. \quad . \quad . \quad . \quad (23)$$

The old quantum theory gives for the energy of the stable states ·

$$E_n = nh\omega. \quad . \quad . \quad . \quad . \quad (24)$$

In the new mechanics the differential equation for the amplitude is:

$$\frac{d^2a}{dx^2} + \frac{8\pi^2m}{h^2}(E - \tfrac{1}{2}kx^2)a = 0. \quad . \quad (25)$$

Let

$$A = \frac{8\pi^2m}{h^2}, \qquad B = \frac{4\pi^2mk}{h^2} = \frac{16\pi^4m^2\omega^2}{h^2}, \quad . \quad (26)$$

so that (25) becomes ·

$$\frac{d^2a}{dx^2} + (AE - Bx^2)a = 0. \quad . \quad (27)$$

Change the variable to q where:

$$q = B^{\frac{1}{4}}x \quad . \quad . \quad . \quad (28)$$

and let

$$\frac{AE}{\sqrt{B}} = \lambda, \quad . \quad . \qquad (29)$$

then

$$\frac{d^2a}{dq^2} + (\lambda - q^2)a = 0. \quad . \qquad (30)$$

The proper values of this equation will be shown to be

$$\lambda = 1, 3, 5, \ldots (2n + 1) \quad . \quad . \qquad (31)$$

After making the substitution .

$$a = e^{-\frac{1}{2}q^2}u \quad . \quad . \quad . \quad . \qquad (32)$$

in (30), we obtain :

$$\frac{d^2u}{dq^2} - 2q\frac{du}{dq} + (\lambda - 1)u = 0 \quad . \quad . \qquad (33)$$

Since u must be uniform, finite and continuous it can be expressed in the form of a series of positive powers of q

$$u = c_0 + c_1q + \ldots + c_nq^n + \ldots \qquad (34)$$

By substitution in (33) and equating to zero the coefficient of q^n it is found that :

$$c_{n+2} = \frac{2n + 1 - \lambda}{(n + 1)(n + 2)}c_n. \quad . \quad . \qquad (35)$$

All the c's with an even suffix can be expressed in terms of c_0, those with an odd suffix in terms of c_1. The constants c_0 and c_1 are the constants of integration of the equation (33). Let it be supposed in the first instance that λ is an odd number $(2k + 1)$, where k is, of course, even or odd. If k is even let c_1 be taken equal to zero and let c_0 have any value ; if k is odd let c_0 be zero and let c_1 have any value. In this way we obtain for u a polynomial of degree k known as the kth polynomial of Hermite and denoted by $H_k(q)$ The function $a = e^{-\frac{1}{2}q^2}H_k$ is uniform, finite and continuous, and has the value zero for $q = \pm\infty$, it is a proper function of equation (30). If c_0 and c_1 be chosen in any other way a finite number of terms will be obtained with an exponent of a particular parity and an infinite number with an exponent of opposite parity, and as u then tends to infinity more rapidly than $e^{\frac{q^2}{2}}$ as

q increases indefinitely, the corresponding function a is not a proper function.

If it be supposed that λ is not equal to an odd integer, whatever the values of c_0 and c_1 a series is obtained for u which becomes infinite more rapidly than $e^{\frac{q^2}{2}}$ as q increases indefinitely, and the corresponding function a is unsuitable. In short, the differential equation has only a uniform, finite and continuous solution which vanishes at infinity when $\lambda = 2k + 1$, k being zero or a positive integer. The corresponding proper functions are

$$a_k(q) = e^{-\frac{q^2}{2}} \mathrm{H}_k(q). \quad . \quad . \quad . \quad (36)$$

It is known from the theory of these polynomials that the functions a_k are orthogonal, but this follows from the general theorem on the orthogonality of proper functions of equations of the type (30). It can also be shown that .

$$\int_{-\infty}^{\infty} \mathrm{H}_n^2 e^{-q^2} dq = 2^n \underline{|n} \sqrt{\pi}, \quad . \quad (37)$$

so that when the functions are normalised :

$$a_k(q) = \frac{1}{\pi^{\frac{1}{4}} \sqrt{2^k \underline{|k}}} e^{-\frac{q^2}{2}} \mathrm{H}_k(q) \quad (38)$$

Returning to the problem of quantisation, it follows from these results that the proper values of (27) are given by :

$$\mathrm{E}_k = (2k + 1)\frac{\sqrt{\mathrm{B}}}{\mathrm{A}} = (2k + 1)\frac{h\omega}{2} = \left(k + \frac{1}{2}\right)h\omega. \quad (39)$$

This result is remarkable, for we obtain in this way the half quantum expression which was suggested by experiment but which could not be deduced from the old quantum theory. The normalised proper function of (27) corresponding to E_k is

$$a_k(x) = \frac{1}{\pi^{\frac{1}{4}} \sqrt{2^k \underline{|k}}} e^{-\frac{2\pi^2 m\omega}{h} x^2} \mathrm{H}_k\left(2\pi \sqrt{\frac{m\omega}{h}}\, x\right), \quad . \quad (40)$$

and the stationary wave of order k is .

$$\psi_k(x, t) = \frac{1}{\pi^{\frac{1}{4}} \sqrt{2^k \underline{|k}}} e^{-\frac{2\pi^2 m\omega}{h} x^2} \mathrm{H}_k\left(2\pi \sqrt{\frac{m\omega}{h}}\, x\right) e^{\frac{2\pi i}{h}\left(k + \frac{1}{2}\right)\omega t}. \quad (41)$$

When the state of the oscillator is represented by ψ_k, the probability elements are at rest and the probability of occurrence at the point x is :

$$\frac{1}{2^k|\underline{k}\sqrt{\pi}}\, e^{-\frac{4\pi^2 m\omega}{h}x^2}\, H_k^2\left(2\pi\sqrt{\frac{m\omega}{h}}\,x\right)$$

The particle can occupy any position along Ox, but the probability that it is far from the origin is very small In the old mechanics the motion took place along a limited portion of Ox, the extremities of this limited strip being the points where the particle turned back along its path. There is thus a great difference in this respect between the old and new mechanics A harmonic oscillator may be considered in two or three dimensions ; in the latter the particle can be displaced in three directions and with a suitable choice of rectangular axes the potential energy may be written in the form ·

$$F = \tfrac{1}{2}(k_1x^2 + k_2y^2 + k_3z^2). \qquad . \quad (42)$$

Write :

$$\psi(x, y, z, t) = a_1(x)\, a_2(y)\, a_3(z)\, e^{\frac{2\pi i}{h}(E_1 + E_2 + E_3)t} \qquad . \quad (43)$$

The wave equation divides into three equations of the form :

$$\frac{d^2a_1}{dx^2} + \frac{8\pi^2 m}{h^2}\left(E_1 - \frac{k_1x^2}{2}\right) a_1 = 0. \qquad . \quad (44)$$

From the result obtained for the linear oscillator it follows that the quantised energy values are .

$$E_{n_1 n_2 n_3} = E_1 + E_2 + E_3 = (n_1 + \tfrac{1}{2})h\omega_1 + (n_2 + \tfrac{1}{2})h\omega_2 + (n_3 + \tfrac{1}{2})h\omega_3, \quad (45)$$

where

$$\omega_i = \frac{1}{2\pi}\sqrt{\frac{k_i}{m}}. \quad (i = 1, 2, 3) \qquad . \quad . \quad (46)$$

The amplitude of the stationary ψ-waves is expressed as a product of Hermite's polynomials.

If two of the constants k_i are equal, there is partial degeneration ; if all are equal there is complete degeneration and the oscillator is isotropic. In both cases several quantised energy values coincide ; in other words, there are several stable states for a single proper energy value.

4. The Hydrogen Atom

We now consider the very important case of the hydrogen atom formed by a fixed nucleus of charge $+e$ and of a planetary electron of charge $-e$. We will take a system of spherical co-ordinates about the nucleus; $\alpha =$ the longitude, $\theta =$ the colatitude, $r =$ the radius vector. In spherical co-ordinates we have, for the line element:

$$ds^2 = dr^2 + r^2 d\theta^2 + r^2 \sin^2\theta \, d\alpha^2, \qquad (47)$$

whence

$$\left.\begin{aligned} g_{11} &= 1, \quad g_{22} = r^2, \quad g_{33} = r^2 \sin^2\theta, \quad g_{ik} = 0 \text{ when } i \neq k, \\ g^{11} &= 1, \quad g^{22} = \frac{1}{r^2}, \quad g^{33} = \frac{1}{r^2 \sin^2\theta}, \quad g^{ik} = 0 \text{ when } i \neq k, \\ g &= r^4 \sin^2\theta \end{aligned}\right\} \qquad (48)$$

The equation for a is therefore:

$$\frac{1}{\sqrt{g}} \sum_{ik} \frac{\partial}{\partial q_i}\left(\sqrt{g}\, g^{ik} \frac{\partial a}{\partial q_k}\right) + \frac{8\pi^2 m}{h^2}\left(\mathrm{E} + \frac{e^2}{r}\right) a = 0, \qquad (49)$$

which becomes in this case:

$$\frac{\partial^2 a}{\partial r^2} + \frac{2}{r}\frac{\partial a}{\partial r} + \frac{1}{r^2 \sin^2\theta}\frac{\partial}{\partial\theta}\left(\sin\theta \frac{\partial a}{\partial\theta}\right) + \frac{1}{r^2 \sin^2\theta}\frac{\partial^2 a}{\partial \alpha^2} + \frac{8\pi^2 m}{h^2}\left(\mathrm{E} + \frac{e^2}{r}\right) a = 0. \qquad (50)$$

Schrödinger has shown that this equation possesses uniform, finite and continuous solutions, vanishing at infinity, for all positive values of E and for the negative values:

$$\mathrm{E}_n = -\frac{2\pi^2 m e^4}{n^2 h^2}, \quad (n = \text{an integer.}) \qquad (51)$$

The positive proper values correspond to the hyperbolic trajectories of the old mechanics, the negative values correspond to the stable states already obtained by Bohr, for the formula (51) is identical with the fundamental formula of Bohr's theory.

It should be noted that we have a continuous series of proper values prolonging a discontinuous series and we have mentioned that this state of affairs can arise when the domain

D of the problem of proper vibrations is infinite, which is the case here.

The problem presents a case of degeneration; several proper functions correspond to each proper value (51), each requiring for its complete determination two integers, k and k_1, such that:

$$0 \leqslant k < n, \quad 0 \leqslant k_1 \leqslant k. \qquad . \qquad . \quad (52)$$

According to Schrodinger's calculations, the stationary wave corresponding to the three integers n, k, k_1, is given by:

$$\psi_{nkk_1}(r, \theta, \alpha, t) = (\mathrm{A} \cos k_1\alpha + \mathrm{B} \sin k_1\alpha)\mathrm{P}_k^{k_1}(\cos \theta)x^k e^{-x}\mathrm{L}_{n+k}^{2k+1}(x)\, e^{\frac{2\pi i}{h}(\mathrm{E}_n t + \gamma)}, \quad (53)$$

A, B and γ being constants, and x denoting the quantity $\frac{4\pi^2 me^2}{n^2h^2}r$. The polynomials $\mathrm{P}_k^{k_1}$ (cos θ) were defined in § 2 of this chapter, and the function $\mathrm{L}_{n+k}^{2k+1}(x)$ is a polynomial in x which depends upon the polynomials of Laguerre, which we will not explain further here.

The probability elements associated with ψ_{nkk_1} are at rest and the density of the probability cloud is proportional to the square of the amplitude. It should be noted that, as in the case of the oscillator, the electron has a certain probability of being at any distance from the nucleus, but the probability diminishes rapidly with the distance. In the old dynamics, on the other hand, the electron with negative energy E_n could not lie outside the sphere of radius:

$$\mathrm{R}_n = -\frac{e^2}{\mathrm{E}_n}, \qquad . \qquad . \qquad . \quad (54)$$

because outside this sphere the kinetic energy would have to be negative, and this would be impossible.

A large number of stable monochromatic waves can be obtained by combining stationary waves of the type (53). It suffices to add together several ψ_{nkk_1} corresponding to the same value of n, but with different values of k and k_1 or with different orientations of the polar axis. One of the simplest combinations is

$$\psi'_{nkk_1} = \mathrm{A}'\mathrm{P}_k^{k_1} (\cos \theta)x^k e^{-x}\mathrm{L}_{n+k}^{2k+1}(x)e^{\frac{2\pi i}{h}\left(\mathrm{E}_n t \pm \frac{k_1 h}{2\pi}\alpha + \gamma\right)}. \quad (55)$$

The probability elements associated with the stable wave (55) describe circles about the polar axis with a velocity related to r and θ by the formula :

$$v = -\frac{1}{m}|\text{grad}\ \phi| = -\frac{1}{mr\sin\theta}\frac{\partial\phi}{\partial\alpha} = \pm\frac{k_1 h}{2\pi mr\sin\theta} \qquad (56)$$

which is to be compared with $mvr = \frac{k_1 h}{2\pi}$ applied by the old quantum theory to the particle itself.

CHAPTER XIX

THE MEANING OF THE ψ-WAVES OF QUANTISED SYSTEMS

1. Application of General Principles to Quantised Systems

THE general wave equation for a system subject to no perturbations is

$$\frac{1}{\sqrt{\mu}} \sum_{ik} \frac{\partial}{\partial q_i} \left(\sqrt{\mu}\, \mu^{ik} \frac{\partial \psi}{\partial q_k} \right) - \frac{8\pi^2}{h^2} F\psi = \frac{4\pi i}{h} \frac{\partial \psi}{\partial t} \quad . \quad (1)$$

and if the system consists of a single particle as in the cases studied in the last chapter, this reduces to:

$$\frac{1}{m} \nabla^2 \psi - \frac{8\pi^2}{h^2} F\psi = \frac{4\pi i}{h} \frac{\partial \psi}{\partial t} \quad . \quad . \quad (2)$$

Both equations are satisfied by all the linear combinations of the stationary ψ-waves having frequencies equal to the proper values, E_k divided by h, conversely any uniform, finite and continuous function vanishing at infinity can be expanded as a series of fundamental functions. It is therefore always possible to write:

$$\psi(q_i, t) = \sum_k c_k a_k (q_i)\, e^{\frac{2\pi i}{h}(E_k t + \gamma_k)}, \quad . \quad (3)$$

the functions a_k being orthogonal and supposed normalised.

The c_k's will be supposed to be chosen in such a way that $\sum_k c_k^2 = 1$, which is always possible, since ψ contains a disposable constant factor. In order to explain the meaning of the ψ-wave we must make use of the two fundamental principles: the principle of interference and of spectral distribution.

According to the former the probability of occurrence of the particle in space or of the representative point in generalised space is :

$$\psi\psi^* = \sum_{kl} c_k c_l a_k a_l e^{\frac{2\pi i}{h}\{(E_k - E_l)t + \gamma_k - \gamma_l\}}$$

$$= \sum_{k,} c_k^2 a_k^2 + 2\sum_{k<l} c_k c_l a_k a_l \cos\frac{2\pi}{h}\{(E_k - E_l)t + \gamma_k - \gamma_l\}. \quad (4)$$

It is rather remarkable that this expression contains exactly the frequencies $\frac{E_k - E_l}{h}$ which occur in Bohr's theory, and which give the frequencies of the lines of an atomic spectrum as differences of the spectral terms $\frac{E_k}{h}$.

The expression (4) gives the absolute probability for on integration :

$$\int \psi\psi^* \, d\tau = 1, \quad . \quad . \quad . \quad (5)$$

on account of the relations :

$$\int a_k a_l \, d\tau = 0, \quad \int a_k^2 \, d\tau = 1, \quad \sum_k c_k^2 = 1 \quad . \quad . \quad (6)$$

How must we state the principle of spectral distribution in this case ? Born's view is that c_k^2 is the probability that the quantised system, of which the associated wave has the form (3), is to be found after an observation in the stationary state of index k. In fact, the intensity $c_k^2 a_k^2$ of the spectral component of frequency $\frac{E_k}{h}$ in the series (3) is variable from point to point but the total intensity of this component $\int c_k^2 a_k^2 \, d\tau$ is equal to c_k^2, since the a_k are normalised and it is therefore natural to regard the c_k^2 as the relative probabilities of the various states of the system associated with the wave (3).

This statement of the principle of spectral distribution for quantised systems appears at first sight to raise a difficulty which it is interesting to examine. We can consider it in its application to a single particle which we will suppose is in any one of its stable states. The probability that it is in the state E_k is c_k^2, but when it is in this state the probability that it will be found at the point (x, y, z) is a_k^2, thus by the theorems of total and combined probabilities the probability that the particle is at (x, y, z) is equal to $\sum_k c_k^2 a_k^2$. But this is not equal to $\psi\psi^*$, for in (4) the frequency terms occur in addition to this term. It follows that there is a contradiction between the two fundamental principles.

This is the nature of the objection, and to remove it the exact meaning attributed to the ψ-wave by the theory of Bohr and Heisenberg must be remembered. Our information regarding a quantised system may be summed up in the form of the ψ-wave of formula (3), but that does not mean that the system is actually in one of the quantised states The probability the energy state E_k exists is c_k^2 A knowledge of the ψ-wave only tells us that if we make an experiment allowing us to assign a position to the particle in the quantised system the possibility that it lies in the element $dx\,dy\,dz$ is $\psi\psi^*\,dx\,dy\,dz$, and if, on the other hand, we make an experiment permitting us to assign an energy state to the particle, there is a probability c_k^2 of finding it in the state E_k But it is the essence of the view of Bohr and Heisenberg to admit that these two experiments will affect the initial state of affairs and will affect it in different ways. This is why the application of the theorem of compound probability is not justified. If to determine the position of the particle we begin by finding its energy state and then its position, the probability of finding the particle at (x, y, z) will be $\sum_k c_k^2 a_k^2$, but there is no reason why this should be the probability of finding the particle at (x, y, z) by a direct measurement of the position from its initial state since the preliminary determination of the energy disturbs the situation. In short, the interest of this objection is that it shows that if we wish to maintain side by side the two principles of interference and of spectral distribution it is necessary to admit that a quantised system is disturbed by all processes of measurement and of observation.

2. The Influence of Perturbations on a Quantised System

We shall suppose that the system is subject to an external perturbation which may depend on the time. The potential energy $F(q_i, t)$ consists now of two terms, a term $V(q_i)$ arising from reactions in the component parts of the system and a term $R(q_i, t)$ from the external perturbing field.

When this perturbation is absent Schrodinger's equation is :

$$\frac{1}{\sqrt{\mu}}\sum_{ik}\frac{\partial}{\partial q_i}\left(\sqrt{\mu}\,\mu^{ik}\frac{\partial a}{\partial q_i}\right) + \frac{8\pi^2}{h^2}(E - V)a = 0. \qquad (7)$$

The most general ψ-wave for the system is

$$\psi = \sum_k c_k\, a_k\, e^{\frac{2\pi i}{h}(E_k t + \gamma_k)}, \quad . \quad . \quad . \quad (8)$$

where the a's are supposed normalised and c_k and γ_k are real constants.

When the perturbation is present the equation is .

$$\frac{1}{\sqrt{\mu}}\sum_{ik}\frac{\partial}{\partial q_i}\left(\sqrt{\mu}\,\mu^{ik}\frac{\partial \psi}{\partial q_k}\right) - \frac{8\pi^2}{h^2}(V + R)\psi = \frac{4\pi i}{h}\frac{\partial \psi}{\partial t}. \qquad (9)$$

The simplest method of obtaining solutions of this equation is to substitute :

$$\psi = \sum_k c_k\, a_k\, e^{\frac{2\pi i}{h}(E_k t + \gamma_k)}, \quad . \quad . \quad (10)$$

and suppose that c_k and γ_k depend on the time , this is Dirac's method of variation of the constants Substituting (10) in (9) we obtain

$$\frac{4\pi i}{h}\sum_k a_k\, e^{\frac{2\pi i}{h}(E_k t + \gamma_k)}\left(\dot{c}_k + \frac{2\pi i}{h}c_k\dot{\gamma}_k\right) + \frac{8\pi^2}{h^2}R\sum_k c_k\, a_k\, e^{\frac{2\pi i}{h}(E_k t + \gamma_k)} = 0. \qquad (11)$$

If we multiply by $a_l\, d\tau$ and integrate over the generalised space we obtain .

$$\frac{4\pi i}{h}\left(\dot{c}_l + \frac{2\pi i}{h}c_l\dot{\gamma}_l\right)e^{\frac{2\pi i}{h}(E_l t + \gamma_l)} + \frac{8\pi^2}{h^2}\sum_k c_k\, e^{\frac{2\pi i}{h}(E_k t + \gamma_k)}\int R\, a_k\, a_l\, d\tau = 0 \qquad (12)$$

The integral is the element (kl) of the matrix which corresponds to the operation of multiplication by R, and we denote it by

$R_{kl}(t)$. Thus:

$$\dot{c}_l + \frac{2\pi i}{h} c_l \dot{\gamma}_l = \frac{2\pi i}{h} \sum_k R_{kl} c_k e^{\frac{2\pi i}{h}\{(E_k - E_l)t + \gamma_k - \gamma_l\}} \qquad (13)$$

and the conjugate complex expression is:

$$\dot{c}_l - \frac{2\pi i}{h} c_l \dot{\gamma}_l = -\frac{2\pi i}{h} \sum_k R_{kl} c_k e^{-\frac{2\pi i}{h}\{(E_k - E_l)t + \gamma_k - \gamma_l\}}. \qquad (14)$$

By addition and subtraction of (13) and (14) we obtain the real equations.

$$\dot{c}_l = -\frac{2\pi}{h}\sum_k R_{kl} c_k \sin \frac{2\pi}{h}\{(E_k - E_l)t + \gamma_k - \gamma_l\} \qquad (15)$$

$$c_l\dot{\gamma}_l = \sum_k R_{kl} c_k \cos \frac{2\pi}{h}\{(E_k - E_l)t + \gamma_k - \gamma_l\}. \qquad (16)$$

From these simultaneous equations c_l and γ_l can be determined if their initial values are known

According to Born the quantity c_k^2 gives the probability that the system is in the energy state E_k at time t. $\sum_k c_k^2$ is supposed equal to unity at the beginning of the perturbation and must remain equal to unity throughout. It is easy to verify this, for by (15):

$$\sum_l c_l \dot{c}_l = \sum_l \frac{1}{2}\frac{d}{dt}(c_l^2)$$

$$= -\frac{2\pi}{h}\sum_{kl} R_{kl} c_k c_l \sin \frac{2\pi}{h}\{(E_k - E_l)t + \gamma_k - \gamma_l\}. \qquad (17)$$

and the right-hand side is zero, since a change of sign occurs in any term when the indices k, l are interchanged, thus $\sum_l c_l^2$ is constant and maintains its initial value unity.

Born's hypothesis in the form we have stated it raises a little difficulty The functions $\psi_k = a_k e^{\frac{2\pi i}{h}(E_k t + \gamma_k)}$ represent the stationary waves corresponding to the value of the potential energy when the perturbation is non-existent, but at an instant τ during the perturbation the potential energy is $V(q_i)+R(q_i, \tau)$

he proper values and functions at this instant are those of quation ·

$$\sum_{ik} \frac{\partial}{\partial q_i}\left(\sqrt{\mu}\,\mu^{ik}\frac{\partial a}{\partial q_k}\right) + \frac{8\pi^2}{h^2}\{E - V(q_i) - R(q_i, \tau)\}a = 0, \quad (18)$$

e τ is regarded as a constant parameter. The proper s E_k^τ of this equation must be considered as the energies e stable states at the time τ. If an experiment is made ne τ to determine the energy of the system, one of the s E_k^τ may be found, but there can be no reason why one e values E_k corresponding to the absence of the perturba- hould be found. Let a_k^τ denote one of the proper functions sponding to E_k^τ for equation (18), then ψ must be expanded eries of proper functions in the form :

$$\psi = \sum_k d_k a_k^\tau e^{\frac{2\pi i}{h}(E_k^\tau t + \delta_k)} \quad . \quad . \quad (19)$$

he quantity d_k^2 will determine the probability that the n is in the energy state E_k^τ at time τ (Fock).

the perturbation has a limited duration beginning at 0 ending at T, $R(q_i, 0) = R(q_i, T) = 0$, and consequently $E_k^0 = E_k^T$ The coefficients c_k of (8) may therefore be to determine the probability that at the end of the per- tion the system is in the state E_k, the probability being

this case the difficulty disappears because the proper s of equation (8) have resumed their original values at nd of the perturbation. It will be possible in this way to late, as Born does, the probability that the perturbation e system has attained a particular state. We shall not into the developments and applications of these general which might well form the subject of a complete volume ; ices to point out how the principle of spectral distribution application in this case.

3. The Probability Cloud and the Heisenberg Matrices

is impossible to develop here Schrödinger's theory of the on of radiation by atoms and the method of the Heisen- matrices. We shall content ourselves with showing how the matrix elements can be introduced in the simple case of the hydrogen atom by considering the probability cloud associated with the ψ-wave. In the hydrogen atom there is a single particle and it is sufficient to take three rectangular co-ordinates (q_1, q_2, q_3). We shall define the six operations Q^i and P^i by the formulæ

$$\left.\begin{aligned} Q^i &= \text{multiplication by } q_i \\ P^i &= \frac{h}{2\pi i}\frac{\partial}{\partial q_i} \quad (i = 1, 2, 3.) \end{aligned}\right\} \quad . \quad (20)$$

From the definition of the matrix elements corresponding to an operator (Chap. XVII (61)) we obtain the elements with indices k, l of the six matrices corresponding to Q^i and P^i as follows

$$Q^i_{kl} = \int a_k\, a_l\, q_i\, d\tau, \quad . \quad (21)$$

$$P^i_{kl} = \int a_k \frac{h}{2\pi i}\frac{\partial a_l}{\partial q_i} d\tau, \quad . \quad (22)$$

the a_k being normalised proper functions for the hydrogen atom.

Let the wave function for the atom in question be supposed to be :

$$\psi = \sum_k c_k\, a_k\, e^{2\pi i(\nu_k t + \gamma_k)} \quad . \quad . \quad (23)$$

The density of the corresponding probability cloud is :

$$\rho = a^2 = \sum_k c_k^2 a_k^2 + 2\sum_{k<l} c_k c_l a_k a_l \cos 2\pi\{(\nu_k - \nu_l)t + \gamma_k - \gamma_l\} \quad (24)$$

and by (37) Chapter IX, the q_i-component of velocity of the probability elements is .

$$v_i = -\frac{1}{m}\frac{\partial\phi}{\partial q_i} = -\frac{h}{4\pi i m}\,\frac{\psi^*\dfrac{\partial\psi}{\partial q_i} - \psi\dfrac{\partial\psi^*}{\partial q_i}}{a^2}$$

$$= \frac{h}{2\pi m a^2}\sum_{k<l} c_k c_l\left(a_k\frac{\partial a_l}{\partial q_i} - a_l\frac{\partial a_k}{\partial q_i}\right)\sin 2\pi\{(\nu_k - \nu_l)t + \gamma_k - \gamma_l\}. \quad (25)$$

Let the electric charge of the electron be supposed equally divided amongst the probability elements so that the total charge is:

$$\int \rho e \, d\tau = e.$$

We may say that the density represents the average probable density of electricity in the atom and the q_i-component of the electric moment of the probability cloud is:

$$M_i = \int \rho e q_i d\tau = 2\sum_{k<l} c_k c_l e \int a_k a_l q_i \cos 2\pi\{(\nu_k - \nu_l)t + \gamma_k - \gamma_l\} d\tau. \quad (26)$$

This component contains terms varying periodically with frequencies $(\nu_k - \nu_l)$, which are the Bohr frequencies, and the amplitude corresponding to the frequency $(\nu_k - \nu_l)$ is proportional to Q^i_{kl}. This indicates a possible physical interpretation of the elements of Heisenberg's matrix Q^i.

Since the electric density of the cloud varies with the time it is the seat of electric currents The q_i-component of the current within the cloud is:

$$J_i = \int \rho e v_i d\tau \quad . \quad (27)$$

and by (25),

$$J_i = \frac{he}{2\pi m}\int \sum_{k<l} c_k c_l \left(a_k \frac{\partial a_l}{\partial q_i} - a_l \frac{\partial a_k}{\partial q_i}\right) \sin 2\pi\{(\nu_k - \nu_l)t + \gamma_k - \nu_l\} d\tau$$

= the real part of:

$$\frac{2e}{m}\sum_{k<l} c_k c_l \frac{h}{4\pi i}\int \left(a_k \frac{\partial a_l}{\partial q_i} - a_l \frac{\partial a_k}{\partial q_i}\right) e^{2\pi i\{(\nu_k - \nu_l)t + (\gamma_k - \gamma_l)\}} d\tau. \quad (28)$$

The components of the current are thus decomposed into periodic terms with Bohr frequencies and with amplitudes proportional in a typical case to:

$$\frac{h}{4\pi i}\int \left(a_k \frac{\partial a_l}{\partial q_i} - a_l \frac{\partial a_k}{\partial q_i}\right) d\tau = \frac{h}{2\pi i}\int a_k \frac{\partial a_l}{\partial q_i} d\tau = P^i_{kl}, \quad . \quad (29)$$

the equality of the two integral terms following from an integration by parts and the vanishing of the a_k at infinity This gives a possible physical interpretation of the Heisenberg matrix components P^i_{kl}

It follows also that if δ denote the electric density of the probability cloud and j_i a typical component of the corresponding current :

$$\delta = \rho e = e\psi\psi^* \quad . \quad . \quad . \quad . \quad . \quad (30)$$

$$j_i = \rho e v_i = -\frac{he}{4\pi i m}\left(\psi^*\frac{\partial\psi}{\partial q_i} - \psi\frac{\partial\psi^*}{\partial q_i}\right) \quad . \quad (31)$$

The formula (30) has been proposed by Schrödinger in his celebrated works on wave mechanics, where he regards δ as an actual electric density. (31) was first given by Gordon in a more general form in his memoir on the Compton effect

INDEX

PRINTED IN GREAT BRITAIN AT THE UNIVERSITY PRESS, ABERDEEN

METHUEN'S GENERAL LITERATURE

A SELECTION OF

MESSRS. METHUEN'S PUBLICATIONS

This Catalogue contains only a selection of the more important books published by Messrs. Methuen. A complete catalogue of their publications may be obtained on application.

PART I. GENERAL LITERATURE

Ashby (Thomas)
SOME ITALIAN FESTIVALS With 24 Illustrations. *Crown 8vo* 7s 6d *net*

Bain (F. W.)
A DIGIT OF THE MOON THE DESCENT OF THE SUN A HEIFER OF THE DAWN IN THE GREAT GOD'S HAIR A DRAUGHT OF THE BLUE AN ESSENCE OF THE DUSK AN INCARNATION OF THE SNOW. A MINE OF FAULTS THE ASHES OF A GOD BUBBLES OF THE FOAM A SYRUP OF THE BEES THE LIVERY OF EVE THE SUBSTANCE OF A DREAM *All Fcap 8vo* 5s *net* AN ECHO OF THE SPHERES *Wide Demy 8vo.* 10s 6d *net*

Balfour (Sir Graham)
THE LIFE OF ROBERT LOUIS STEVENSON *Twentieth Edition In one Volume Cr. 8vo* *Buckram*, 7s 6d. *net*.

Barker (Ernest)
NATIONAL CHARACTER *Demy 8vo* 10s 6d. *net* GREEK POLITICAL THEORY · Plato and his Predecessors. *Second Edition. Demy 8vo* 14s *net*

Belloc (Hilaire)
PARIS THE PYRENEES *Each* 8s 6d *net* ON NOTHING HILLS AND THE SEA ON SOMETHING THIS AND THAT AND THE OTHER. ON. *Each* 6s. *net* FIRST AND LAST. ON EVERYTHING ON ANYTHING EMMANUEL BURDEN *Each* 3s. 6d *net*. MARIE ANTOINETTE 18s. *net* A HISTORY OF ENGLAND In 5 vols Vols. I, II and III. 15s *net each* HILLS AND THE SEA Illustrated in Colour by Donald Maxwell 15s. *net*

Birmingham (George A.)
A WAYFARER IN HUNGARY Illustrated 8s. 6d *net* SPILLIKINS SHIPS AND SEALING-WAX Two Books of Essays *Each* 3s 6d. *net*.

Budge (Sir E. A. Wallis)
A HISTORY OF ETHIOPIA NUBIA AND ABYSSINIA Illustrated In 2 vols. £3 13s 6d *net*.

Bulley (M. H)
ART AND COUNTERFEIT Illustrated 15s *net* ANCIENT AND MEDIEVAL ART. A SHORT HISTORY *Second Edition, Revised Crown 8vo* 10s 6d *net*

Chandler (Arthur), D D.
ARA CŒLI 5s *net* FAITH AND EXPERIENCE 5s *net* THE CULT OF THE PASSING MOMENT 6s *net* THE ENGLISH CHURCH AND REUNION 5s. *net* SCALA MUNDI 4s 6d *net*.

Chesterton (G. K.)
THE BALLAD OF THE WHITE HORSE 3s 6d *net*. Also illustrated by ROBERT AUSTIN. 12s 6d *net* CHARLES DICKENS *Each Fcap. 8vo.* 3s 6d *net* ALL THINGS CONSIDERED TREMENDOUS TRIFLES. FANCIES VERSUS

Grahame (Kenneth)
THE WIND IN THE WILLOWS *Nineteenth Edition Crown 8vo.* 7s. 6d. *net* Also, illustrated by WYNDHAM PAYNE *Small 4to* 7s 6d *net* Also unillustrated *Fcap 8vo* 3s 6d *net.*

Hadfield (J. A.)
PSYCHOLOGY AND MORALS *Seventh Edition Crown 8vo* 6s *net*

Hall (H. R.)
THE ANCIENT HISTORY OF THE NEAR EAST *Seventh Edition Revised Demy 8vo* £1 1s *net* THE CIVILIZATION OF GREECE IN THE BRONZE AGE Illustrated *Wide Royal 8vo* £1 10s *net*

Hamer (Sir W. H.) and Hutt (C. W.)
A MANUAL OF HYGIENE Illustrated *Demy 8vo.* £1 10s *net.*

Heine (Heinrich)
FLORENTINE NIGHTS Translated by C G LELAND Illustrated in Colour by FELIX DE GRAY *Fcap 4to.* £1 5s *net*

Herbert (A. P.)
MISLEADING CASES IN THE COMMON LAW With an Introduction by LORD HEWART. 5s. *net.* THE BOMBER GIPSY 3s 6d *net* LIGHT ARTICLES ONLY Illustrated 6s *net* THE WHEREFORE AND THE WHY "TINKER, TAILOR" Each illustrated 3s 6d *net* THE SECRET BATTLE 3s 6d *net*

Hind (A. M.)
A CATALOGUE OF REMBRANDT'S ETCHINGS Two Vols Profusely Illustrated *Wide Royal 8vo* £1 15s *net*

Holdsworth (W. S)
A HISTORY OF ENGLISH LAW Nine Volumes *Demy 8vo* £1 5s *net each*

Hudson (W. H.)
A SHEPHERD'S LIFE Illustrated *Demy 8vo* 10s 6d *net* Also, unillustrated *Fcap. 8vo.* 3s 6d *net*

Hutton (Edward)
CITIES OF SICILY Illustrated 10s 6d *net* MILAN AND LOMBARDY THE CITIES OF ROMAGNA AND THE MARCHES SIENA AND SOUTHERN TUSCANY VENICE AND VENETIA THE CITIES OF SPAIN. NAPLES AND SOUTHERN ITALY Illustrated *Each,* 8s 6d *net.* A WAYFARER IN UNKNOWN TUSCANY THE CITIES OF UMBRIA. COUNTRY WALKS ABOUT FLORENCE. ROME FLORENCE AND NORTHERN TUSCANY. Each illustrated. 7s. 6d *net.*

Inge (W. R.), D.D., Dean of St Paul's
CHRISTIAN MYSTICISM. (The Bampton Lectures of 1899) *Sixth Edition. Crown 8vo* 7s 6d *net.*

Kipling (Rudyard)
BARRACK-ROOM BALLADS. 246*th Thousand*
THE SEVEN SEAS 180*th Thousand.*
THE FIVE NATIONS 143*rd Thousand*
DEPARTMENTAL DITTIES 111*th Thousand*
THE YEARS BETWEEN. 95*th Thousand*
Four Editions of these famous volumes of poems are now published, viz — *Crown 8vo Buckram,* 7s 6d *net Fcap 8vo Cloth,* 6s *net Leather,* 7s 6d *net* Service Edition Two volumes each book *Square Fcap 8vo* 3s *net* each volume
A KIPLING ANTHOLOGY—Verse *Fcap. 8vo Cloth,* 6s *net* and 3s 6d *net Leather,* 7s 6d *net* TWENTY POEMS FROM RUDYARD KIPLING 458*th Thousand Fcap 8vo* 1s *net* A CHOICE OF SONGS *Second Edition Fcap 8vo* 2s *net*

Lamb (Charles and Mary)
THE COMPLETE WORKS Edited by E V LUCAS A New and Revised Edition in Six Volumes With Frontispieces *Fcap 8vo* 6s *net each*
The volumes are. I MISCELLANEOUS PROSE II ELIA AND THE LAST ESSAYS OF ELIA III BOOKS FOR CHILDREN IV. PLAYS AND POEMS. V. and VI. LETTERS
SELECTED LETTERS Chosen and Edited by G T CLAPTON *Fcap 8vo.* 3s 6d *net*
THE CHARLES LAMB DAY BOOK. Compiled by E V LUCAS *Fcap 8vo* 6s *net*

Lankester (Sir Ray)
SCIENCE FROM AN EASY CHAIR SCIENCE FROM AN EASY CHAIR Second Series DIVERSIONS OF A NATURALIST. GREAT AND SMALL THINGS Illustrated. *Crown 8vo* 7s 6d *net.* SECRETS OF EARTH AND SEA. Illustrated. *Crown 8vo.* 8s 6d *net.*

Lodge (Sir Oliver)
MAN AND THE UNIVERSE (*Twentieth Edition*). THE SURVIVAL OF MAN (*Seventh Edition*) MODERN PROBLEMS *Each* 7s 6d *net.* RAYMOND (*Thirteenth Edition*). 10s 6d *net.* RAYMOND REVISED. 6s *net.* THE SUBSTANCE OF FAITH (*Fourteenth Edition*) 2s *net* RELATIVITY (*Fourth Edition*). 1s. *net.*

Lucas (E. V.)
THE LIFE OF CHARLES LAMB 2 Vols *£1 1s net* EDWIN AUSTIN ABBEY, R A 2 Vols *£6 6s net* THE COLVINS AND THEIR FRIENDS 12s *6d net* VERMEER OF DELFT 10s *6d net* A WANDERER IN ROME A WANDERER IN HOLLAND A WANDERER IN LONDON LONDON REVISITED (Revised) A WANDERER IN PARIS A WANDERER IN FLORENCE A WANDERER IN VENICE *Each* 10s *6d net* A WANDERER AMONG PICTURES 8s *6d net* E V LUCAS'S LONDON *£1 net* INTRODUCING LONDON INTRODUCING PARIS *Each* 2s *6d net* THE OPEN ROAD 6s *net* Also, illustrated by CLAUDE A SHEPPERSON, A R W S 10s *6d net* Also, India Paper *Leather*, 7s *6d net* THE JOY OF LIFE 6s *net* *Leather Edition* 7s *6d net* Also India Paper *Leather* 7s *6d net* FIRESIDE AND SUNSHINE CHARACTER AND COMEDY *Each* 6s *net* THE GENTLEST ART 6s *6d net* *And* THE SECOND POST 6s *net* Also, together in one volume 7s *6d net* HER INFINITE VARIETY GOOD COMPANY ONE DAY AND ANOTHER OLD LAMPS FOR NEW LOITERER'S HARVEST CLOUD AND SILVER A BOSWELL OF BAGHDAD 'TWIXT EAGLE AND DOVE THE PHANTOM JOURNAL GIVING AND RECEIVING LUCK OF THE YEAR ENCOUNTERS AND DIVERSIONS ZIGZAGS IN FRANCE EVENTS AND EMBROIDERIES 365 DAYS (AND ONE MORE) A FRONDED ISLE A ROVER I WOULD BE *Each* 6s *net* URBANITIES Illustrated by G L STAMPA 5s *net* YOU KNOW WHAT PEOPLE ARE Illustrated by GEORGE MORROW. 5s *net* THE SAME STAR A Comedy in Three Acts 3s *6d net* LITTLE BOOKS ON GREAT MASTERS *Each* 5s. *net* ROVING EAST AND ROVING WEST 5s *net* PLAYTIME AND COMPANY 7s *6d net* *Mr Punch's* COUNTY SONGS Illustrated by E H SHEPARD 10s *6d net* "THE MORE I SEE OF MEN . . ." OUT OF A CLEAR SKY *Each* 3s *6d net* See also **Dolls' House (The Queen's)** and **Lamb (Charles).**

Lucas (E. V.) and Finck (Herman)
TWELVE SONGS FROM "PLAYTIME AND COMPANY" Words by E V LUCAS. Music by HERMAN FINCK *Royal 4to* 7s *6d net*

Lynd (Robert)
THE LITTLE ANGEL 6s *net* THE GOLDFISH. THE PLEASURES OF IGNORANCE OLD FRIENDS IN FICTION. *Each* 5s *net* THE BLUE LION THE PEAL OF BELLS THE MONEY BOX THE ORANGE TREE. *Each* 3s *6d net*

McDougall (William)
AN INTRODUCTION TO SOCIAL PSYCHOLOGY (*Twenty-first Edition*) 10s *6d net* NATIONAL WELFARE AND NATIONAL DECAY 6s *net* AN OUTLINE OF PSYCHOLOGY (*Fourth Edition*) 10s *6d net* AN OUTLINE OF ABNORMAL PSYCHOLOGY 15s *net* BODY AND MIND (*Sixth Edition*) 12s *6d net* CHARACTER AND THE CONDUCT OF LIFE (*Third Edition*) 10s *6d net* ETHICS AND SOME MODERN WORLD PROBLEMS (*Second Edition*) 7s *6d net*

Mackenzie (W Mackay)
THE MEDIÆVAL CASTLE IN SCOTLAND (The Rhind Lectures on Archæology 1925–6) Illustrated *Demy 8vo* 15s *net*

Mallet (Sir C. E)
A HISTORY OF THE UNIVERSITY OF OXFORD In 3 vols Illustrated *Demy 8vo* *Each £1 1s net*

Maeterlinck (Maurice)
THE BLUE BIRD 6s *net* Also, illustrated by F CAYLEY ROBINSON 10s *6d net* DEATH 3s *6d net* OUR ETERNITY 6s *net.* THE UNKNOWN GUEST 6s *net* POEMS 5s *net* THE WRACK OF THE STORM 6s *net* THE MIRACLE OF ST ANTHONY 3s *6d net* THE BURGOMASTER OF STILEMONDE 5s *net.* THE BETROTHAL 6s *net* MOUNTAIN PATHS 6s *net* THE STORY OF TYLTYL *£1 1s net* THE GREAT SECRET 7s *6d net* THE CLOUD THAT LIFTED and THE POWER OF THE DEAD 7s *6d net* MARY MAGDALENE 2s *net*

Masefield (John)
ON THE SPANISH MAIN 8s *6d net* A SAILOR'S GARLAND 6s *net* and 3s. *6d net* SEA LIFE IN NELSON'S TIME 5s *net.*

Methuen (Sir A.)
AN ANTHOLOGY OF MODERN VERSE 137*th Thousand*
SHAKESPEARE TO HARDY An Anthology of English Lyrics 19*th Thousand*
Each Fcap 8vo Cloth, 6s. *net* *Leather,* 7s *6d net*

Milne (A. A.)
NOT THAT IT MATTERS IF I MAY THE SUNNY SIDE THE RED HOUSE MYSTERY ONCE A WEEK THE HOLIDAY ROUND. THE DAY'S PLAY *Each* 3s. *6d net* WHEN WE WERE VERY YOUNG. *Sixteenth Edition.* 169*th*

Thousand. WINNIE-THE-POOH *Sixth Edition 91st Thousand* NOW WE ARE SIX *Fourth Edition 109th Thousand* THE HOUSE AT POOH CORNER Each illustrated by E. H SHEPARD. *7s 6d net Leather, 10s 6d net* FOR THE LUNCHEON INTERVAL *1s 6d net*

Milne (A. A.) and Fraser-Simson (H.)
FOURTEEN SONGS FROM "WHEN WE WERE VERY YOUNG" *Twelfth Edition 7s 6d net* TEDDY BEAR AND OTHER SONGS FROM "WHEN WE WERE VERY YOUNG" *7s 6d net* THE KING'S BREAKFAST *Third Edition 3s 6d net* SONGS FROM "NOW WE ARE SIX" *Second Edition 7s 6d net* MORE SONGS FROM "NOW WE ARE SIX" *7s 6d net* Words by A. A MILNE. Music by H FRASER-SIMSON Decorations by E H SHEPARD

Montague (C. E.)
DRAMATIC VALUES. *Cr 8vo 7s 6d net.*

Morton (H. V.)
THE HEART OF LONDON *3s 6d net* (Also illustrated, *7s 6d net*) THE SPELL OF LONDON THE NIGHTS OF LONDON *Each 3s 6d net* THE LONDON YEAR. IN SEARCH OF ENGLAND THE CALL OF ENGLAND. Each illustrated *7s 6d net*

Oman (Sir Charles)
A HISTORY OF THE ART OF WAR IN THE MIDDLE AGES, A D. 378–1485 *Second Edition*, Revised and Enlarged 2 Vols Illustrated. *Demy 8vo. £1 16s net*

Oxenham (John)
BEES IN AMBER. *Small Pott 8vo 2s net* ALL'S WELL THE KING'S HIGHWAY THE VISION SPLENDID THE FIERY CROSS. HIGH ALTARS HEARTS COURAGEOUS ALL CLEAR! *Each Small Pott 8vo Paper, 1s 3d net. Cloth, 2s net.* WINDS OF THE DAWN. *2s. net*

Perry (W. J.)
THE ORIGIN OF MAGIC AND RELIGION THE GROWTH OF CIVILIZATION *Each 6s net.* THE CHILDREN OF THE SUN. *£1 1s net*

Petrie (Sir Flinders)
A HISTORY OF EGYPT In 6 Volumes. Vol I FROM THE IST TO THE XVITH DYNASTY *11th Edition, Revised 12s net.* Vol II THE XVIITH AND XVIIITH DYNASTIES *7th Edition, Revised 9s net.* Vol. III XIXTH TO XXXTH DYNASTIES *3rd Edition 12s net* Vol. IV. EGYPT UNDER THE PTOLEMAIC DYNASTY By EDWYN BEVAN *15s net.* Vol V. EGYPT UNDER ROMAN RULE. By J G MILNE. *3rd Edition, Revised 12s net* Vol. VI. EGYPT IN THE MIDDLE AGES By STANLEY LANE POOLE *4th Edition 10s net*

Ponsonby (Arthur), M P.
ENGLISH DIARIES *£1 1s net* MORE ENGLISH DIARIES *12s 6d net* SCOTTISH AND IRISH DIARIES *10s 6d net*

Raleigh (Sir Walter)
THE LETTERS OF SIR WALTER RALEIGH Edited by LADY RALEIGH Two Vols. Illustrated *Second Edition Demy 8vo 18s net* SELECTED LETTERS. Edited by LADY RALEIGH *7s 6d net*

Smith (C. Fox)
SAILOR TOWN DAYS SEA SONGS AND BALLADS. A BOOK OF FAMOUS SHIPS SHIP ALLEY *Each*, illustrated, *6s net.* FULL SAIL Illustrated *5s net* TALES OF THE CLIPPER SHIPS A SEA CHEST *Each 5s net* THE RETURN OF THE "CUTTY SARK" Illustrated *3s 6d net* A BOOK OF SHANTIES ANCIENT MARINERS *Each 6s net.*

Stevenson (R. L.)
THE LETTERS Edited by Sir SIDNEY COLVIN 4 Vols *Fcap 8vo. Each 6s net.*

Surtees (R. S.)
HANDLEY CROSS. MR. SPONGE'S SPORTING TOUR ASK MAMMA MR FACEY ROMFORD'S HOUNDS PLAIN OR RINGLETS? HILLINGDON HALL. *Each* illustrated, *7s 6d net* JORROCKS'S JAUNTS AND JOLLITIES. HAWBUCK GRANGE *Each*, illustrated, *6s net*

Taylor (A. E)
PLATO THE MAN AND HIS WORK *Second Edition Demy 8vo £1 1s. net*

Tilden (William T.)
THE ART OF LAWN TENNIS. SINGLES AND DOUBLES THE TENNIS RACKET *Each*, illustrated, *6s net* THE COMMON SENSE OF LAWN TENNIS MATCH PLAY AND THE SPIN OF THE BALL. Illustrated. *5s net*

Tileston (Mary W.)
DAILY STRENGTH FOR DAILY NEEDS *32nd Edition 3s 6d. net.* India Paper *Leather, 6s net*

Trapp (Oswald Graf)
THE ARMOURY OF THE CASTLE OF CHURBURG. Translated by J. G. MANN. Richly illustrated *Royal 4to.* Limited to 400 copies *£4 14s. 6d net.*

Underhill (Evelyn)
MYSTICISM (*Eleventh Edition*). *15s. net.*

THE LIFE OF THE SPIRIT AND THE LIFE OF TO-DAY (*Sixth Edition*) 7s 6d *net* MAN AND THE SUPERNATURAL 7s 6d *net* CONCERNING THE INNER LIFE (*Fourth Edition*) 2s. *net.*

Urwick (E J.)
THE SOCIAL GOOD. *Demy* 8*vo*. 10s. 6*d net*

Vardon (Harry)
HOW TO PLAY GOLF. Illustrated 19*th Edition* *Crown* 8*vo*. 5s *net*

Waterhouse (Elizabeth)
A LITTLE BOOK OF LIFE AND DEATH 23*rd Edition* *Small Pott* 8*vo* 2s 6d *net*

Wilde (Oscar)
THE WORKS In 17 Vols *Each* 6s. 6d. *net*
I. LORD ARTHUR SAVILE'S CRIME AND THE PORTRAIT OF MR. W. H. II THE DUCHESS OF PADUA III POEMS IV LADY WINDERMERE'S FAN V. A WOMAN OF NO IMPORTANCE VI AN IDEAL HUSBAND. VII. THE IMPORTANCE OF BEING EARNEST. VIII A HOUSE OF POMEGRANATES IX INTENTIONS X. DE PROFUNDIS AND PRISON LETTERS XI ESSAYS XII. SALOME, A FLORENTINE TRAGEDY, and LA SAINTE COURTISANE XIII A CRITIC IN PALL MALL XIV. SELECTED PROSE OF OSCAR WILDE. XV ART AND DECORATION. XVI FOR LOVE OF THE KING. (5s. *net*) XVII VERA, OR THE NIHILISTS.

Williamson (G. C.)
THE BOOK OF FAMILLE ROSE Richly Illustrated *Demy* 4*to* £8 8s *net*

PART II. A SELECTION OF SERIES

The Antiquary's Books
Each, illustrated, *Demy* 8*vo* 10s 6d *net*

The Arden Shakespeare
Edited by W J CRAIG and R H CASE *Each, wide Demy* 8*vo* 6s *net*
The Ideal Library Edition, in single plays, each edited with a full Introduction, Textual Notes and a Commentary at the foot of the page Now complete in 39 Vols

Classics of Art
Edited by J H W LAING *Each*, profusely illustrated, *wide Royal* 8*vo* 15s *net to* £3 3s *net*
A Library of Art dealing with Great Artists and with branches of Art.

The Connoisseur's Library
With numerous Illustrations Wide Royal 8*vo* £1 11s 6*d net each vol.*
EUROPEAN ENAMELS FINE BOOKS GLASS GOLDSMITHS' AND SILVERSMITHS' WORK. IVORIES JEWELLERY. MINIATURES MEZZOTINTS PORCELAIN. SEALS. MUSSULMAN PAINTING WATCHES

English Life in English Literature
General Editors. EILEEN POWER, M A, D Lit, and A W. REED, M A, D Lit *Each, Crown* 8*vo*, 6s *net*
A series of source-books for students of history and of literature

The Faiths: VARIETIES OF CHRISTIAN EXPRESSION. Edited by L. P. JACKS, M.A., D D., LL.D. *Each, Crown* 8*vo*, 5s *net* each volume The first volumes are. THE ANGLO-CATHOLIC FAITH (T. A. LACEY); MODERNISM IN THE ENGLISH CHURCH (P GARDNER), THE FAITH AND PRACTICE OF THE QUAKERS (R M JONES), CONGREGATIONALISM (W B SELBIE), THE FAITH OF THE ROMAN CHURCH (C C MARTINDALE), THE LIFE AND FAITH OF THE BAPTISTS (H WHEELER ROBINSON), THE PRESBYTERIAN CHURCHES (JAMES MOFFATT); METHODISM (W BARDSLEY BRASH), THE EVANGELICAL MOVEMENT IN THE ENGLISH CHURCH (L ELLIOTT BINNS), THE UNITARIANS (HENRY GOW).

The Gateway Library
Fcap. 8*vo* 3s 6d. each volume.
Pocketable Editions of Works by HILAIRE BELLOC, ARNOLD BENNETT, E F BENSON, GEORGE A. BIRMINGHAM, MARJORIE BOWEN, G K CHESTERTON, A CLUTTON-BROCK, JOSEPH CONRAD, J H CURLE, GEORGE GISSING, GERALD GOULD, KENNETH GRAHAME, A P. HERBERT, W H HUDSON, RUDYARD KIPLING, E V KNOX, JACK LONDON, E V LUCAS, ROBERT LYND, ROSE MACAULAY, JOHN MASEFIELD, A. A MILNE, ARTHUR MORRISON, EDEN PHILLPOTTS, MARMADUKE PICKTHALL, CHARLES G D ROBERTS, R L. STEVENSON, and OSCAR WILDE.

A History of England in Seven Volumes
Edited by SIR CHARLES OMAN, K B E, M P, M A, F S A. With Maps. *Demy* 8*vo* 12s 6*d net* each volume
ENGLAND BEFORE THE NORMAN CONQUEST (SIR C. OMAN), ENGLAND UNDER THE NORMANS AND ANGEVINS (H. W. C.

CPSIA information can be obtained at www.ICGtesting.com
Printed in the USA
LVOW121924140812

294322LV00015B/212/P

9 781178 623116